# Leadership Ethics
*An Introduction*

Are leaders morally special? Is there something ethically distinctive about the relationship between leaders and followers? Should leaders do whatever it takes to achieve group goals?

*Leadership Ethics* draws on both moral theory and empirical research in psychology to evaluate the reasons everyday leaders give to justify breaking the rules. Written for people without a background in philosophy, it introduces readers to the moral theories that are relevant to leadership ethics: relativism, amoralism, egoism, virtue ethics, social contract theory, situation ethics, communitarianism, and cosmopolitan theories such as utilitarianism and transformational leadership.

Unlike many introductory texts, *Leadership Ethics* does more than simply acquaint readers with different approaches to leadership ethics. It defends the Kantian view that everyday leaders are not justified in breaking the moral rules.

Terry L. Price is associate professor and associate dean for academic affairs at the Jepson School of Leadership Studies at the University of Richmond. He is the author of *Understanding Ethical Failures in Leadership* and co-editor of *The Values of Presidential Leadership, The Quest for Moral Leaders,* and the three-volume reference work *The International Library of Leadership.*

# Leadership Ethics

## An Introduction

TERRY L. PRICE
*University of Richmond*

CAMBRIDGE
UNIVERSITY PRESS

Hm
1261
.P75
2008

CAMBRIDGE UNIVERSITY PRESS
Cambridge, New York, Melbourne, Madrid, Cape Town, Singapore, São Paulo, Delhi

Cambridge University Press
32 Avenue of the Americas, New York, NY 10013-2473, USA

www.cambridge.org
Information on this title: www.cambridge.org/9780521699112

First published 2008

Printed in the United States of America

*A catalog record for this publication is available from the British Library.*

*Library of Congress Cataloging in Publication Data*

Price, Terry L., 1966–
Leadership ethics : an introduction / Terry L. Price.
    p.   cm.
Includes bibliographical references and index.
ISBN 978-0-521-87583-7 (hardback) – ISBN 978-0-521-69911-2 (pbk.)
1. Leadership – Moral and ethical aspects.   I. Title.
HM1261.P75   2008
174–dc22         2008001678

ISBN   978-0-521-87583-7 hardback
ISBN   978-0-521-69911-2 paperback

*For Lori, Harper, and Bernard*

# Contents

# Acknowledgments

This book represents ten years of thinking about leadership ethics and of teaching the subject to undergraduates. My greatest debt is to the students in my classes. Their contributions and feedback have greatly influenced the way I teach leadership ethics and the approach I take in this book. I am particularly grateful to students in my fall 2007 Ethics and Leadership course for reading and critiquing draft chapters.

I owe a special institutional debt. I am fortunate to have a faculty appointment at the Jepson School of Leadership Studies at the University of Richmond, which allows me to concentrate all of my intellectual efforts on leadership ethics. I thank the Jepson School for research funding, a sabbatical year, and an additional visiting year in the Department of Philosophy at the University of North Carolina at Chapel Hill.

I have wonderful colleagues at the Jepson School and the University of Richmond. Because of them, there is no better place to do interdisciplinary work in leadership ethics. This book was especially influenced by the work and advice of our psychologists: Scott Allison, Don Forsyth, George ("Al") Goethals, and – most importantly – Crystal Hoyt. Crystal collaborated with me on the empirical study described in Chapter 6, and she deserves great thanks for all the work she did in the analysis and interpretation of the results – as well as for her suggestions for summarizing our general findings. On more than one occasion, I referred to myself as "Crystal's other honors student." Alyson Emrick administered the survey as an attachment to the questionnaire for her senior honors thesis, and I want to thank her, too.

I also received helpful advice and comments on the text from Joanne Ciulla, Sandra Peart, Thaddeus Williamson, and Karen Zivi. Douglas Hicks merits a special mention for carefully working through the final draft of the manuscript.

In response to presentations of this work, conference participants at the Association for Practical and Professional Ethics and the International Leadership Association raised important criticisms and, in their kindness, offered excellent advice on how to strengthen the arguments. I cannot mention all commentators by name, but I particularly want to acknowledge Edwin Hartman, David Levy, Ronald Riggio, and Daniel Wueste.

Chapter 1 is a reworked version of my paper "Abuse, Privilege, and the Conditions of Responsibility for Leaders," which was previously published as Chapter 4 in *The Quest for Moral Leaders: Essays in Leadership Ethics*, edited by Joanne B. Ciulla, Terry L. Price, and Susan E. Murphy (Cheltenham, UK, and Northampton, MA, USA: Edward Elgar, copyright © 2005), 65–79. I have adapted this work with permission from Edward Elgar and my co-editors, Joanne Ciulla and Susan Murphy, and I thank them for their courtesy.

I relied on many people to assist with research, check the quotes and citations, collect references, and proofread the text. Lorie Gillis, Christine Most, Cassie Price, and Tammy Tripp supported this project as staff members of the Jepson School, and Allison Rosser and Ashley Prime served as my student assistants. When deadlines were looming, Allison arrived early on Saturday mornings to complete the job. Ashley's wonderful eye for detail made her an invaluable partner in the indexing and editing process. Lucretia McCulley at the University of Richmond Library somehow managed to track down news stories on very little – and sometimes incorrect – information. Will Moore graciously shared his gift for editing and expertly worked through a draft of the manuscript.

Cambridge University Press has once again put its faith in my work. Beatrice Rehl, my editor at Cambridge, encouraged me in this project, adapted deadlines so that I could improve the book, and exercised what can only be described as genuine editorial wisdom. Responsiveness may be uncommon in publishing today, but you would not know it working with Beatrice. I sincerely appreciate my relationship with her and Cambridge.

Ronald Cohen, who edited my last book for Cambridge, was enthusiastic about working with me again on this project. The book reflects his good sense, excellent ear, and respect for the English language.

I have dedicated this book to Lori Speagle, Harper Speagle-Price, and Bernard Speagle. I owe them much more than this. They overlooked my grumpiness on the days when the writing did not go well, and they were always ready to celebrate even minor victories such as a completed chapter. Although Bernard did not lie at my feet while I wrote this book, I should give him reinforcement for this behavior anyway. I forgot to acknowledge him in my last book after he dutifully kept me company in the early morning hours. Lori, Harper, and Bernard also put their lives in Richmond on hold so that I could spend a year writing and teaching in Chapel Hill. I am a truly lucky partner and father.

# Introduction

## BETWEEN THE VILLAIN AND THE HERO

Students of leadership ethics, whatever the particular context of study, face no shortage of examples. Politics offers bad leaders such as Richard Nixon. It also brings us murderous leaders such as Hitler and Stalin, each of whom was responsible for the deaths of millions of innocent people. From religion come not only charlatans such as Jim and Tammy Faye Bakker, but also destructive prophets such as Jim Jones and David Koresh, two leaders who ultimately led their followers to suicidal showdowns with the outside world. In business, the stakes are usually lower,[1] but this context has its fair share of villains, too, with newcomers joining the list almost by the day: WorldCom's Bernie Ebbers, Tyco's Dennis Kozlowski, and Enron's Jeff Skilling.

Negative exemplars from politics, religion, and business make for frequent contrasts with leaders on the positive side of the ethical divide. Although there are sometimes disagreements about the real heroes of the moral story, Abraham Lincoln and Franklin Roosevelt are regularly cited for their moral accomplishments as presidents, and Martin Luther King Jr. has a central place in our understanding of ethical leadership for social change. All of these examples – the bad and the good – are standard fare in our day-to-day discussions of ethical

---

[1] This is not to trivialize the moral importance of death or suffering from dangerous products, unjust working conditions, and corporate theft.

leadership. But is working from villainous and heroic leadership the best way to think about leadership ethics in everyday life?[2]

Advocates of this approach to leadership ethics – what we might call *the ethics of the extreme case* – charge everyday leaders to be less like the Nixons and Kozlowskis of the world and more like the Lincolns and Kings. What this approach misses, however, is the fact that villainous and heroic leaders have something in common, and the commonality proves to be more important for everyday leadership ethics than any differences between them. The commonality is that both villainous and heroic leaders sometimes have to break – or, at least, *think* they have to break – the rules to achieve their ends. We readily acknowledge this fact about villainous leaders. Watergate, which exposed the political "dirty tricks" of the Nixon administration, now serves as a paradigm of bad leadership. Tyco's Kozlowski, once the poster child for corporate immorality, allegedly misused Tyco money to support a very lavish lifestyle – including, among other things, a million-dollar birthday party for his wife.

However, the heroic Lincoln broke the rules as well – for example, suspending habeas corpus during the Civil War. Other presidents have similarly used wartime as a pretext for breaking the rules.[3] Historians generally agree that Franklin Roosevelt systematically deceived the American public in order to lead the country into World War II, yet Roosevelt's role in this war remains a central part of the story of his heroism. Finally, rule breaking constituted a critical piece of King's heroic leadership in the civil rights movement. To achieve the ends of equality, King advocated breaking not only the unjust law

---

[2] In an introductory section called "Of Heroes and Villains," Craig Johnson suggests that we should focus less on the heroes of leadership and more on the villains of leadership (Craig E. Johnson, *Meeting the Ethical Challenges of Leadership: Casting Light or Shadow* [Thousand Oaks, CA: Sage Publications, 2001], 3–5). For other views of leadership ethics that work from examples of either villainous or heroic leadership, see James MacGregor Burns, *Leadership* (New York: Harper and Row Publishers, 1978); Bernard M. Bass and Paul Steidlmeier, "Ethics, Character, and Authentic Transformational Leadership Behavior," *Leadership Quarterly* 10 (1999): 181–217; James MacGregor Burns, *Transforming Leadership: A New Pursuit of Happiness* (New York: Atlantic Monthly Press, 2003); Barbara Kellerman, *Bad Leadership: What It Is, How It Happens, Why It Matters* (Boston: Harvard Business School Press, 2004); and Jean Lipman-Blumen, *The Allure of Toxic Leaders: Why We Follow Destructive Bosses and Corrupt Politicians – and How We Can Survive Them* (Oxford: Oxford University Press, 2005).

[3] It may be too soon to tell whether George W. Bush has done so in his war on terrorism and, if he did, whether this makes him a hero or a villain.

but also the law that was "just on its face and unjust in its application."[4]

Part of the appeal of thinking about leadership in terms of villains
and heroes is its simplicity. Whereas villains use their leadership positions to feed desires for excessive power and luxury, heroes exercise
leadership to achieve group ends and, sometimes, the ends of society
more broadly.[5] The simplicity of this approach can find its way into our
thinking about everyday leadership. Given the nature of the wrongs
committed by villainous leaders, it is quite easy for everyday leaders to
distance themselves from their own immorality.

Equally problematic is the ease with which everyday leaders identify
with heroic leaders. After all, everyday leaders – like heroic leaders –
are typically committed to the importance of the group ends they seek
to achieve. As a result of what seems to be a straightforward distinction
between villainous and heroic leadership, the ethics of everyday leadership can also seem straightforward. An everyday leader can rationalize
this way: "Unlike the behavior exhibited by villainous leaders, my
rule-breaking behavior is part of a long tradition of heroic leadership."

There are thus two general risks of thinking about everyday leadership ethics in terms of the sharp line often drawn between villainous
and heroic leadership. On the one hand, working from examples of
villainous leadership demands too little of the student of leadership
ethics. For instance, inordinate attention in business school classes to
the Kozlowskis of the world may lead students to see the daily behavior
of many leaders as morally acceptable because it does not cross the
line that leaders such as Kozlowski crossed. By focusing on wrongs
that are rare in everyday leadership, villainous leadership turns our
attention away from other, more common ethical failures in leadership.[6] On the other hand, the risk of working from examples of heroic

4 King, "Letter from Birmingham City Jail," in *A Testament of Hope: The Essential Writings of Martin Luther King, Jr.* ed. James Melvin Washington (San Francisco: Harper and Row Publishers, 1986), 294.
5 See Bass and Steidlmeier, "Ethics, Character, and Authentic Transformational Leadership Behavior." For a critique of this view, see Terry L. Price, "The Ethics of Authentic Transformational Leadership," *Leadership Quarterly* 14 (2003): 67–81.
6 One implication of using villainous leadership as a pedagogical tool in applied ethics is a preoccupation with the incentive structures necessary to get people to behave morally. This preoccupation is evident in business school classes that mistake business law for business ethics. The law sets only a bare minimum that we can expect of people, promising extrinsic costs for people who do not live up to it.

leadership is that students of leadership will model their behavior on these exemplars, even though everyday leaders do not face relevantly similar crises.

When we put these two points together, it turns out that avoiding the moral failures of very bad leaders is not sufficient for ethical leadership in everyday life, and making the hard choices that some good leaders have had to make may not be necessary for it. The subject of everyday leadership ethics falls somewhere between the moral problems of the villain and the hero.

## THE MORAL PSYCHOLOGY OF LEADERSHIP

If the immorality of everyday leaders is hardly so grievous, and the moral demands on them hardly so grand, what then do these leaders have in common with villainous and heroic leaders? This book assumes that what is common to all leaders is the *moral psychology of leadership.* A central component of the moral psychology of leadership is a belief about justification – namely, that leaders are sometimes justified in doing what others are not allowed to do. As we have seen, even the leaders we hold in the highest esteem sometimes break the rules in the service of group ends. Still, not even heroic leaders have a moral license to break whatever rules they want to break. They must be able to justify their behavior.

Leadership ethics thus brings with it a distinctive demand for justification. If ethical leadership is consistent with rule breaking, then there must be a convincing reason or set of reasons for leaders to behave in ways that are proscribed for the rest of us. This makes the ethics of everyday leadership particularly complicated. Everyday leaders are engaged in a social activity closely associated with assumptions about rule breaking; however, when such leaders act on these assumptions, their behavior rarely falls neatly into categories of "villainous" and "heroic." The student of everyday leadership ethics therefore has the much more difficult task of sorting and weighing different claims of justification.

What reasons might everyday leaders use to justify their behavior? In the chapters to follow, I consider several lines of justification, most of which are variations on the reasons any person might give for breaking rules that apply more generally to others. The morally relevant difference is that leaders who appeal to these reasons seem to be in a relatively better position to build a special case for their rule-breaking behavior. Consider, for example, the leader who lies to followers. What might the response be to questions about why the leader behaved this way? Some plausible responses include the following: the leader did it . . .

> because he has his own morality.
> because she does not care about morality.
> because he could.
> because she is special.
> because we said he could.
> because she had to.
> because he has special obligations to his group.
> because it was for a higher cause.

Again, any of these responses could be similarly applied by one of the rest of us in an attempt to justify our own behavior. What distinguishes an appeal to these reasons in the leadership context, however, is that the rule breaker's standing as a leader generally gives (at least the impression of) greater substance to the justification. More so than the rest of us, leaders may well be in a position to develop a convincing argument based on one or more of these reasons.

First, the defense of the leader who acts as he does "because he has his own morality" points to the fact that leadership seems to function with its own set of norms. One team of leadership consultants conveys this idea on its website gutsyleaders.com by selling T-shirts with the logo "We Ain't No . . . Face Savin', Excuse Makin', Rule Followin', Fun Squelchin', Permission Seekin', Status Quo Protectin' Clock Punchers." A more sophisticated way to make this point is to say that leadership is *normatively differentiating*. Different norms for leaders and followers evolve out of the process of leader emergence within groups.[7] In virtue of this feature of leadership, we might say that leaders have their own code of ethics.

As we will see, normative differentiation is driven by another commonly accepted feature of leadership – namely, that leadership is *instrumentalist*. Leadership aims to achieve something considered to be valuable and worth achieving, and the success of leaders depends to

---

[7] See E. P. Hollander, *Leaders, Groups, and Influence* (New York: Oxford University Press, 1964).

a large extent on actual achievement of these ends.[8] Accordingly, leaders attribute significant priority to their goals, and the value of their goals can compete with morality. We should not be surprised, then, if a leader sometimes acts as she does "because she does not care about morality." This possibility leaves us with an important moral question. Can morality rein in the behavior of everyday leaders if it fails to generate reasons for people who do not care – or do not care *enough* – about morality? Put another way, does the strong commitment of everyday leaders to their ends justify their acting against morality's demands?

A second set of reasons from the list of potential justifications focuses on the resources that leaders have at their disposal or – at least – that others have only to a lesser extent. Leadership is *power conferring*. Because leadership is a relationship of influence between people, leaders are able to exercise power over others in ways that make it possible for leaders to get away with doing what others cannot do. So, when a leader uses his power to break a rule that applies to the rest of us, there may be some truth to the claim that he did it "because he could." For example, President Bill Clinton famously said of his affair with Monica Lewinsky that he did it "just because [he] could."[9]

There is also a respectable intellectual tradition committed to the idea that leaders are endowed with personal qualities that make them different from followers. According to this way of thinking about leadership, leaders acquire and maintain their positions because of characteristics that contribute to effectiveness. This view thus holds that leadership *depends on traits*. If the trait view of leadership is correct, then we may be able to say that the leader – unlike the rest of us – acts as she does "because she is special." For this justification to work, it would have to show both that the trait view is correct in its claims that there are actual differences between leaders and followers and that these differences are relevant to moral evaluation.

A third set of reasons from the list of potential justifications looks to notions such as consent and necessity. These notions play important roles in common understandings of justification. For example, a boxer has no legitimate moral complaint against the opponent who breaks his nose with a fairly laid punch. Nor can the boxer make a moral

---

[8] See, for example, Burns, *Leadership*, 22.
[9] Howard Kurtz, "Bill Clinton's very personal reflections: In '60 Minutes' interview, ex-president calls affair 'terrible moral error,'" *Washington Post* (June 17, 2004).

charge against the doctor who causes him some degree of pain in an effort to treat the broken nose. In this case, we say that any "harm" done to the boxer is justified by either consent or necessity. Similarly, one might suggest that consent and necessity justify rule-breaking behavior by leaders. As leadership is to some extent *consensual*, this justification holds that followers can hardly complain when their leader does what he can to achieve the ends to which he has consistently pledged commitment. Ultimately, the leader acts as he does "because we said he could."

A leader can also believe that the goals of the group are so important that, as Michael Walzer puts it, he must do "within rational limits whatever is necessary" to achieve them.[10] Here, we should notice that even everyday leaders appeal to necessity for justification. For instance, after learning that a supervisor in Chesterfield County, Virginia, had been arrested, another county official spent more than $18,000 to charter a jet to return from a vacation. The official and his champions defended his behavior this way:

"My judgment was I needed to get back there immediately, to use whatever resources I could to get back... [I]f you consider the circumstances – we had just had our board chairman arrested and had no idea what was going on, and I need to get back to the county."

"You had a crisis in the county and the man had to get back to be the administrator and be in control. You can't do that from far away."

"It was a unique situation, the first time that anybody had been in this predicament before."[11]

In this situation and others like it, defenders of a leader's behavior say that leadership must be *responsive to necessity*. Advancing group goals in the face of necessity sometimes requires a leader to do what the rest of us cannot do. When she does it, we say that she did it "because she had to."

A fourth and final set of reasons from the list of potential justifications moves away from the claim that rule breaking is justified by

---

[10] Michael Walzer, "Political Action: The Problem of Dirty Hands," *Philosophy and Public Affairs* 2 (1973): 165.

[11] Julian Walker, "Chesterfield official paid $18,000 for flight," *Richmond Times-Dispatch* (February 21, 2006).

the importance of a particular group's goals. We can admit that the goals of any particular group do not stand out as sufficiently special – and, so, cannot alone justify rule breaking – without denying that a leader ought nevertheless to do what he can to achieve the group's goals. According to this view, leadership is necessarily *partial.* Leaders are expected to put the goals of their group, organization, or society ahead of the goals of others. But this is not because group ends somehow lend themselves to validation by disinterested third parties. Rather the importance of a leader's ends is grounded in the moral relationship between the leader and his group. Because he is the leader of this collective body rather than some different group of people, some say that he ought to do what he can to achieve his group's goals and not the goals of others. The justificatory version of this claim implies that the leader sometimes has to break the rules "because he has special obligations to his group."

An opposing view of leadership suggests that we should adopt a more inclusive understanding of what constitutes the group as a whole. We are all members of particular groups – for example, families, churches, corporations, civic associations, and countries. But we are also members of humanity or the global society. According to this view, leadership must be significantly *impartial.* Impartiality also makes room for the argument that rule breaking can be justified. Leaders can have a justification for rule-breaking behavior when the exception serves society at large or the common good, not the partisan interests of their particular groups. In these cases, we might be inclined to say that the leader did what she did "because it was for a higher cause."

THE PLAN OF THE BOOK

The reasons just described are simply *potential* justifications for rule breaking. All of them may fail to provide *actual* justifications for rule-breaking behavior by everyday leaders. Determining whether they constitute successful justifications is the primary task of this book. To carry out this task, I devote a chapter to each potential justification. Each potential justification also links up with a particular moral theory.

Part I, "Leader-Centric Approaches," focuses on moral theories that give particular weight to the beliefs, desires, ends, and characteristics of leaders. Chapter 1 uses the theory of *moral relativism* to articulate the leader's belief that he is justified in his behavior "because he has his own morality." Moral relativism captures the idea that a leader's rule-breaking behavior might be justified by his own moral beliefs or those of his society.

Chapter 2 investigates whether *amoralism* characterizes the moral psychology of the everyday leader. The amoral leader breaks the rules "because she does not care about morality." Amoralism comes up as a response to the claim that the demands of morality are categorical in nature. The primary historical advocate of the categorical nature of moral demands is Immanuel Kant, who holds that morality applies to individuals independently of their particular desires and ends.[12] This chapter's discussion of Kantian ethics and the moral psychology of everyday ethical failure serves as the theoretical foundation for the remainder of the book. Kantian ethics also plays a prominent role in Chapter 7, and in Chapter 9, which serves as the conclusion of the book.

Chapter 3 takes up the argument that leaders should conform their behavior to the demands of *egoism*. This view privileges the desires and ends of the everyday leader, essentially encouraging him to use his power as a leader to break the rules "because he can."

Chapter 4 considers the moral theory most closely identified with the idea that a leader acts as she does "because she is special" – namely, *virtue ethics*. According to this view, because morality is more about *being* than *doing*, a person can be virtuous without an unyielding commitment to the moral rules. Indeed, morality may require rule breaking.

Part II, "Group-Centric Approaches," gives greater attention to the ways in which a leader's moral psychology is shaped by the collective nature of leadership. Chapter 5 appeals to *contractarianism* to examine the idea that a leader sometimes breaks the rules "because we said he could." Because this moral theory sees consent as central to justification, it proves to be a particularly good candidate for thinking about the ethical relationship between leaders and followers in the organizations and institutions that comprise modern, democratic society.

Chapter 6 evaluates the everyday leader's claim that she broke the rules "because she had to." In so doing, it exposes beliefs leaders have

---

[12] Immanuel Kant, *Groundwork of the Metaphysic of Morals*, trans. H. J. Paton (New York: Harper and Row Publishers, 1964).

about the objective importance of group goals. These beliefs support the *moral situationism* that sometimes characterizes leadership behavior. If everyday leadership cannot sustain the relevant attributions of importance to group goals, we must reject moral situationism.

Chapter 7 examines an alternative to the idea that the ends of a leader's group are special because of their objective importance. *Communitarianism* makes sense of the leader's claim that he broke the rules "because he has special obligations to his group." Drawing on this moral theory, we can see a leader's commitment to group ends as being justified by reasons that are internal to the community of which he is the leader.

Chapter 8 revives the argument that a leader's ends can be justified by reasons that apply to rational actors more broadly. *Cosmopolitanism* refers to a cluster of moral theories that denies that groups – for example, nation-states – can justifiably privilege their own particular ends. It replaces these particular ends with more general ends such as the welfare of humanity. In so doing, cosmopolitan moral theory serves as perhaps the best way to understand the claims of a leader who says she broke the rules "because it was for a higher cause."

In coverage, then, the book constitutes an introduction to the moral theories that are relevant to everyday leadership ethics. But there are three main respects in which this book is different from other introductory texts in applied moral philosophy. First, the discussion of the moral theories covered in the book is motivated by the central problem of this applied context. The rule-breaking behavior associated with leadership cries out for justification, so moral theory is needed to determine the appropriate response. In other words, the moral theories come up as answers to a particular question, which is different from their being introduced and then *applied* to the list of moral problems that leaders face.

Second, the book defends a particular answer to the basic question it raises. My analysis of the potential justifications for rule breaking relies heavily on the Kantian view of morality introduced in Chapter 2, and I conclude in Chapter 9 that everyday leaders are not justified in breaking the rules. So the text is not neutral in the way that some introductions simply acquaint the reader with different ways of thinking about ethics, ultimately leaving all conclusions up for grabs. It is rather a *guided* introduction to leadership ethics.

Third, because this book is about moral psychology, it aims to tell us something about the way leaders think about their personal qualities and the importance of their goals, especially the importance of their groups' goals. Accordingly, it is meant to be a work not only in applied philosophical ethics but also in the emerging field of "empirical philosophy."[13] Chapter 4 draws on empirical research in psychology on leader traits and on psychological phenomena such as the so-called better-than-average effect. If we are to examine the thesis that leaders are justified in breaking the rules because they have special characteristics, then we should first determine whether they really are special and, if so, in what ways. Trait studies are crucial to this task because they test how leaders compare with followers in terms of characteristics such as belief, motivation, and morality.

In everyday life, our comparisons with others are complicated by the better-than-average effect. Psychological research shows that what people generally believe about their personal characteristics conflicts with reality.[14] Simply put, not everyone can be better than average. But there is much less empirical research on people's beliefs about the importance of their personal goals and the goals of their group.[15] Given the centrality of such beliefs to the moral psychology of leadership, this book includes a discussion of the results of an original empirical study of student leaders at the university level.[16] Our objective in this study was to see whether psychological phenomena related to the better-than-average effect apply to a leader's beliefs about the importance of her personal goals and her group's goals.

Evidence for a "more-important-than-average effect" on leaders' beliefs about the importance of their personal goals would give us reason to question the claims of the egoistic leader discussed in Chapter 3.

---

[13] This empirical element is in keeping with the dominant approach in business schools and in many leadership studies programs.

[14] See, for example., M. D. Alicke and O. Govorun, "The Better-than-Average Effect," in *The Self in Social Judgment*, eds. M. D. Alicke, D. A. Dunning, and J. I. Krueger (New York: Psychology Press, 2005), 85–106.

[15] There is an extensive psychological literature on people's tendency to value what they have more than what they do not have. For an introductory discussion of the "endowment effect" and scholarly references, see Daniel Gilbert, *Stumbling on Happiness* (New York: Alfred A. Knopf, 2006), 145–146.

[16] Crystal L. Hoyt, Terry L. Price, and Alyson Emrick, "Leadership and the More-Important-Than-Average Effect." Manuscript in preparation.

If leaders generally overestimate the importance of their *personal* goals, then this finding would encourage us to discount such ends when considering a case for the justification of rule-breaking behavior. Support for the claim that the more-important-than-average effect also applies to leaders' beliefs about the importance of *group* goals would pose a similar challenge to attempts to use these goals to justify the behavior of the leader who breaks the rules to advance collective ends.

My main thesis – that rule breaking is not justified in everyday leadership – garners support from both moral theory and empirical research in psychology. To the extent that moral theory allows rule breaking, it does so only in cases that are best characterized as "heroic." Everyday leadership, by definition, cannot be exceptional in this way. The difficulty for the practice of leadership is that normal human psychology tends to compete with what turns out to be the best moral analysis. Leaders may be especially prone to see themselves as exceptional, as they are typically thought to stand out both in terms of their personal qualities and in terms of the importance of the goals to which they are committed.

Hence the central question of leadership ethics: *Do the distinctive features of leadership justify rule-breaking behavior?* In the context of everyday leadership, an answer to this question must be informed by our best understanding of moral theory and an accurate view of the way everyday leaders think about themselves and the importance of their goals. The answer will tell us how everyday leaders *should* think about morality and their place in the moral community.

PART I

# LEADER-CENTRIC APPROACHES

# 1

# Relativism and Exceptionalism

## EXPLANATION AND JUSTIFICATION

Leaders often act as though they have their own code of ethics.[1] Actions that are wrong for the rest of us, it seems, can be right for them. One way to think about this phenomenon is to understand leadership ethics in terms of the theory of *moral relativism*. This is the view that what is right or wrong differs either from person to person or from society to society. Applied to leadership ethics, this view of morality permits leaders to act as they or their cultures see fit. In other words, a leader – as an individual or as a member of a particular society – can claim justification "because he has his own morality."

We can call the first version *personal relativism* and the second version *cultural relativism*. Personal relativism privileges the moral beliefs of the individual, whereas cultural relativism yields to the moral commitments within a person's society. For both versions of this theory, morality is determined by reference to the beliefs of particular people, not by reference to some objective standard. What is right or wrong is a matter of subjective perceptions, either at the individual or at the collective level. For example, relativism holds that lying can be moral for

---

[1] This chapter is a substantially revised version of Terry L. Price, "Abuse, Privilege, and the Conditions of Responsibility for Leaders," in *The Quest for Moral Leaders: Essays in Leadership Ethics*, eds. Joanne B. Ciulla, Terry L. Price, and Susan E. Murphy (Cheltenham, UK, and Northampton, MA, USA: Edward Elgar, 2005), ch. 4, 65–79. It is used in adapted form with the permission of Edward Elgar.

some individuals but immoral for other individuals, or that lying can be permissible in one culture but impermissible in another culture.

Relativism makes for a subtle but important contrast with a different way of thinking about the claim that leaders have their own code of ethics. *Moral exceptionalism* holds that there is something morally special about leaders or leadership. Perhaps leaders or the situations they face are distinctive from a moral point of view. Or, there may be something special about the relationship between leaders and followers or about the connection leaders have to the particular ends they are trying to achieve. Whatever the differences, as long as these differences are relevant to moral justification, they suggest an alternative grounding for the claim that leaders have their own code of ethics. Morality provides an objective standard for behavior, but the flexibility of this standard allows us to respond to morally relevant differences between people, situations, and relationships. One consequence of this flexibility is that leaders can be justified in doing things that the rest of us would not be justified in doing.

As we will see in later chapters, many standard moral theories can accommodate the exceptionalist version of the claim that leaders have their own code of ethics.[2] Justification ultimately rests on objective differences associated with being a leader or exercising leadership behavior. What these theories cannot accommodate, however, is the relativist view that a leader's behavior is right or wrong simply because he or his society believes it to be right or wrong. One important function of standard moral theories is to adjudicate between subjective opinions of what ethics requires. As a consequence, these theories can hardly countenance opposing behaviors for different individuals or societies – at least not in the absence of morally relevant differences between them. In fact, if morality is determined simply by whatever a person or his society thinks, then there would be little need for the moral direction that such theories are meant to provide. Figuring out what constitutes moral behavior would require only that we look to ourselves to see what behaviors are accepted – by us or by our societies – and are therefore acceptable.

---

[2] Traditional Kantian ethics is an exception here. For a discussion of Kant's absolutism, see Chapters 2 and 7.

This feature of moral relativism prompts the common criticism that it is most plausible as a descriptive theory, not a normative theory.[3] Although relativism *explains* why people behave as they do, it hardly *justifies* their behavior. People's moral beliefs are explanatory because they are part of a description of the circumstances that contribute to our understanding of why people act as they do. But the fact that people hold particular moral beliefs – any more than the fact that they hold particular non-moral beliefs – does not give us reason to think that their beliefs are correct. And if we cannot conclude that the moral beliefs people currently hold are true, we certainly cannot conclude that people are justified in acting on these beliefs.

Nonetheless, students of ethics are often very attracted to relativism. Part of the attraction is in the fact that relativism seems to be a sensible response to intractable moral disagreement. Given that we cannot prove that our own moral beliefs are correct, we are hardly in a solid position to judge the moral beliefs of others. This sentiment is an admirable one, and its exploration in the leadership context is the focus of this chapter. Perhaps we should not be too hard on leaders – say, by blaming them – when their behavior can be understood in terms of their commitment to moralities that differ radically from our own. Blame can strike us as inappropriate when we are able to explain a leader's behavior by the fact that it conforms to "his morality," even though the behavior certainly does not conform to "our morality." For example, descriptive facts about a leader's upbringing or culture potentially help us understand, and perhaps forgive, immoral leadership behavior such as false imprisonment, the killing of innocents, and even torture.

By highlighting the fact that explanation can be relevant to moral assessment, relativism grounds a potentially viable strategy for arguing that a leader ought not to be held responsible for his rule-breaking behavior. We are hesitant to blame him because – through no fault of his own – he holds mistaken views about the moral permissibility of such behaviors. This way of thinking about immoral leadership relies on relativism only as a part of a causal explanation of the leader's

---

3 See James Rachels, *The Elements of Moral Philosophy* (New York: Random House, 1986), 15–17.

behavior. In so doing, it offers a potential excuse for leaders who break the moral rules.

This chapter considers explanations for the moral beliefs of leaders, focusing primarily on two kinds of upbringing that might contribute to mistaken moral beliefs. First, we might think that leaders can be mistaken about morality because they were subjected to a deprived or abusive upbringing. A second, less obvious cause of mistaken moral beliefs – but one that has greater relevance in a discussion of leadership ethics – is the childhood of privilege or entitlement. Both explanations help us understand the behavior of some leaders without also making their behavior morally right. In other words, explaining leader immorality does not justify it. The chapter concludes, however, with the claim that the notions of privilege and entitlement can be extended to show that leaders may have their own code of ethics in the justificatory sense advocated by moral exceptionalism.

### "UNFORTUNATE FORMATIVE CIRCUMSTANCES"

In a famous paper called "Freedom and Resentment," P. F. Strawson claims that "peculiarly unfortunate . . . formative circumstances" sometimes undermine moral responsibility.[4] For Strawson, a bad upbringing can cause an agent to be "psychologically abnormal" or "morally underdeveloped."[5] In such cases, we often come to see the agent as "exempted" from the moral rules that apply to other individuals.[6] Because of the agent's unfortunate formative circumstances, it simply expects too much of him to treat him as though he is responsible for his behavior.

Susan Wolf fashions a hypothetical example that allows us to consider the effects of formative circumstances on the moral beliefs of leaders:

---

[4] Peter Strawson, "Freedom and Resentment," in *Perspectives on Moral Responsibility*, eds. John Martin Fischer and Mark Ravizza (Ithaca, NY: Cornell University Press, 1988), 52. Much of the literature cited in this section is about the nature of responsibility, but one assumption of these authors is that moral cognition can be corrupted by upbringing.

[5] Strawson, "Freedom and Resentment," 52.

[6] Gary Watson, "Responsibility and the Limits of Evil: Variations on a Strawsonian Theme," in *Responsibility, Character, and the Emotions: New Essays in Moral Psychology*, ed. Ferdinand Schoeman (Cambridge: Cambridge University Press, 1987), 260.

JoJo is the favorite son of Jo the First, an evil and sadistic dictator of a small, underdeveloped country. Because of his father's special feelings for the boy, JoJo is given a special education and is allowed to accompany his father and observe his daily routine. In light of this treatment, it is not surprising that little JoJo takes his father as a role model and develops values very much like Dad's. As an adult, he does many of the same sorts of things his father did, including sending people to prison or to death or to torture chambers on the basis of whim.[7]

Wolf concludes that leaders with background experiences such as JoJo's may lack "the ability to know the difference between right and wrong . . . [A] person who, even on reflection, cannot see that having someone tortured because he failed to salute you is wrong plainly lacks the requisite ability."[8] JoJo therefore fails to meet the conditions for responsible agency.

How can leaders claim ignorance of the fact that practices such as torture are wrong? Their immoral behavior hardly lends itself to a *cultural* explanation.[9] Many leaders engage in these behaviors not only in the face of political opposition but also against general moral prohibitions within their society. For example, even in JoJo's society, we might assume that torture is not a commonly acceptable form of behavior.

JoJo's willingness to resort to this measure is better explained by *personal* values passed down to him from his father, not in terms of more widespread cultural values. It is JoJo, much more so than his society, who is misguided. JoJo's case, then, is not perfectly analogous to that of "persons who, though acting badly, act in ways that are strongly encouraged by their societies – the slaveowners of the 1850s, the Nazis of the 1930s, and many male chauvinists of our fathers' generation."[10] Despite the fact that JoJo holds mistaken moral beliefs that were transmitted to him directly from his father, not unlike racist or sexist beliefs that are sometimes transmitted from father to son,

---

7 Susan Wolf, "Sanity and the Metaphysics of Responsibility," in *Responsibility, Character, and the Emotions: New Essays in Moral Psychology*, ed. Ferdinand Schoeman (Cambridge: Cambridge University Press, 1987), 53–54.
8 Susan Wolf, "Sanity and the Metaphysics of Responsibility," 56.
9 For a discussion of the relevant empirical questions, see Michelle Moody-Adams, "Culture, Responsibility, and Affected Ignorance," *Ethics* 104 (1994): 291–309.
10 Susan Wolf, "Sanity and the Metaphysics of Responsibility," 56–57.

the idiosyncrasy of JoJo's morality distinguishes his case from cases in which whole societies or majorities within them are committed to moralities that we find problematic.

In this respect, JoJo is much closer to the individuals that Strawson exempts from moral responsibility because of "peculiarly unfortunate . . . formative circumstances."[11] Unfortunate formative circumstances put only some individuals outside the norm. Saying that a particular individual is unfortunate in his circumstances is a relative claim; it is a claim about his fortune compared with others within his society.[12] The relativism at issue is therefore personal, not cultural. Accordingly, if we conclude that such reasons explain JoJo's behavior, it is because his upbringing makes him different from other people within his society, not because his upbringing inculcates generally accepted, but mistaken, moral beliefs.

In what ways are the formative experiences of leaders such as JoJo different from the formative experiences of most others within their society? One answer is that the childhoods of these leaders are deprived or, more strongly, abusive. Indeed, there is some evidence to suggest, for instance, that the villainous leaders Arnold Ludwig calls "the infamous five" had childhoods that might be characterized in this way:

Hitler, Mao, Mussolini, Stalin, and Pol Pot . . . were alienated, estranged, or openly hostile toward their fathers. Joseph Stalin's father, who periodically beat him and his mother, was a violent alcoholic and was eventually killed in a brawl when Stalin was eleven years old. Pol Pot's parents sent him to live with an older brother and his wife, who adopted him when he was six, so his relationship with his parents was distant or resentful at best, despite his brother's claim about the lack of open conflicts with them. Adolph Hitler's father, who died when he was eight, drank heavily and was brutally violent toward his family. Mussolini's father drank too much, womanized, and was intermittently employed. Mao Zedong hated his father for beating him and his brothers and for shaming him in front of others, and constantly bucked his authority.[13]

---

[11] Strawson, "Freedom and Resentment," 52.
[12] Douglas Hicks has pointed out to me that this use of "fortune" does not imply that such circumstances are outside of human control.
[13] Arnold M. Ludwig, *King of the Mountain: The Nature of Political Leadership* (Lexington: University of Kentucky Press, 2002), 152.

Some immoral leaders, we might be inclined to say, received a "special education" in the exercise of power and domination.[14]

But is such an education sufficient to explain the inability of leaders "to know the difference between right and wrong?"[15] It is not at all clear why a deprived or abusive upbringing would cause an agent to hold mistaken beliefs about morality, especially about the *content* of morality. Content mistakes are mistaken beliefs about what types of behavior are morally right and what types of behavior are morally wrong – for example, whether it is right or wrong to engage in acts of false imprisonment, killing, and torture.[16] First, experiencing a deprived or abusive upbringing might equally be said to make one peculiarly aware of the wrongness of this kind of behavior. For example, Bill Clinton's experiences as a child in a troubled home quite possibly served as the source of his empathy for others.

Second, moral education is hardly limited to the relationship between parent and child. This is particularly true in a society in which the values of one's parents are radically different from more general social values. In such a society, even children with deprived or abusive upbringings would be exposed to values that roundly condemn the behavior of their parents. In this respect, the argument that personal deprivation and abuse impedes moral knowledge is weaker than the argument that a bad culture can make a person unable to know the difference between right and wrong. Generally speaking, it is more difficult to distinguish morally right behaviors from morally wrong behaviors in a society in which people are *systematically* mistaken about the content of morality.

However, not all mistaken moral beliefs are about the content of morality. Leaders can also be mistaken about its *scope* – the application of moral rules. These mistakes come in two varieties: mistakes about who is *bound* by moral rules and mistakes about who is *protected* by these

---

[14] Wolf, "Sanity and the Metaphysics of Responsibility," 53.

[15] Wolf, "Sanity and the Metaphysics of Responsibility," 56.

[16] For a discussion of the distinction between content and scope mistakes, see Terry L. Price, *Understanding Ethical Failures in Leadership* (New York: Cambridge University Press, 2006), ch. 1; and Terry L. Price, "Explaining Ethical Failures of Leadership," *Leadership and Organization Development Journal* 21 (2000): 177–84 (reprinted with revisions in *Ethics, the Heart of Leadership*, ed. Joanne B. Ciulla, 2nd ed. [Westport, CT: Praeger, 2004], 129–46).

rules. With respect to the first kind of error, the leader mistakenly believes that he is justified in breaking a moral rule because it does not apply to him at all or, at least, not in his situation. With respect to the second kind of error, the leader mistakenly believes that some individuals do not merit the protection of moral rules.

In some cases, beliefs about who is protected by morality will be connected to beliefs about who is bound by morality. For example, *social contract approaches* to morality generally assume that the protection of morality's requirements extends only to those who have the requisite abilities for being bound by them.[17] For thinkers such as Thomas Hobbes, the rationale for extending the protections of morality to an individual in the first place is to create an incentive for him to adhere to the requirements of morality, thus bringing benefits or preempting harms to other parties to the contract.[18]

One thing social contract theorists have right is that it is too much to ask agents to be bound by the rules of morality when they themselves are not protected by these rules. Membership in the moral community minimally entails the protection of moral requirements. Yet a person's upbringing can give him the impression that he does not merit this kind of protection. To see how a leader with a deprived or abusive background might draw the conclusion that he is not bound by morality, consider Watson's claim that an individual's

cruelty [can be] a response to the shattering abuse he suffered during the process of socialization. The objects of his hatred [are] . . . the 'moral order' that mauled and rejected him . . . He defies the demand for human consideration *because he has been denied this consideration himself.* The mistreatment he received becomes a ground as well as a cause of the mistreatment he gives.[19]

In other words, an abused and deprived person can come to see himself as being outside of the moral community. Given the assumption that he is not a member of the moral community, he is not bound by the rules of morality.

[17] Allen Buchanan, "Justice as Reciprocity versus Subject-Centered Justice," *Philosophy and Public Affairs* 19 (1990): 227–52. See Chapter 5 for a discussion of Buchanan's view in the context of a critique of contractarian moral theories.

[18] Thomas Hobbes, *Leviathan,* ed. Richard Tuck (Cambridge: Cambridge University Press, 1991).

[19] Watson, "Responsibility and the Limits of Evil," 277 (emphasis added).

This assumption, of course, is false. Abused and deprived individuals are genuine members of the moral community, fully meriting its protections. In some cases, they simply fail to recognize their moral worth. And we can certainly understand why they are completely ignorant on this point. We can also understand the conclusion that they might draw from it – namely, that they are not bound by the rules of morality either.

Perhaps, then, leaders with deprived and abusive backgrounds are mistaken about the scope of morality, not its content. In other words, they recognize that behaviors such as torture are prohibited by morality, but they fail to see that these rules apply to them. On this understanding of the immorality of leaders, their ruthlessness and brutality is a reaction to a faulty moral system, one that has subjected them to ruthlessness and brutality. Because the system did not protect them as children, they will not be bound by it as adults.

Still, even this way of understanding why leaders might hold mistaken moral beliefs raises important empirical questions.[20] These questions are not about the causal connection between upbringing and moral ignorance. As we have seen, distinguishing between general knowledge about morality's content and more particularized knowledge about its scope allows us to make this causal connection explicit: deprivation and abuse can cause mistakes about the scope of morality. Rather, the empirical questions raised by this view of morally mistaken leaders are about the deprivation and abuse, or the extent of deprivation and abuse, actually experienced by these leaders.

David Jones, for example, considers the "possibility that the development of Hitler's character was 'arrested' by harmful experiences or conditions within the family over which he had no control."[21] Jones rejects this possibility, however, on the grounds that "most accounts tend to describe Hitler's father as having been gruff, but more bluster than bite. In addition, there is ample evidence . . . that Hitler's mother doted on him and that in general he led a carefree and even pampered existence as a youth."[22]

---

[20] It also fails to show what makes leadership ethics different from ethics more generally – why, that is, leaders in particular seem to have their own code of ethics.

[21] David H. Jones, *Moral Responsibility in the Holocaust: A Study in the Ethics of Character* (New York: Rowman and Littlefield, 1999), 137–38.

[22] Jones, *Moral Responsibility in the Holocaust*, 138.

The gravity of the wrongdoing associated with Hitler and other leaders nevertheless seems to cry out for an explanation, one that makes some appeal to their beliefs about the world and their place in it.[23] Wolf makes the stronger point that all "severely deviant behavior, such as that of a serial murderer or a sadistic dictator, does constitute evidence of a psychological defect in the agent."[24] Still, an analysis of the moral beliefs of these leaders must locate the cause of the "psychological defect" in conditions other than a deprived and abusive childhood. What else could cause this kind of defect in leaders?

### PRIVILEGED LEADERS

It is no doubt true that many leaders came from very rough beginnings. Ludwig says of the Central African Republic's Salah Eddine Ahmed Bokassa that "it seems reasonable to assume that his traumatic childhood must have warped his psyche. His father, who was the local headsman of his tribe, was jailed and then beaten to death by company officials . . . "[25] Shortly thereafter, Bokassa's mother killed herself. Similarly, Manuel Noriega's mother "died a couple of days after he was born, and his father abandoned him when he was five."[26] Ludwig adds that "Saddam Hussein also had a difficult childhood. His father had died before he was born, and his mother essentially abandoned him to be raised by his uncle."[27]

But a deprived or abusive background is hardly necessary for one to become an adult who engages in ruthless and brutal conduct.[28] As Watson notes,

[S]omeone who had a supportive and loving environment as a child, but who was devoted to dominating others, who killed for enjoyment, would not be vicious in the way [the deprived or abused individual who sees himself as being

---

[23] On the issue of moral ignorance, biographer Hugh Trevor-Roper claims that "Hitler was convinced of his own rectitude" (quoted in Ron Rosenbaum, *Explaining Hitler: The Search for the Origins of His Evil* [New York: Random House, 1998], 69).

[24] Wolf, "Sanity and the Metaphysics of Responsibility," 61.

[25] Ludwig, *King of the Mountain*, 143.

[26] Ludwig, *King of the Mountain*, 143.

[27] Ludwig, *King of the Mountain*, 144.

[28] Nor is it sufficient. See, for example, Watson's claim that "the force of [such] example[s] does not depend on a belief in the *inevitability* of the upshot" ("Responsibility and the Limits of Evil," 275).

outside the moral community] is, since he or she could not be seen as striking back at "society"; but such a person could be just *as* vicious. In common parlance, we sometimes call such people "bad apples," a phrase that marks a blank in our understanding. In contrast to [the individual] whose malice is motivated, the conduct of "bad apples" seems inexplicable . . . However, do we not suppose that *something* must have gone wrong in the developmental histories of these individuals, if not in their socialization, then "in them" – in their genes or brains?[29]

In the absence of evidence for deprivation or abuse, Watson moves rather quickly to more *natural* explanations of the behavior of the "bad apples." Here, the suggestion is that the behavior of these individuals can be traced to heredity or neurological abnormalities.

What Watson ignores is that other considerations of *nurture* might explain the behavior of some "bad apples." One alternative appeal to nurture holds that mistaken moral beliefs can also be caused by peculiarly *fortunate* formative circumstances. According to this argument, a particularly privileged upbringing can contribute to a leader's mistaken belief that he is outside of the scope of morality.

Many future leaders, even particularly immoral ones, were raised in rather supportive environments, not under especially difficult, much less deprived and abusive, conditions. For example, Augusto Pinochet of Chile "was the first of six children and his mother's favorite," and Haiti's Jean-Claude Duvalier, or "Baby Doc," was a "spoiled child" whose mother "came up with the clever idea of special tutoring for Jean-Claude with somebody else taking notes while he slept."[30] Indonesia's Sukarno "spent much time during his childhood with his grandmother, who believed he was a saint with supernatural powers."[31]

In fact, the childhoods of many leaders are more than supportive. The upbringings of these future leaders are properly described as *privileged.* Probably no leader was more privileged as a child than Egypt's King Farouk I, who reigned from 1936 to 1952. According to Ludwig, Farouk

grew up in palatial splendor, with nursemaids and servants devoted to making all of his infantile wishes come true. As the only son of his parents, King Faud I

---

[29] Watson, "Responsibility and the Limits of Evil," 277–278.
[30] Ludwig, *King of the Mountain*, 138, 147.
[31] Ludwig, *King of the Mountain*, 150.

and Queen Nazri, and with only two half-sisters, he was the natural heir to the throne . . . Bored by her life in her husband's harem, [Farouk's mother] turned all her attention on her precious son . . . He was pampered, prettified, doted on, fawned on, and indulged by his mother and the other women in the harem . . . At the appropriate age, [his] parents secured a private tutor for him, since attending school with children of lesser rank would be unseemly for a future ruler. To prepare him for wisely ruling his kingdom, his tutor taught him about his divine right to rule and his genealogical connections with the Prophet Muhammad . . . [32]

It is hard to imagine that this kind of environment would have no effect on Farouk's behavior as a child. As we might expect, "[Farouk was] occasionally given to rages when he didn't get his way. He also liked to throw things. One of his favorite games was to smash rare vases or to grab his pet kitten by the tail and toss it around the room."[33]

It is equally hard to imagine that this kind of environment would have no effect on Farouk's behavior as an adult. Again, in keeping with our expectations, "he also loved to play practical jokes, the more embarrassing to people the better."[34] After becoming king at the age of sixteen, Farouk's "gluttony helped him to grow to over 330 pounds. With the reputation of a playboy, he soon became renowned throughout the world for his womanizing, partying, and extravagances."[35] Ultimately, according to the *Encyclopedia of Heads of States and Governments 1900 through 1945*, "His regime was . . . viewed as corrupt, and the King's self-indulgent playboy lifestyle did little to endear him to the Egyptian people. [In 1952] Farouk was forced to abdicate in favor of his infant son."[36] Egypt became a republic a year later.

How do we explain King Farouk's behavior? One relatively straightforward explanation is that he was reared to see himself as outside of the scope of morality. Throughout his childhood, "[a]s the object of all

---

[32] Ludwig, *King of the Mountain*, 129–131.
[33] Ludwig, *King of the Mountain*, 130. Ludwig also notes that one of Saddam Hussein's "favorite amusements was to heat the bar he carried for protection over a fire and then stab an animal in the stomach as it passed by. With practice he became so good at this that he could rip the animal open and almost split it in half with one stroke" (145).
[34] Ludwig, *King of the Mountain*, 130.
[35] Ludwig, *King of the Mountain*, 136–137.
[36] Harris M. Lentz III, *Encyclopedia of Heads of States and Governments, 1900 through 1945* (Jefferson, NC: McFarland and Company, 1999), 139–140.

this attention, he already was preparing for his later role as king . . . "[37] It would not be surprising, then, if he came to believe that generally accepted moral rules applied to him neither as a child nor as an adult, even though these rules applied to others.

Here, unlike leaders whose deprivation and abuse lead them to see themselves as "being beyond the boundaries of moral community,"[38] leaders such as Farouk see themselves as being *above* the moral community, not *beneath* it. In other words, the mistaken moral beliefs in question are fundamentally mistakes about who is bound by its moral requirements. These mistaken moral beliefs are not derived from an assumption on the part of leaders that they are not good enough to be protected by morality. The foundational moral mistake of such leaders is thinking that they are too good, too important, or too special to be subject to the rules. After all, they are not the *subjects*! As we will see, this feature is characteristic of the general moral psychology of leadership.

If the upbringing of leaders is to be used to support a claim of moral ignorance, then the best causal story appeals directly to a particular kind of mistake – about the scope of morality – with a particular kind of childhood cause – privilege. First, identifying the relevant mistake as an error about the scope of morality allows us to firm up the causal connection between childhood experiences and moral ignorance. Compared with mistakes about the content of morality, scope mistakes are much easier to explain by appeals to upbringing.

Second, identifying privilege as the particular childhood cause answers empirical questions that arise in those cases in which deprivation and abuse are absent. Jones's claim that "there is ample evidence . . . that Hitler's mother doted on him and that in general he led a carefree and even pampered existence as a youth"[39] need not detract from efforts to trace "a psychological defect"[40] to his upbringing. In fact, a sense of entitlement, much more than deprivation and abuse, would seem apt to produce the critical moral mistake Jones assigns to Hitler: "Only I and my interests count in the world; everything else is of secondary importance or of no value."[41] This belief

---

[37] Ludwig, *King of the Mountain*, 130.
[38] Watson, "Responsibility and the Limits of Evil," 271.
[39] Jones, *Moral Responsibility in the Holocaust*, 138.
[40] Wolf, "Sanity and the Metaphysics of Responsibility," 61.
[41] Jones, *Moral Responsibility in the Holocaust*, 139.

does not represent the worldview of someone who doubts whether he is good enough to be protected by morality; rather, it is the belief of someone who does not see himself as bound by its rules.

We can similarly explain the mistaken moral beliefs of Wolf's hypothetical leader, JoJo. There is no need to assume that JoJo's moral ignorance is so extensive that he fails to recognize commonly accepted moral rules against false imprisonment, killing, and torture. We need only assume that he is ignorant of the application of these rules to his own behavior. Surely a large part of the explanation for why JoJo thinks that he is not bound by commonly accepted rules is that he was reared to see himself as special. His mistakes of scope can be traced to a particularly privileged childhood, which encouraged him to believe that he deserved exceptions when it came to the application of these rules. Instead of underestimating his moral worth as a person, he overestimated it. Our causal story thus looks no further than to JoJo's father's "special feelings" and the "special education" JoJo received as a child.[42] JoJo was taught that ordinary rules applied only to ordinary people. In effect, he was taught that the rules of morality do not apply to dictators.

This explanation of leaders' mistaken moral beliefs also raises empirical questions – for example, about the prevalence and extent of this kind of privilege. These questions are not unlike the questions that were raised earlier about claims of deprivation and abuse. For some leaders, empirical questions of either kind will be quite easy to answer. With respect to questions about deprivation and abuse, we know that leaders such as Bill Clinton were reared under relatively difficult conditions. Clinton's father died before Clinton was born, and his stepfather was a violent alcoholic.[43] Likewise, we might characterize the upbringing of leaders reared within politically powerful families such as the Kennedys and the Bushes as childhoods of privilege.[44] These early influences lend themselves to an explanation of

---

[42] Wolf, "Sanity and the Metaphysics of Responsibility," 53.

[43] See, for example, Jonathan Alter and Eleanor Clift, "You didn't reveal your pain: Clinton reflects on the turmoil of his childhood," *Newsweek* (March 30, 1992); and Gary Wills, "Clinton's forgotten childhood," *Time* (June 8, 1992).

[44] At the 1988 Democratic National Convention, Ann Richards, state treasurer and soon-to-be governor of Texas, famously said of George H. W. Bush: "Poor George, he can't help it – he was born with a silver foot in his mouth" (Ann Richards, "Transcript

personal exception making on the part of Clinton and some members of the Kennedy family, as well as the public exception making on the part of George W. Bush and his administration.[45]

The problem with these explanations, however, is that neither a deprived and abusive upbringing nor a privileged upbringing is necessary for a leader to believe that he has his own morality. Many leaders, even those notorious for their ethical failings, were reared in surprisingly conventional families. This is especially true for leaders in democratic societies.[46] With respect to most democratic leaders, we can be fairly confident that their childhoods were neither particularly abusive and deprived nor particularly privileged. Richard Nixon, for example, "was raised in a relatively joyless lower-middle-class household located in the small town of Whittier, California."[47] Indeed, according to Ludwig, "Nixon typifies the kind of childhood...commonly found in leaders of established democracies...Like Nixon, the greatest proportion of democratic rulers came from middle-class backgrounds."[48] Why, then, do some of these leaders act as if they have their own code of ethics?

## THE CIRCUMSTANCES OF LEADERSHIP

If the notion of privilege is to play a general role in explaining why leaders have their own moralities, then this notion will have to be extended to include more than family background. To see the promise of this

---

of the keynote address by Ann Richards, the Texas treasurer," *New York Times* [July 19, 1988]).

45 Here, in particular, I have in mind Bush administration statements on the applicability of the Geneva Conventions to prisoners of war in Afghanistan and Iraq, as well as the administration's efforts to keep U.S. soldiers outside the jurisdiction of the International Criminal Court. We might also think about myriad controversies during the Bush presidency over the application of rules to Vice President Dick Cheney and Attorney General Alberto Gonzales.

46 Ludwig, *King of the Mountain,* 165.

47 Ludwig, *King of the Mountain,* 163.

48 Ludwig, *King of the Mountain,* 165. It is worth noting that research does suggest that leaders are generally more privileged than followers. On Bernard Bass's analysis, "taken as a whole, the evidence presented in studies from a wide variety of leadership situations indicated that leaders tend to come from a socioeconomic background that is superior to that of their followers" (Bernard M. Bass, *Bass and Stogdill's Handbook of Leadership: Theory, Research, and Managerial Applications,* 3rd ed. [New York: Free Press, 1990], 71).

approach, notice that even if a leader was reared in a conventional family setting, the experiences that contributed to the development of his moral beliefs may not themselves be conventional. A leader's view of himself and his place in the world may have its roots in sources well beyond parenting and the household. As a result, leadership can have a much broader association with privilege and entitlement.

Ludwig's research makes clear that many future leaders are set apart not by their family backgrounds but rather by the status they achieve within groups as children.[49]

The inclination of these children and youths to show leadership abilities even shows up in how they play games . . . As a teenager, [Indira Gandhi] organized her own party, called the monkey brigade, and recruited many children to it. She drilled them, marched them, and issued orders to them about their duties . . . As a child, Charles de Gaulle . . . often played tin soldiers with his brothers and other relatives [to whom Charles made political and military assignments] . . . Charles always would be the king of France and commander of the French army. Whenever anyone else wanted to trade positions with him, Charles would indignantly protest, 'Never! France is mine!'[50]

Yassir Arafat was like Indira Gandhi and Charles de Gaulle: "By the time [Arafat] was ten years old, [he] was training and drilling all the children in the neighborhood to become Arab guerrilla fighters, and, by the time he was in college, he assumed authority over all aspects of Palestinian students' lives."[51] The tendencies exemplified by these future leaders are indicative of a behavioral characteristic Ludwig refers to as "[b]ureaucratizing the group."[52]

In addition, future leaders exhibit what Ludwig calls "contrariness": they rebel against their parents, confront school officials, defy religious creeds, question the party's authority, and disregard social traditions.[53] Fidel Castro, for example, "organized a group of workers against his father, who owned a sugar plantation, because he felt his father was exploiting them," and "Mao was one of the first students to cut off his pigtail to signify his independence."[54] As a teenager, Mao also

---

[49] For a litany of examples, see Ludwig, *King of the Mountain*, 166.
[50] Ludwig, *King of the Mountain*, 166–167.
[51] Ludwig, *King of the Mountain*, 328.
[52] Ludwig, *King of the Mountain*, 327.
[53] Ludwig, *King of the Mountain*, 330–333.
[54] Ludwig, *King of the Mountain*, 331, 329.

"began shocking his schoolmates by wearing eccentric, outlandish outfits; interrupting boring teachers with nasty remarks; revolting against all forms of discipline; and reveling in his rebelliousness."[55] What was the result of Mao's acts of contrariness? "[H]is fellow students voted him 'student of the year' and elected him secretary to the Student Society."[56]

The leadership behavior exhibited by future leaders such as Castro and Mao thus contrasts sharply with *rule following*. In fact, it is better described as *rule breaking* or, as in the childhoods of Indira Gandhi, de Gaulle, and Arafat, as *rule making*.[57] This feature of leadership is just what we should expect given what it means to *rule*: "to control, guide, direct, exercise sway or influence . . ."[58] It is the *ruled*, not the *rulers*, who are "subjected to control, guidance, or discipline."[59]

The experience of having this kind of status within the group almost certainly affects the way leaders think about themselves and their place in the moral community. After all, the parental, educational, religious, and social values they violate are regularly aligned with morality. There is little reason to question the sincerity of their beliefs about justified rule breaking. Given their particular leadership experiences and, more specifically, the successful nature of these experiences, leaders can come to believe that they have their own code of ethics.

Advocates of this way of thinking about leadership can find easy inspiration in Jean-Jacques Rousseau's (1712–1788) account of the origins of inequality. According to Rousseau's view of the creation of civil society:

They accustomed themselves to assemble before their huts round a large tree; singing and dancing, the true offspring of love and leisure, became the amusement, or rather the occupation, of men and women thus assembled together with nothing else to do. Each one began to consider the rest, and to wish to be considered in turn; and thus a value came to be attached to

55 Ludwig, *King of the Mountain*, 329.
56 Ludwig, *King of the Mountain*, 329.
57 See, for example, E. P. Hollander, *Leaders, Groups, and Influence* (New York: Oxford University Press, 1964).
58 "Rule," def. 1a, *The Oxford English Dictionary*, 2nd ed. (Oxford: Oxford University Press, 1989).
59 "Ruled," def. 1a, *The Oxford English Dictionary*, 2nd ed. (Oxford: Oxford University Press, 1989).

public esteem. Whoever sang or danced best, whoever was the handsomest, the strongest, the most dexterous, or the most eloquent, came to be of most consideration; and this was the first step towards inequality, and at the same time towards vice.[60]

In other words, it was the recognition of differences among individuals that originally gave rise to differences in status. To achieve status, people needed "qualities capable of commanding respect" or, at least, had an "interest... [in appearing] what they really were not."[61] Because status is based on this perception of difference, it ultimately does not matter whether an individual actually has the differentiating qualities or is only *seen* to have the qualities.

In the twentieth century, E. P. Hollander elucidates the notion of status in everyday leadership by appeal to what he calls *idiosyncrasy credit*.[62] Idiosyncrasy credit marks the status of particular individuals within the group and tracks the attainment and maintenance of leadership influence. How do leaders acquire this kind of status?

People do not... possess status as an immutable personal attribute. It rests foremost in the eyes of one or more perceivers; and, whether directly or indirectly, it is these others who in some sense accord status... [A] differentiated perception, with effects upon interpersonal expectancies, conditions a particular behavioral approach to the object person. Since the expectancies applicable to the behavior of this person are in some way special, he is perceived, reacted to, and expected to behave uniquely. Status may thus be considered as some accumulation of positively disposed impressions, residing in the perceptions of relevant others, and having operational significance.[63]

Idiosyncrasy credit can therefore be understood "in terms of the degree to which an individual may deviate from the common expectancies of the group."[64] The perception of differences – specifically, the belief that the leader is somehow special – makes it acceptable for him to behave as if he really is special. Accordingly, "What one member of a group may do with impunity another may not do."[65]

---

[60] Rousseau, *A Discourse on the Origin of Inequality*, in *The Social Contract and Discourses*, trans. G. D. H. Cole (London: J. M. Dent Ltd., 1973), 90.

[61] Rousseau, *A Discourse on the Origin of Inequality*, 95.

[62] Hollander, *Leaders, Groups, and Influence*, 167–169.

[63] Hollander, *Leaders, Groups, and Influence*, 157.

[64] Hollander, *Leaders, Groups, and Influence*, 167.

[65] Hollander, *Leaders, Groups, and Influence*, 205.

Hollander suggests that the differentiated perceptions of some individuals by their group members are a response to two types of behaviors – namely, the exhibition of *conformity* and *competence*.[66] As he puts it, "Within a group framework, two main dimensions appear to be central to this process: the behavior of the object person in accordance with interpersonal expectancies, and his contributions to group goals."[67] By displaying early conformity to the rules and by showing competence with respect to the attainment of group ends, leaders earn idiosyncrasy credit. This credit allows leaders to act as if they have their own morality.

Hollander's experimental research bears him out. In one problem-solving study, initial conformity by a confederate, as well as his special adeptness at "solving" problems for the group, caused group members to acquiesce in the confederate's rule breaking. The confederate was allowed to ignore rules that were designed to regulate the behavior of participants – for example, "by speaking out of prescribed turn, by questioning the utility of majority rule, and by unsupported . . . challenges to the recommendations made by others" – even though the participants created these rules before beginning the problem-solving exercise.[68]

The results of Hollander's experimental research on leader emergence show that the relationship between leadership and rule breaking is much more complicated than we might at first imagine. Individuals who emerge from groups as leaders do not engage in persistent rule breaking or rule making. Rather, these kinds of behavior evolve out of leaders' participation in group processes. For example, it was only when "the confederate began nonconforming *after* the first zone [trials 6–10 of 15] . . . [that] his behavior was accepted with minimal challenge; by the third zone [trials 11–15 of 15], his suggestion that majority rule was faulty yielded a rubber stamping of his choice."[69] As Hollander explains this phenomenon, "conformity serves to maintain or increase status early in interaction, while later, status allows a greater degree of latitude for nonconformity."[70]

[66] Hollander, *Leaders, Groups, and Influence*, ch. 17.
[67] Hollander, *Leaders, Groups, and Influence*, 157.
[68] Hollander, *Leaders, Groups, and Influence*, 199.
[69] Hollander, *Leaders, Groups, and Influence*, 203.
[70] Hollander, *Leaders, Groups, and Influence*, 159.

Matters are more complicated still: a leader "cannot simply continue to redisplay behaviors which were appropriate to the group's earlier expectancies, because the expectancies applicable to him are now altered in keeping with his rising status."[71] So, "while an individual may find it necessary to conform to common group expectancies as he rises to the status of leadership, he may be expected to innovate (and thus, in some sense, nonconform) as a function of his achieved status."[72] In other words, leadership does more than permit rule breaking; it actually *requires* leaders to break the rules.

Why would group members allow, indeed *require*, leaders to do what other group members themselves are not allowed to do? Why, that is, do leaders essentially get to have their own code of ethics? The answer to this question draws our attention to the other type of behavior exhibited by emergent leaders: competence. In Hollander's problem-solving study, subjects consistently gave the confederate high marks on "overall contribution to the group activity."[73] On this criterion, the confederate was ranked first by almost all participants. One plausible explanation of why leaders get to have their own code of ethics, then, appeals to the perceived good that results from allowing leaders to do what other group members are not allowed to do.

This perception also explains why group members demand that leaders break rules that apply more generally to other group members. In the group context, rules themselves have no special moral authority. It is their connection to achievement of group goals that determines whether these rules are binding on group members. So the leader who abides by the rules, despite the fact that so doing conflicts with goal achievement, misidentifies the kind of behaviors necessary to maintain status within the group. Conforming to rules that apply only to others constitutes a display of incompetence by the leader, and this kind of incompetence detracts from the leader's status, potentially returning him to the position of a follower.

Very much in keeping with the more general argument from privilege, Hollander's analysis of leader emergence helps us understand why everyday leaders might act as though they have their own morality.

---

[71] Hollander, *Leaders, Groups, and Influence*, 174.
[72] Hollander, *Leaders, Groups, and Influence*, 188.
[73] Hollander, *Leaders, Groups, and Influence*, 202.

Leadership itself fuels this phenomenon. One defining characteristic of the circumstances of leadership – the conditions in which leaders achieve status and influence within groups – is the expectation of rule breaking and rule making.

Hollander's analysis also gives us clues about potential justifications for the claim that what is right for leaders may be wrong for the rest of us. If Hollander is correct, group members perceive leaders as being relevantly different from other people. Moreover, when leaders break the rules, their behavior is not always at the expense of group members and against their wishes. It is precisely because leaders contribute to group goals that they are both allowed and required to break rules that apply more generally to other group members.

So there may be something to the claim that leaders really do have their own code of ethics. This claim refers to more than a descriptive fact about the behavior of leaders – namely, that they sometimes act as if they are justified in doing what the rest of us should not do. Rather, it is an assertion about a fundamental difference between leaders and the rest of us – that leaders have moral justification for breaking the rules after all. Whether their rule breaking can be justified depends on the possibilities for moral exceptionalism.

## THE POSSIBILITIES FOR MORAL EXCEPTIONALISM

The central question of leadership ethics – *Do the distinctive features of leadership justify rule-breaking behavior?* – derives from the nature of leadership itself. Leadership comes with its own set of rules and requirements. It is in this strong sense that the advocate of moral exceptionalism claims that leadership has its own code of ethics. An examination of the circumstances of leadership thus takes us to the very foundations of morality, suggesting that there may be something morally special about leaders and leadership. If leadership encourages and, moreover, demands rule breaking, moral exceptionalism represents nothing less than an attempt to institute a different morality for leaders.

In contrast, relativist explanations of why leaders act as though they have their own code of ethics do not pose so serious a threat to ordinary morality. If our explanation of unethical leadership behavior were to point to the upbringing of leaders – for instance, whether they grew up in either unfortunate or fortunate conditions – we would not be left with the concern that leadership is a direct challenge to the moral rules. An appeal to family background would help us understand why leaders behave as they do, but the explanation would give us little reason to think that leaders might be justified in doing what others are not allowed to do. It would be an explanation, and little more.[74]

Rule breaking by leaders is of particular concern because it seems to be intrinsic to the process of leadership. We cannot simply abstract away from the nature of leadership, as we might dismiss peculiarities associated with a leader's personality or background. In other words, the moral distinctiveness of leadership cannot be reduced to contingent features of people in leadership positions. Rather, it is central both to the way we think about what it is to be a leader and to the way that leaders think about themselves.

The most straightforward way of addressing the connection between leadership and rule breaking would be to show that a proper understanding of ethics vindicates moral exceptionalism, thereby defending the idea that leadership really is special. As noted at the beginning of this chapter, most moral theories are flexible enough to attend to relevant distinctions in circumstances and, in some cases, to claim that these distinctions ground differential justifications for actors. A contrasting approach to rule-breaking behavior in leadership would show that the correct moral theory does not justify a special code of ethics for leaders. According to this Kantian approach, we need to change the way we think about rule breaking by leaders – at least in everyday contexts. Everyday leaders can no longer act as if they have their own code of ethics.

My conclusion is that we should accept the Kantian approach to rule breaking by everyday leaders. But I make the argument by considering, and ultimately rejecting, particular applications of moral exceptionalism. Each application offers a different distinguishing feature of leaders, circumstances, or relationships that might make moral exceptionalism the correct approach to rule-breaking behavior in everyday leadership.

---

[74] These explanations would have implications for the responsibility of leaders when the conditions of their upbringing make it unreasonable to expect these leaders to conform their behavior to the rules of morality.

Each of the exceptionalist strategies for addressing the connection between leadership and rule breaking falls into one of two categories: *leader-centric* approaches and *group-centric* approaches. Leader-centric approaches appeal to the beliefs, desires, personal goals, or traits of leaders to justify rule-breaking behavior. Group-centric approaches draw on notions of consent, the importance of group ends, the nature of the relationship between leaders and followers, or the greater good to ground the justification of rule breaking.

The next chapter takes up the first exceptionalist attempt to justify rule-breaking behavior in everyday leadership: the amoralist justification. Amoralism comes up as an objection to Kantian ethics, which serves as the theoretical foundation of this book. If amoralism is correct, a leader can be justified in her rule-breaking behavior because the moral rules fail to apply to people when they do not care about morality.

2

# Reason and Amoralism

## THE UNIVERSALITY OF REASON

Are leaders above the law? When people in leadership positions are indicted, found guilty, and sentenced to prison, prosecutors and pundits are quick to remind us that the law applies even to leaders: "The jury has spoken and they have sent an unmistakable message to boardrooms across the country that . . . no matter how rich and powerful you are you have to play by the rules."[1] Proponents of this particular claim usually have in mind the law of the state. But what about the so-called *moral law*? Are leaders also bound by the moral rules that apply to the rest of us?

Immanuel Kant (1724–1804), the primary historical exponent of *deontological ethics*, holds that morality does indeed bind all rational agents, including leaders.[2] According to deontological ethics, what makes an action right or wrong are features of the action itself, not the consequences of the action. So, if Kant is right, leaders cannot justify rule-breaking behavior by appealing to its effects on followers or anyone else for that matter. Reason tells us that some actions simply ought not to be done, and – in this way – it gives us our *duties*. The leader who nonetheless engages in immoral behavior is being unreasonable.

---

[1] Sean M. Berkowitz, director of the Justice Department's Enron Task Force, "Quotation of the Day," *New York Times* (May 26, 2006).

[2] Immanuel Kant, *Groundwork of the Metaphysic of Morals*, trans. H. J. Paton (New York: Harper and Row Publishers, 1964).

38

This is true even of the leader who breaks the rules "because she does not care about morality."

What are our duties on Kant's account? Reason demands that we act only in ways that it would be possible for everyone to act. Although people sometimes mistakenly understand this as "the golden rule," Kant does not say that we should treat others the way we want others to treat us. He holds the stronger view that we should act in ways that we want everyone to act toward everyone else. In other words, it must be possible to *universalize* our actions. Kant puts it this way in the first version of his Categorical Imperative: "Act only on that maxim through which you can at the same time will that it should become a universal law."[3]

The *maxim* of an action is simply a description of what one is trying to do. This description must be used when imagining all others engaging in the action. For example, a leader might think to herself: "I will lie to achieve my ends." A leader's *ends* are the goals for the sake of which she is considering deception, something that the leader sees as having *value*. If it turns out that the leader cannot imagine a world in which all people lie to achieve their ends, then she has a duty not to engage in that behavior. Kant calls the result of a failed attempt at universalization a *contradiction in conception*.[4] The attempt to universalize the action leads to a conceptual impossibility. We cannot even *think* it.

Sometimes when people say, "You can't think that," what they really mean is that it would be morally wrong to think it. Philosophers refer to this set of moral problems in terms of *the ethics of belief*.[5] For example, it has been said that it is wrong to think ill of one's partner – say, that he or she is having an affair.[6] But Kant is not saying that it would be morally wrong to have certain thoughts or to engage in contemplation, even about performing actions that might be morally wrong. He is referring to a stronger kind of impediment to thought. According to Kant, a failure to universalize the maxim of one's actions means that it is *impossible* to imagine a world in which everyone does the wrong action

---

3 Kant, *Groundwork*, 88.
4 Kant, *Groundwork*, 91.
5 See Van A. Harvey, "Is There an Ethics of Belief?" *Journal of Religion* 49 (1969): 41–58.
6 Harvey notes a similar example ("Is There an Ethics of Belief?" 49) from H. H. Price ("Belief and Will," *Aristotelean Society Supplementary Volume* [1954]: 13). See also Jack W. Meiland, "What Ought We to Believe? or The Ethics of Belief Revisited," *American Philosophical Quarterly* 17 (1980): 16.

that one is considering doing. The fact that it cannot even be thought is what makes it morally wrong. Such contradictions in conception give rise to *strict* duties.[7] Under no circumstances is a person permitted to engage in an action that he has a strict duty not to do.

The leader who is about to lie to achieve some end would thus try to imagine a world in which everyone lies to achieve his ends. Kant contends there can be no such world. His reasoning is that lying cannot help us achieve our ends in a world in which everyone uses this strategy. A strategy of deception works only when – and precisely because – people tell the truth for the most part and similarly expect the truth from others. Strategies of deception assume background conditions of honesty. In a world in which no one can be trusted to tell the truth, there is no incentive to tell a lie. The leader who lies to achieve his ends must therefore rely on a system in which everyone else generally tells the truth. In other words, he must make an exception of himself and do what he expects everyone else to refrain from doing. According to Kantian ethics, this is the paradigm of unreasonableness.

Several potential leadership behaviors – when an attempt is made at universalizing them – give rise to contradictions in conception. Promise breaking and cheating are two prominent examples. Promise breaking can sometimes be an effective way for a leader to achieve his ends, but only in a system of widespread promise keeping. If promises were always broken by everyone, this strategy could not be used to advance the leader's ends. The leader would try to make his false promise to encourage an act of cooperation from another, but the potential cooperator would know better. So there would be no incentive to make the false promise in the first place.

Similarly, in a world in which everyone cheats, there is no reason to institute assessments such as exams. The assessments would do nothing more than provide a mechanism for people to cheat in an ultimately doomed attempt to gain a competitive advantage over others. Like the liar, the promise breaker and the cheater must advocate a set of rules that they themselves choose not to follow. What could be more unreasonable than that?

Other kinds of behaviors can be immoral on Kantian ethics despite the fact that an attempt to universalize them does not lead to a

---

[7] Kant, *Groundwork*, 91.

contradiction in conception. This is because, as Kant would put it, they lead to a *contradiction in will*.[8] In these cases, although we can conceive of a world in which everyone acts as we are about to act, we cannot will that there be such a world.

For instance, Kant asks us to think about whether we ought to help others in need.[9] To derive our duties in this case, we should try to conceive of a world in which no one helps anyone. According to Kant, we can imagine such a world. To be sure, it would not be a very attractive place – a world of pure selfishness and a nasty kind of individualism. Nevertheless, thinking of such a world is not impossible in the way that it is impossible to imagine a world of people who lie to achieve their ends. But we cannot will a world in which no one helps anyone. That is, we cannot intend for such a world to exist. For, in a world in which no one helps anyone, no one helps us. Because we need the help of others – no matter what our projects and goals – we must will a world in which people help others. We thus have a duty to help others in need.[10]

Here it is important to recognize the subtlety of Kant's argument. He is not saying that the duty to help others is grounded in the fact that failing to help them now will make it unlikely that they will help us in the future. In other words, the argument is not a *consequentialist* appeal to the importance of reciprocity in human relations. As an advocate of deontological ethics, Kant cannot rely on the *effects* of our actions to determine what duties we have to others. More specifically, he cannot point to the effects that not helping would have on the agent who fails to help others in need.

Rather, the duty to help others is grounded in the inconsistency between two things willed by such an agent – namely, that no one help anyone and that someone help her. It need not even be true that the

---

[8] Kant, *Groundwork*, 91.

[9] Kant, *Groundwork*, 90–91.

[10] In his *Doctrine of Virtue*, Kant writes: "The proof that beneficence is a duty follows from the fact that our self-love cannot be divorced from our need of being loved by others (that is, of receiving help from them when we are in need), so that we make ourselves an end for others. Now our maxim cannot be obligatory for others unless it qualifies as a universal law and so contains the will to make other men our ends too. The happiness of others is, therefore, an end which is also a duty" (adapted from Immanuel Kant, *Doctrine of Virtue: Part II of The Metaphysic of Morals*, trans. Mary J. Gregor [Philadelphia: University of Pennsylvania Press, 1964], 53).

agent expects to need – and, so, must will – the help of others in the *future*. It is enough that the agent wills – as all agents do – that others help her *at some point*, perhaps at some *earlier* point. The universalization – according to which no one helps anyone – applies across time, thereby entailing a contradiction with any past, present, or future instance in which the agent wills the help of another.

Because the duty to help others in need is derived from a contradiction in will, not a contradiction in conception, Kant concludes that it is a *broad* duty, not a strict duty.[11] This means that morality gives us some discretion when it comes to decisions about when to discharge this duty. What kind of discretion does morality allow? Unlike duties not to lie, break promises, or cheat – duties that require conformity under all conditions – the duty to help others in need can be discharged without constant helping behavior. In other words, although there are always people to whom we might offer help, morality does not require that we always be engaged in helping behavior. For one thing, this requirement would be impossible to meet.

Although Kant does not say how regular our helping behavior must be to discharge the duty in question, there is reason to think that Kantians must significantly limit the stringency of the corresponding requirement. The argument for this claim turns on the derivation of broad duties. The duty to help others in need is ultimately grounded in our own ends, the ends we intend – or have intended or will intend – to achieve. The contradiction in will is generated by the fact that we must will the help of others to achieve these ends. Because we will that others help us achieve our ends, we cannot consistently will that no one help anyone. However, if the duty to help others is too strong, so strong that discharging it occupies all our time and energies, it will undermine our capacity to pursue our own ends. And it is our ends that give rise to the duty to help others in the first place.

As Kant puts it:

The law says only that I should sacrifice a part of my well-being to others without hope of requital, because this is a duty; it cannot assign determinate limits to the extent of this sacrifice. These limits will depend, in large part, on what a person's true needs consist of in view of his temperament, and it must be left to each to decide this for himself. For a maxim of promoting

---

[11] Kant, *Groundwork*, 91.

another's happiness at the sacrifice of my own happiness, my true needs, would contradict itself were it made a universal law. Hence this duty is only a *wide* one: since no determinate limits can be assigned to what should be done, the duty has in it a playroom for doing more or less.[12]

Without our ends, there is nothing for the sake of which we must will the help of others and, as a consequence, there would be nothing to prevent us from universalizing non-helping behavior. In other words, there would be no contradiction in willing a world in which no one helps anyone. Therefore, frequent or even occasional helping behavior suffices on Kantian ethics. We must be able to discharge the duties derived from contradictions in will by engaging in the required behaviors without undermining the ends to which we are committed as rational agents.

Broad duties are best exemplified by the general duty to help others in need. This duty lends itself to concrete instantiation in the leadership context. Since Kantian ethics does not specify the exact recipients of our helping behavior, it is up to us – given the circumstances in which we find ourselves – to find ways to discharge the duty. First, the leadership context typically delineates a group of individuals, most often followers, with respect to which the leader can exercise moral discretion to help people in need, thereby discharging her more general duty. The most obvious, but by no means the only, recipients of a leader's helping behavior, then, would be group members.

Second, leadership often brings with it the power and resources to provide this kind of help. What we morally *ought* to do depends – to some extent – on what we are *able* to do, and leaders are certainly able to do what others are often unable, or less able, to do. For example, because of what others have done for them, leaders have a more concrete Kantian duty to mentor followers than do non-leading group members. We know that leaders themselves must have relied on the support of others in their rise to positions of power and influence, because no one is able to achieve success on her own. To the extent that leaders willed the means to their success, they cannot also will a world in which no one provides the support of a mentor. They therefore have a Kantian duty to mentor other potential leaders.[13]

---

[12] Adapted from Kant, *Doctrine of Virtue*, 53–54.
[13] I return to these issues in Chapter 7.

RESPECT FOR RATIONAL AGENCY

Respect for the development of other people – particularly their development as rational, autonomous agents – is central to Kantian ethics. Kant makes this clear in his second version of the Categorical Imperative, which he understands as an alternate formulation of the first version: "Act in such a way that you always treat humanity, whether in your own person or in the person of any other, never simply as a means, but always at the same time as an end."[14] This formulation tells us, first and foremost, that morality prohibits bypassing the rational faculties of agents. Lying and promise breaking are morally wrong, for example, because they are strategies for getting people to do things without appealing to their reason. According to Kant, this tactic treats people as mere instruments or things, not as the rational agents they really are.

Does Kant think that it is wrong for leaders to ask followers to carry out a task because so doing treats followers as means? After all, a central component of leadership is getting people to do things as a means to goal achievement. Properly understood, the second version of the Categorical Imperative does not imply that it is morally wrong to get others to engage in behaviors directed at the achievement of some end. Everyday leadership would not be possible without this kind of influence. As we shall see, getting followers to carry out a task is not the same thing as treating them as a *mere* means.

The notion of *consent* is critical to any discussion of the issue of using people. When followers are given the opportunity to engage their own reason and to make choices to do what leaders ask them to do, they are being treated not as *mere* means but "at the same time as an end." In other words, they are being treated as rational agents with value in themselves. So the behavior of the leader who gets a follower to carry out a task by convincing the follower that it should be done is morally different from the behavior of the leader who uses physical force to make a follower carry out the task. In fact, the use of coercion in the second case may cause us to think that this relationship does not constitute leadership at all. For example, the master–slave relation is

[14] Kant, *Groundwork*, 96.

not a leadership relation precisely because there is nothing consensual about it.

In contrast, the use of consent in the typical leadership case reflects the facts that followers are valuable as rational agents and that they have their own goals. Followers are not simply means to the achievement of the leader's goals. To be sure, leaders – like everyone else – will also see their own goals as having value; otherwise, we would not expect leaders to have these goals. What the second version of the Categorical Imperative tells us is that leaders must also give proper weight to the value of other individuals and, in this case, to the value of followers. Followers are valuable regardless of any contribution they might make to the achievement of the leader's goals. In fact, Kant holds that nothing could exceed the value that rational agents have in themselves. As he puts it, they have "dignity" but no "price."[15]

Questions arise, of course, about how much choice followers must have on Kant's account. Given differences in power between leaders and followers, we will sometimes have reason to doubt whether real choice lies behind follower behavior. In fact, this power differential threatens to undermine consent altogether. Leadership is often about getting people to do things they might not otherwise do. In some cases, followers do not care about whether the end is achieved; in other cases, they would like to see the end achieved but do not particularly care to be the ones to make it happen. How much power, then, can a leader exert on followers to get them to do what he wants them to do?

For instance, is it permissible on a Kantian account to threaten to fire employees if they fail to do as they are directed? French and Raven refer to this kind of ability to punish, sanction, or otherwise impose costs on followers as *coercive* power.[16] They also identify its companion, *reward* power – the ability to make benefits available to followers.[17] As Gary Yukl puts it, reward power includes "the authority to give pay increases, bonuses, or other economic incentives... [and] is derived also from control over other tangible benefits such as a promotion, a better job, a better work schedule, a larger operating

---

[15] Adapted from Kant, *Groundwork*, 102.
[16] John R. P. French Jr. and Bertram Raven, "The Bases of Social Power," in *Studies in Social Power*, ed. Dorwin Cartwright (Ann Arbor, MI: Institute for Social Research, 1959), 157–158.
[17] French and Raven, "The Bases of Social Power," 156–157.

budget, a larger expense account, and status symbols such as a larger office or a reserved parking space."[18] It might seem, then, that the close association between leadership and power undermines the kind of follower choice that is necessary on a Kantian account.

If we accept the principle that an agent's behavior is based on choice only if he is not motivated by good or bad consequences, it will turn out that much of our behavior is not based on choice. This principle makes it impossible to choose to do something for any kind of consequentialist reasons. Now Kant does believe that actions have *moral worth* only if they are done from a sense of duty, not because of the consequences that follow for the agent or anyone else.[19] This understanding of moral worth implies that the agent who behaves morally only because he wants to avoid criticism from his mother or to impress a potential employer gets no moral credit for his behavior. Because his choice to do (what turns out to be) the moral action is independent of the morality of the action – that is, he would have done it anyway (as long as his doing it has the expected effects) – it makes no sense to give him any moral credit for the action.

Yet this certainly does not mean that he did not *choose* to do the action. It means that he chose to do it based on what Kant calls *heteronomous* influences.[20] Although Kant contrasts behavior based on these influences with *autonomous* behavior, which is done out of respect for the moral law, he cannot claim that we are responsible agents only when we act autonomously in this strong sense. This claim would entail our being responsible agents only when we behave morally!

Autonomy is indeed threatened, however, when we act primarily on the rational agency of others. Accordingly, more morally dangerous for the Kantian than French and Raven's coercive power is *referent* power, where a leader's power rests on intense feelings of attraction or identification on the part of followers.[21] In the most morally dangerous cases, followers can identify with the leader to such an extent that they forego their own agency and substitute the agency of the

[18] Yukl, *Leadership in Organizations*, 6th ed. (Upper Saddle River, NJ: Prentice Hall, 2006), 151.
[19] Kant, *Groundwork*, 66.
[20] Kant, *Groundwork*, 108.
[21] French and Raven, "The Bases of Social Power," 161–163. See also Yukl, *Leadership in Organizations*, 153–155.

leader. Leaders who play on the non-rational feelings of followers in this way bypass the rational agency of those they lead. In so doing, they violate the Kantian requirement that they not treat others as mere means. *Charismatic* leaders such as Adolf Hitler, Jim Jones, and Charles Manson relied heavily on referent power in their relationships with followers.[22]

This is not to say, of course, that feelings of respect and loyalty cannot be rational. Leaders are sometimes the objects of these feelings precisely because they have *earned* the respect and loyalty of followers. However, in cases in which the feelings have no justification and leaders draw on these feelings to get followers to act, followers are treated as mere means.[23]

One way to ground follower feeling in rationality is to trace it back to another kind of power identified by French and Raven – namely, *legitimate* power.[24] Leaders have this kind of power in virtue of their positions of leadership. Here we can put a finer point on French and Raven's notion of legitimate power by distinguishing between *de facto* legitimacy and *de jure* legitimacy. *De facto* legitimacy implies only that the leader has power in virtue of his place in the organizational or constitutional structure. Why is he justified in exercising power over followers? It is simply because he is the executive director, the CEO, or the president.

But this kind of power does not get us very far in a Kantian justification of leadership because it makes no appeal to the rational faculties of followers. What we need is *de jure* legitimacy, which implies that power is exercised over followers by *right*. Real legitimacy derives not from a leader's position but rather from followers' consent. The justified exercise of this kind of power requires that followers consent to be in the relation of leadership.

To the extent that legitimate power appeals to the rational agency of followers, it can thus be distinguished from pure referent power. Followers identify with the agency of leaders, but not simply out of

[22] Charles Lindholm, *Charisma* (Cambridge, MA: Basil Blackwell, 1990).
[23] For an opposing view, see Robert C. Solomon, "Ethical Leadership, Emotions, and Trust: Beyond 'Charisma,'" in *Ethics, the Heart of Leadership*, ed. Joanne B. Ciulla, 2nd ed. (Westport, CT: Praeger, 2004), 83–102. Solomon defends the idea of "giving" trust over earning it.
[24] French and Raven, "The Bases of Social Power,"158–161.

feelings of attraction. Instead, they rationally decide to act on the agency of another person. Whatever feelings they have for the leader are grounded in a rational assessment of the relationship.

A similar Kantian justification works for coercive power and reward power. Followers who respond to sanctions and rewards make their choices based on rational assessments of consequences. The utilization of power, then, need not always be understood as treating followers as mere means. When power engages the rational agency of actors, it can be distinguished from behavior such as lying and promise breaking – behaviors that paradigmatically treat others as mere means. Neither lying nor promise breaking leaves room for this kind of rational assessment on the part of the followers to whom a lie is told or for whom a promise is broken. The liar and promise breaker overtakes the rational agency of followers and substitutes the leader's own agency to get them to do what she wants.

This Kantian account of power is not immune to challenge. The most serious objection concedes that the exercise of power by leaders is not analogous to lying and promise breaking. Still, according to this objection, choice does not guarantee respect for the rational agency of followers. Even the person with the proverbial gun to his head has a choice. He can rationally decide to do what he is told to do, or he can choose to be defiant and risk being killed. We nonetheless say that the person in this situation is clearly the object of coercion.

Likewise, so the objection goes, the employee who has "consented" to join an organization and will be fired if she disobeys her supervisor really has no choice. Perhaps this is the only job she could find and, if she loses it, her family is likely to suffer greatly because of her unemployment. She *had* to take this job and she *had* to do what she was told to do. Therefore, according to this objection, the "choice" to accept the authority of a leader or to act in ways that will avoid sanctions is not sufficient for overcoming moral worries about power in the leader-follower relation.

Is there a way to respond to this objection? Sometimes when a person claims that she had "no choice," what she really means is that there were no good choices. This is true of the employee in the situation just described. But would we not blame the employee if she obeys her supervisor and engages in immoral behavior? Imagine, for example, that she is asked to destroy the results of a safety test showing that the company's product is dangerous to consumers? Surely we cannot let her off the moral hook in this case, even if her family's financial security is the reason that she acquiesces in her boss's plan. Destroying the safety test puts the health and lives of others at serious risk.

The fact that we blame this employee, even though she faced a very hard choice, means that her rational agency is not undermined by the hard choice she has to make. Of course, we would also blame the employer for concocting the scheme and for putting the employee in this difficult situation. But there is enough blame to go around.[25] Follower agency is undermined in this kind of case only if it would be unreasonable to expect the follower to do what she morally ought to do. This necessary condition is satisfied in the gun-to-the-head case. It is not satisfied in everyday cases involving the exercise of power.

The prevalence of cases in which followers have no choice is probably exaggerated. What followers have more often are hard choices, sometimes very hard choices. This distinction allows us to embrace the claim "following orders is no excuse," a claim consistently affirmed in the Nuremberg Trials of 1945–1949 and in the trial of Adolf Eichmann in 1961.[26] The Nuremberg Trials prosecuted representative Nazi war criminals, and Eichmann was tried for his role in the Final Solution. Most cases in which leaders exercise their power do not involve followers' being asked to engage in immoral behavior, let alone the kind of behavior carried out by the Nazis. We can nevertheless assess follower agency in everyday cases by asking a hypothetical question: would it be appropriate to blame obedient followers if the followers' behavior actually *were* immoral?[27]

---

[25] See Michael J. Zimmerman, "Moral Responsibility and Ignorance," *Ethics* 107 (1997): 410–426.

[26] See Terry L. Price, "Responsibility," in *Leadership: The Key Concepts*, eds. Antonio Marturano and Jonathan Gosling (London: Routledge, 2008), 143. United States soldiers also claimed they were "just following orders" in the massacre at My Lai. For a discussion, see Jonathan Glover, *Humanity: A Moral History of the Twentieth Century* (New Haven, CT: Yale University Press, 2000), ch. 9.

[27] See Peter Strawson, "Freedom and Resentment," in John Martin Fischer and Mark Ravizza, *Perspectives on Moral Responsibility* (Ithaca, NY: Cornell University Press, 1993), 45–66.

An affirmative answer to this question suggests that the followers' agency has not been undermined by the leader's exercise of power. When the obedience of followers does not constitute any kind of wrongdoing, there is nothing for which to blame them. However, the fact that we would be in a position to blame followers *were* their actions wrong assumes that the followers could be reasonably expected to do otherwise. The fact that the followers could be reasonably expected to do otherwise assumes that the followers had sufficient agency and were not treated as mere means.

What this Kantian analysis of power does not imply is that leaders should be unconcerned with the kinds of choices followers have. Leaders have not succeeded on moral fronts if they simply leave followers with bad choices. Here it is important to notice that the second version of the Categorical Imperative has both a negative and a positive component. The negative component requires that leaders not treat followers as mere means. The positive component requires that leaders act in ways that *promote* the autonomy of followers. As Kant explains, it is not enough "to agree negatively and not positively with humanity as an end in itself."[28]

Promotion of the autonomy of followers requires that leaders help followers to pursue their ends. A precondition for the rational pursuit of ends by followers is the *development* of their autonomy, and the development of autonomy ultimately requires the exercise of choice-making capacities. The positive component of the Categorical Imperative is therefore not satisfied in situations in which followers relinquish their agency to leaders, even though leaders with *de jure* legitimacy do not violate the negative component in these situations. Because followers can hardly develop their autonomy without a rich set of choices, leaders have a duty to create an environment of choice in their organizations so that followers might exercise their skills and talents as rational agents.

As a result of such efforts on the part of leaders, followers will have even greater choice in their professional lives – for example, to pursue other job opportunities and, in some cases, to take on leadership roles themselves. This outcome is a welcome side effect of an environment of choice, and it should serve to ameliorate any remaining

---

[28] Adapted from Kant, *Groundwork*, 98.

concerns about whether Kantian ethics is appropriately sensitive to the importance of follower choice in its analysis of the exercise of power in leadership. When leaders respect the positive component of the Categorical Imperative, there will be little room to question whether followers were coerced into making the choices they must sometimes make.

In the end, the prevalence of real alternatives for followers provides the best proof that their leaders have *de jure* legitimacy. It also supports the strongest kind of follower consent to the exercise of coercive and reward power by leaders. Because an environment of choice gives followers real options, obedience in such an environment implies that followers have other reasons besides avoiding sanctions and acquiring benefits for acting on leaders' directives.

## THE "PROBLEM" OF AMORALISM

As we have seen, Kantian ethics is ultimately grounded in the value of reason. Here, Kant is not referring to particular reasons for action – for example, that doing the right thing would achieve some end, thereby giving us a reason to do it. This feature of the Kantian account therefore creates something of a puzzle: If a leader cannot appeal to particular reasons to justify action, then what is left to ground morality? According to Kant, the answer is that we behave morally, not for the consequences of doing the right thing, but out of respect for the law-like nature of reason: "Since I have robbed the will of every inducement that might arise for it as a consequence of obeying any particular law, nothing is left but the conformity of actions to *universal law as such*, and this alone must serve the will as its principle. That is to say, I ought never to act except in such a way that I can also will that my maxim should become a universal law."[29]

As the reader will have noticed, Kant's answer appeals to the first version of the Categorical Imperative. Morality requires respect for the formal structure of reason itself. The second version of the Categorical Imperative also articulates the kind of respect morality demands that we give to reason. In the second version, the rationality of autonomous agents, not the formal structure of reason, is the focus of our respect.

[29] Kant, *Groundwork*, 70 (emphasis added).

The two versions of the Categorical Imperative imply that leaders – out of respect for reason – should not make exceptions of themselves or use followers as mere instruments to achieve their ends. More than this, they have a duty to advance the rationality of followers.

Kant famously holds that these moral imperatives are categorical in nature.[30] Unlike hypothetical imperatives, categorical imperatives apply unconditionally. Because morality does not rest on any particular reason for action, no change in circumstances could undermine the authority of a categorical imperative. For example, the prohibition on lying applies regardless of the consequences of not lying for the potential liar, or anyone else for that matter.

In contrast, the application of a hypothetical imperative depends importantly on the desires and interests of the actor to whom the imperative applies. The claim that a particular student *should* study for an exam holds only if there is some connection to that student's desires and interests. Specifically, she must care about making a good grade on the exam, or it must plausibly matter for her well-being in some long-term or objective sense. If we learn that the student is planning to drop the course or drop out of college to pursue her music career, we may also be inclined to drop our statement about what she ought to do. The claim that she should study, then, applies only hypothetically; it applies only *if* doing well on the exam is dictated by her other desires and interests.

There is nothing the student can tell us, however, to cancel the authority of a categorical imperative. The prohibition on lying holds regardless of whether telling a lie is consistent with her career plans, even if it is a necessary component of these plans. This absolute prohibition makes no room for a hypothetical *if* statement allowing such an exception. Simply put, she should not tell a lie – period. The universality of the requirement applies to her and everyone else, regardless of their circumstances.

Can reason itself support this kind of universality? Does everyone, including leaders, have a reason to follow the moral rules? Philosophers such as Phillipa Foot have questioned the Kantian view that moral imperatives are categorical in nature, claiming that "the

---

[30] Kant, *Groundwork*, 82.

problem is to find proof for this further feature of moral judgments."[31] In her famous paper "Morality as a System of Hypothetical Imperatives," Foot compares morality to the demands of etiquette or the rules of a club.[32] As Foot points out, etiquette and club rules look categorical in the sense that their normative force does not seem to turn on a connection between meeting these demands and satisfying the desires and interests of the person to whom they allegedly apply.

To take one example, the putative authority of the etiquette *should*-statement "one should put one's napkin in one's lap only after one's hostess has done so" is not diminished in the least by the fact that one would prefer to unfurl one's napkin before the hostess has done so or that one would prefer to leave one's napkin on the table throughout the entire meal. But clearly table manners as such have no independent normative force. They give us reasons to act – they *really* apply to us – only if we care about this sort of thing. Drawing on the claim that the demands of morality are similarly hypothetical in nature, Foot concludes that we have reason to be moral only insofar as we care about morality. In other words, *amoralism* does not entail irrationality. The leader who does not care about morality has no reason to be moral.

The character who sees himself as lacking a reason to be moral is no stranger to the philosophical literature. Historically, he has been given very serious consideration. In Plato's (428–348 BCE) *Republic*, Glaucon defends the view, which must have been common even in the ancient world, that morality does not apply when individuals are immune to the costs of immorality and are no longer dependent upon morality's benefits.[33] To make his case, Glaucon tells Socrates and others the story of the shepherd Gyges, who finds a ring that makes him invisible. On Glaucon's telling, as soon as Gyges realizes what the ring will allow him to do, "he at once arranged to become one of the messengers sent to report to the king. And when he arrived there, he seduced the king's wife, attacked the king with her help, killed him, and took over the kingdom."[34]

---

31  Foot, "Morality as a System of Hypothetical Imperatives," in her *Virtues and Vices and Other Essays in Moral Philosophy* (Oxford: Basil Blackwell, 1978), 160.
32  Foot, "Morality as a System of Hypothetical Imperatives," 160.
33  Plato, *Republic*, trans. G. M. A. Grube (Indianapolis: Hackett Publishing Company, 1992), 35–36 [359d–360b].
34  Plato, *Republic*, 35–36 [360a–b].

Socrates' answer to the question "Why be moral?" is that morality is an intrinsic component of well-being.[35] As such, its value is not dependent upon instrumental punishments and rewards associated with immorality and morality, respectively. That is, morality in the individual does not *lead to* happiness as a separate state of the mind or soul; morality in the individual *is* happiness.

Thomas Hobbes's *Leviathan* also takes up the question that Socrates and his interlocutors addressed.[36] For Hobbes, "Why be moral?" is the question asked by the fool: "The Fool hath said in his heart, there is no such thing as justice; and sometimes also with his tongue, seriously alleging that every man's conservation and contentment being committed to his own care, there could be no reason why every man might not do what he thought conduced thereunto: and therefore also to make, or not make; keep, or not keep covenants, was not against reason when it conduced to one's benefit."[37] In contrast to Socrates, Hobbes takes a markedly instrumentalist approach, responding to the fool that it is "against the reason of his preservation" to break his covenants because the fool needs the support of his confederates and cannot trust his security to the chance that they will remain ignorant of his deception.[38] Even the fool, that is, has a reason to be moral.[39]

Neither of these responses to the basic challenge to morality is entirely successful. For one thing, as Plato's most famous student – Aristotle – objects, we would not count as happy the virtuous person who "suffer[s] the worst evils and misfortunes," no matter how virtuous this person is.[40] According to Aristotle, no one would do so, "except to defend a philosopher's paradox."[41] For another thing, Socrates' view ignores – because it did not have access to – modern developments in anthropology, psychology, and sociology. Some immoral individuals

---

[35] See Plato, *Republic*, pp. 28–31 [352–353] and the book's argumentative appeal to the parts of the state corresponding to the parts of the soul.

[36] Thomas Hobbes, *Leviathan*, ed. Richard Tuck (Cambridge: Cambridge University Press, 1991).

[37] Adapted from Hobbes, *Leviathan*, 101.

[38] Hobbes, *Leviathan*, 103.

[39] See Chapter 3 of this book for a discussion of egoism.

[40] Aristotle, *Nicomachean Ethics*, trans. Terence Irwin (Indianapolis: Hackett Publishing Company, 1985), 8 [1096a1].

[41] Aristotle, *Nicomachean Ethics*, 8 [1096a3].

to whom we put the Socratic question, "How can you sleep at night?" may well offer the reply that they sleep just fine![42] Likewise, Hobbes is probably overly optimistic in his claim that everyone has a reason to be moral in all circumstances. It is simply unbelievable that we can never rely on the supposition that others will remain ignorant of our deceptive or otherwise immoral behaviors.

Foot's analysis of Kantian categorical imperatives thus combines with standard objections to the Socratic and Hobbesian responses, essentially exhausting the possibilities on which one might claim that it is always against reason to be immoral. According to Foot, it is illegitimate to assume that

the amoral man, who agrees that some piece of conduct is immoral but takes no notice of that, is inconsistently disregarding *a rule of conduct* that he has accepted; or again of thinking it inconsistent to desire that others will not do to one what one proposes to do to them. The fact is that the man who rejects morality because he sees no reason to obey its rules can be convicted of *villainy* but not of inconsistency. Nor will his action necessarily be irrational. Irrational actions are those in which a man in some way defeats his own purposes, doing what is calculated to be disadvantageous or to frustrate his ends. Immorality does not *necessarily* involve any such thing.[43]

This conclusion, if true, has important implications for moral theory.

But the implications of Foot's point for everyday leadership ethics are less clear. Even if we concede that not everyone has a reason to be moral, we cannot draw the stronger inference – namely, that for many or most people it is not against reason to be immoral. Determining the extent of the problem of amoralism for everyday leadership ethics will depend on the *moral psychology* behind unethical behavior in everyday life. Accordingly, we should worry about the amoralist only if it turns out that the ordinary culprit of unethical leadership is the leader who does not care about morality.

---

[42] See the discussion of "sleep-test ethics" in Joseph L. Badaracco Jr., *Defining Moments: When Managers Must Choose between Right and Right* (Boston: Harvard Business School Press, 1997), ch. 4.

[43] Foot, "Morality as a System of Hypothetical Imperatives," 161–162 (first two emphases added).

## EXCEPTION MAKING BY LEADERS IN EVERYDAY LIFE

How should we understand the moral psychology of the leader who makes an exception of herself in everyday life? That is, how is she motivated and how does she think about her behavior? This individual is the leader who tells a lie or breaks a promise to advance her ends, but she is also the leader who arrives late for meetings, uses her cell phone as others try to enjoy a public musical performance, takes credit for the work of other employees, breaks the queue at the airline customer-service desk, or drives in the emergency lane in a traffic jam.

A standard Kantian analysis would hold that these everyday behaviors are unethical in the same way that lying and promise breaking are unethical. The liar and the promise breaker cannot universalize their actions, because lying and promise breaking are possible only in a world in which people tell the truth and keep their promises. For Kant, lying and promise breaking are against reason – in fact, *conceptual* contradictions – because lying can have no purpose in a world in which no one can be trusted to tell the truth, and there would be no incentive to make or accept a promise in a world in which no promises are kept.

The parallel argument against lateness concedes that this behavior can be a time-saver for the leader who is late, as it ensures that her time is not wasted waiting for others to arrive for the start of the meeting. But this strategy is morally problematic because it must assume that everyone else arrives on time. Not everyone can engage in this behavior, any more than everyone in a group can be a "free rider" on the work of others.[44] Similarly, there is no musical performance to enjoy if all members of the audience are using their cell phones, there is no queue in a world in which everyone unfailingly moves straight ahead

---

[44] One qualification on this claim: there can be a norm in a culture or organization according to which everyone can be "late." The Peruvian government recently mounted a campaign against the culture of lateness. As it turns out, officials in charge of the campaign were thirty minutes late to its ceremonial beginning, and the Associated Press received its invitation to the ceremony over two hours after it had started! See Leslie Josephs, "Peru trying to turn fashionably late into hopelessly passé," *Raleigh News and Observer* (February 25, 2007); Carla Salazar, "This just in: Peru battles chronic lateness," *The Seattle Times* (March 3, 2007); and Thomas Catan, "Late-running nation told to wake up and start living in English time," *The Times of London* (February 28, 2007).

to the customer-service desk, and there would be no emergency lane if we were to universalize the behavior of leaders who drive in it.

What do these leaders have to say for themselves? What can they be thinking? One response might be that much of this behavior is not unethical after all. The leader's style may be rude or inconvenient for others, but a charge of immorality is surely too strong. However, the apologist's appeal to leadership style wrongly assumes that an action cannot be both rude or inconvenient and, at the same time, immoral. Lateness, free riding, cell phone use, and queue cutting – unlike violations of norms about when to put one's napkin in one's lap or what fork to use – also show a more serious kind of inconsideration that clearly makes them moral issues. This is truer still with violations of the norm against driving in the emergency lane. The lack of consideration shown by the violator of this norm extends not only to the convenience of other drivers but also to the survival of possible victims of an accident that may have caused the traffic delay.

Moral norms can thus coincide with the norms of etiquette, just as they can coincide with legal norms – in fact, the features that make actions such as murder and rape illegal are the same features that make them immoral. Similarly, what makes behaviors rude can also make them unethical, even if we leave open questions about their moral gravity. In these cases, the behaviors in question are immoral in addition to being rude or inconvenient, which is different from being *merely* rude or inconvenient. Honking your horn in a traffic jam is merely rude, and the traffic jam itself is merely inconvenient. The leader who drives in the emergency lane to get to his appointments and is always late when he arrives stands accused of more than having a rude or inconvenient style. On the Kantian account at least, his behavior is also immoral.

In an exercise in moral psychology, however, the most important question is not whether such exception-making behavior is morally wrong, but rather what the individuals who engage in it think about its morality. If it turns out that such behavior is not unethical in the end, then that is all the more reason to doubt that the leaders who engage in it see their behavior as immoral. In other words, there is no need to characterize these individuals as amoralists to explain behavior that might be morally permissible in the first place.

This possibility suggests a related, and more plausible, explanation: perhaps leaders believe that such behavior is not immoral when *they* engage in it.[45] This explanation, too, is importantly different from explanations that appeal to amoralism. We can see this by considering behaviors such as lying and promise breaking. The liar and the promise breaker need not be seen as adopting the amoralist stance and proclaiming, "You be moral and I'll not." Whereas the amoralist sees himself as permanently beyond the scope of morality, the claim of the everyday liar or promise breaker can be that he is justified in telling a lie or breaking a promise *in the circumstances in which he finds himself.* In other words, his rule breaking is discriminating and therefore does not reflect the blanket exemption to morality that characterizes the amoralist stance.

As long as the leader concedes that his justification would equally extend to others similarly situated, his claim that he is justified in making an exception of himself is consistent with the idea that he really does care about morality. Whereas Foot's amoralist avoids the charge of inconsistency because he does not value morality, the everyday unethical leader, whom we can assume does value morality, avoids the inconsistency by claiming that his behavior is not immoral after all. This kind of leader believes he has a justification for his behavior.

In this respect, the everyday leader who makes an exception of himself is like the author of this letter:

**Dear Abby:** I'm writing about cell phone conversations in a public eatery. Granted, most of the time it can be avoided – and should be. However, there are exceptions, and bystanders should not be so judgmental. I'm a hospice nurse and am often on call, yet not at the office. I must take the calls I receive and often work through complex problems on the phone, no matter where we are or what we are doing. Sometimes the calls are quite lengthy; sometimes there are none at all.

Bystanders who might judge my cell phone use do me a great disservice, and likewise people in other professions. My family is just glad that I can go out and enjoy time with them, even when I'm "working." They appreciate what I do and are proud that I give these worthy patients attention when they need

---

[45] See Terry L. Price, *Understanding Ethical Failures in Leadership* (New York: Cambridge University Press, 2006).

it. Please consider that when you are a bystander, you might not know the "rest of the story." – **Nurse in Ada, Okla**[46]

Perhaps the hospice nurse is justified in taking calls when dining out, even though we might still wonder why the *conversation* has to be carried out in public. Engaging in phone calls outside of the dining area would be one way to minimize disruption for other patrons of the restaurant. The problem, however, is that many people hold positions of importance and come to believe that their businesses or legal practices or research labs cannot survive their absence even during a meal. We need only look around at almost any restaurant to see them!

Very few people actually see their own behavior as rude, let alone sufficiently exceptional as to constitute an instance of immorality. For instance, an Associated Press/Ipsos poll on people's views about rudeness found that only 8 percent of respondents admitted that they used their cell phones in a "loud or annoying manner in public . . . in the last few months."[47] However, 85 percent claimed that others do so either frequently (55 percent) or occasionally (30 percent).[48] A compelling explanation for this phenomenon is that when people are thinking about their own cell phone behavior, their attention is focused on the calls they receive, not on any annoying side effects these calls might have for others. When they are thinking about the cell phone behavior of others, they again focus on their own experience of the calls, not on any benefits to the people using their cell phones. Unlike the cell phone user, outsiders have access to one side of a conversation that, in all likelihood, is completely irrelevant to their own lives and what they care about.

This appeal to differences in auditory experience parallels a similar explanation social psychologists use to understand the phenomenon

---

[46] "Dear Abby: Rude cell phone patrons should learn etiquette," *Richmond Times-Dispatch* (November 22, 2005). Interestingly, the author's tone is one that Kurt Eichenwald finds to be common in corporate scandals: "'You don't understand' is a phrase that has emerged in every single one of these cases where you would see people raising warning signals, raising flags early on, and the response of senior management is, 'You don't understand'" (Kurt Eichenwald, "Kurt Eichenwald discusses the collapse of energy giant Enron," *Fresh Air* [January 17, 2002]).

[47] Associated Press/Ipsos, "The decline of American civilization, or at least its manners," October 14, 2005. Available from Polling the Nations (poll.orspub.com).

[48] Associated Press/Ipsos, "The decline of American civilization."

of *actor–observer divergence*.[49] Differences in the visual cues to which we have access can lead actors to see their own behavior as a response to the *situation* and lead observers to see the behavior of these actors as caused by features of the *actors*, features such as their character traits. This explanation of actor–observer divergence highlights the fact that the *situation* is the visual focus of the actors' attention, whereas the *actors* are the visual focus of attention for observers.

Differences in experiences are part of the explanation for the contrast between the way people see their own behavior and the way they see the behavior of others. But these differences fail to give us the whole story. Another difference is in the way people judge *the importance of their own behavior* compared with *the importance of the behavior of others*.[50] Notice that public cell phone use by others would be annoying even if we were privy to both sides of the conversation. Our own behavior tends to matter more to us than the behavior of others. Leaders may be especially susceptible to these divergent attitudes about importance. Their positions often demand that they focus their attention nearly exclusively on the goals they are trying to achieve. This kind of focus cannot help but feed leaders' beliefs about the importance of their goals and the importance of their own behavior in achieving them. Technological advances such as the cell phone and e-mail, which make it possible for leaders to be perpetually involved in their leadership activities, have certainly done little to keep leaders from overestimating their own importance.

One objection to this general way of thinking about exception-making behavior in everyday life is to question the extent to which people are generally committed to standard moral prohibitions such as the prohibition against lying and promise breaking. According to the recent work of Alan Wolfe, "The defining characteristic of the moral philosophy of the Americans can...be described as the principle of moral freedom."[51] For example, Wolfe appeals to the fact that 60 percent of survey respondents agreed that "lying is sometimes

---

[49] Edward E. Jones and Richard E. Nisbett, "The Actor and the Observer: Divergent Perceptions of the Causes of Behavior," in *Attribution: Perceiving the Causes of Behavior*, eds. Edward E. Jones, David E. Kanouse, Harold H. Kelley, Richard E. Nisbett, Stuart Valins, and Barnard Weiner (Morristown, NJ: General Learning Press, 1972), 85.

[50] See my discussion in Chapter 6.

[51] Alan Wolfe, *Moral Freedom* (New York: W. W. Norton and Company, 2001), 195.

necessary, especially to protect someone's feelings,"[52] and he suggests that people "know that one cannot always be honest, but instead of concluding that one can never tell the truth, they try to create informal rules that govern when truth is required and when it is not."[53] In effect, "people [have got] it into their heads that they can determine for themselves when to be honest and when not to be ... "[54]

The idea that people can decide morality for themselves, Wolfe thinks, "is so radical an idea... that it has never had much currency among any but a few of the West's great moral theorists."[55] According to Wolfe, even Kant – autonomy's chief exponent – holds that "we can be autonomous... only to the degree that we act in accord with timeless moral precepts not chosen by us. Moral action, in [Kant's] view, was the exact opposite of a do-as-you-please affair."[56] Wolfe's claim, then, is that people behave as they do in everyday life because they see themselves as free to do as they please. Like the amoralist, they see themselves as free from morality.

On the whole, of course, people's behavior can look relatively amoral. The actions of one person in an everyday moral situation can be quite different from those of another person in the same situation. Behavior can range from what we would expect from an absolute prohibition on lying to what we would expect from no prohibition at all. But it certainly does not follow from this kind of behavioral variety that the individuals in these moral situations see themselves as free from morality. To many individuals, we might assume, their behavior is ultimately the result of their efforts to figure out the right answer, an answer that would also apply to other individuals in the same situation.

In fact, there is something very Kantian about this kind of moral individualism. Of course, Kant himself would not be comfortable with the practice that Wolfe describes this way: "for nearly all of them, when

[52] Wolfe, *Moral Freedom*, 104. Poll conducted by Blum and Weprin Associates, Inc., on March 13–16, 2000 for the *New York Times*, "The inner life of Americans: Views on spirituality, identity, sexuality, anxiety, and more," http://asnic.utexas.edu/~bennett/__310/Wolfe-poll.htm.

[53] Wolfe, *Moral Freedom*, 225.

[54] Wolfe, *Moral Freedom*, 127.

[55] Wolfe, *Moral Freedom*, 200.

[56] Wolfe, *Moral Freedom*, 202.

a moral decision has to be made, they look into themselves – at their own interests, desires, needs, sensibilities, identities, and inclinations – before they choose the right course of action."[57] It is capitulation to these particularities of human nature that often leads to exception making – for instance, to behaviors such as lying to protect someone's feelings. Still, a central feature of Kant's moral philosophy is that individuals have the capacity to determine what morality requires. It is not obvious that the subjects of Wolfe's interviews are engaged in a project any more radical than this.

Moral freedom would imply a view closer to what philosopher Susan Wolf identifies as the existentialist position of Martin Heidegger (1889–1976) and Jean-Paul Sartre (1905–1980): "the belief that one's actions and values are wholly one's own, ultimately unsupportable by anything but one's own unjustifiable choice."[58] If this view were widely held, it would certainly give credence to the amoralist explanation of people's behavior. But is there any reason to attribute Alan Wolfe's radical idea of moral freedom to everyday leaders?

Wolfe's own survey data, which serves as part of the foundation of his argument, gives us reason to think that this attribution would be unwise. Of survey respondents, 47 percent "think what is shown on television today is less moral than American society"; 49 percent agree with the statement, "The growing income gap in America between those at the top and those at the bottom is morally wrong"; and 90 percent "think grown children have a moral responsibility to take care of their parents."[59] These are hardly the views of people who think they are free from morality. Wolfe's analysis thus shows only that people see themselves as free to act on what they believe morality requires or allows, not that they see themselves as free to do as they please when it comes to issues of morality.

## MORAL GROUNDS FOR EXCEPTION MAKING

If the moral psychology behind everyday exception making cannot be characterized in terms of freedom *from* morality, maybe it can be

---

[57] Wolfe, *Moral Freedom*, 196.
[58] Susan Wolf, *Freedom Within Reason* (Oxford: Oxford University Press, 1990), 65.
[59] Blum and Weprin Associates, Inc., "The inner life of Americans."

understood instead in terms of freedom *within* morality.[60] According to this view, exception-making behavior is justified not because morality fails to apply to individuals when they do not care about it, but rather because morality itself makes room for exceptions to moral rules. The justification of rule breaking by leaders thus rests on the remaining prospects for the doctrine of *moral exceptionalism*, which was introduced in the previous chapter.

Here, an examination of moral theories outside the Kantian tradition is in order. Although amoralism fails to ground a radical kind of moral exceptionalism in everyday leadership, the advocate of moral exceptionalism nevertheless has a wealth of additional resources upon which she might draw. In fact, not only amoralism but also most standard moral theories reject the Kantian fascination with rules that apply universally to all rational agents.

Examples include theories that privilege self-interest – thereby allowing leaders to use their own goals and projects to justify exceptional behavior – as well as theories that favor *being* (having particular characteristics) over *doing* (following rules). According to these theories, personal ends or virtues can make a leader truly exceptional. Examples of non-Kantian approaches to morality also include theories that defend rules generated by agreement, where the resulting rules need not apply equally to all parties to the contract. Finally, still other theories hold that the rules of morality are overridden by particular circumstances, group membership, or the greater good. The question, then, is whether any of these moral grounds actually justify rule-breaking behavior by leaders.

Leadership serves as perhaps the best applied context for an examination of the case for moral exceptionalism. As we will see, all of the moral theories have something to contribute to a proper understanding of leadership ethics. For instance, advocates of egoism are right that the pursuit of self-interest can be morally permissible and that leaders need not sacrifice their own personal goals and projects. Advocates of communitarianism are correct that leaders can have special obligations to the group and a morally important connection to

---

[60] My way of putting this point makes obvious appeal to Wolf's *Freedom Within Reason*. However, she is referring to the freedom to act according to the moral rules, whereas I have in mind the freedom to act – albeit for moral reasons – against the moral rules.

group goals, both as a result of the relationship between leaders and followers.

Still, as we will also see, each of these theories presents serious ethical challenges for everyday leaders. Even what would initially seem to be the most compelling argument for exception making by leaders – namely, an appeal to the greater good – does not have an easy case to make for rule-breaking behavior in everyday leadership. Do these difficulties vindicate Kantian opposition to moral exceptionalism? To answer this question, we now consider each of the remaining approaches to the connection between leadership and rule breaking.

# 3

## Power and Self-Interest

The English author Kingsley Amis once proudly said, "I want more than my share before anyone else has had any."[1] Had Amis been a child when he made this statement, it might strike us as humorous. But coming from an adult, Amis's statement seems to reflect a morally deficient attitude.[2] Beneficiaries of successful parenting and socialization appreciate the fact that what is best for them sometimes conflicts with what is best for others. For example, while our interests might be served by eating half the cocktail shrimp ourselves, blaming the manager of another department for something he did not do, or stealing an idea from a subordinate, such behavior certainly does not serve the respective interests of the other people at the party, the falsely accused co-worker down the hall, or the follower who did not get credit for what was rightfully his.

Most of us also learn early on to abide by moral rules to resolve such conflicts of interest when they occur. We morally ought to "share and

---

[1] Quoted in Zachary Leader, *The Life of Kingsley Amis* (New York: Pantheon Books, 2006), 424.

[2] Amis's son Philip says that we should expect nothing less (or more) from a child called "Kingsley" (Leader, *The Life of Kingsley Amis*, 505). Similarly known for his bad behavior, American literary maverick Norman Mailer was born "Norman Kingsley Mailer." His "mother's favorite," Mailer was "[p]ampered and doted on" (Charles McGrath, "Norman Mailer, towering writer with a matching ego, dies at 84," *New York Times* [November 11, 2007]).

share alike," take responsibility for our actions by telling the truth when we have behaved badly, and respect the property – including the intellectual property – of others. One purpose of these rules is to constrain our behavior so that we do not inappropriately privilege our own interests. In fact, without the motivation of self-interest, there is a question as to whether we would need moral rules at all.[3]

Conventional understandings of morality, as well as our day-to-day discussions of ethics, emphasize the tension between acting in self-interest and doing the right thing. As one prosecutor describes a former university president accused of financial malfeasance, "[She] had her own set of rules – if she wanted it, [she] was going to buy it."[4] This approach to evaluating behavior also has a direct parallel in the leadership literature.[5] Here, the overwhelming tendency of scholars is to associate immoral leadership with self-interest and moral leadership with altruism. When leaders fail ethically, selfishness is the obvious culprit. Immoral leaders put their own selfish interests ahead of what is good for group members. The failed CEO jeopardizes stockholder investment for personal gain, the reckless military leader risks the lives of his troops for personal glory, and the disloyal politician turns her back on her party or constituents for political power.[6]

In contrast, according to the standard view in the literature, moral leaders resolve conflicts between self-interest and morality in the right way – namely, by putting collective ends and the interests of group members ahead of their own selfish desires. For example, Ethan Berman, CEO of RiskMetrics, surprisingly requested that the decisions of his company's compensation committee properly reflect

---

[3] But see Chapter 8 for a critical discussion of the collective pursuit of the greater good. See also Allen E. Buchanan, *Ethics, Efficiency, and the Market* (Totowa, NJ: Rowman and Allanheld, 1985), 71–73.

[4] Ralph Blumenthal, Maureen Balleza, and Audrey La, "Ex-university head in Texas on trial for money misuse," *New York Times* (September 17, 2007).

[5] See Robert K. Greenleaf, *Servant Leadership: A Journey into the Nature of Legitimate Power and Greatness* (New York: Paulist Press, 1977); Jane M. Howell and Bruce J. Avolio, "The Ethics of Charismatic Leadership: Submission or Liberation?" *Academy of Management Executive* 6, 2 (1992): 43–54; and Rabindra N. Kanungo and Manuel Mendonca, *Ethical Dimensions of Leadership* (Thousand Oaks, CA: Sage Publications, 1996).

[6] For a critique of this account of ethical failure, see my *Understanding Ethical Failures in Leadership* (New York: Cambridge University Press, 2006).

performance, first, by not increasing his salary and, second, by

looking . . . to broaden its definition of "leaders" beyond employees with significant managerial or financial responsibilities to those who display time and time again the values that we as a company believe in and therefore "lead" others by example not by mandate. That, as much as any other attribute, will create value in the long run.[7]

In other words, Berman recommends putting others first for the sake of the group as a whole.

An alternative approach to ethics – generally referred to as *egoism* – rejects the assumption that there is something morally problematic about the pursuit of self-interest. Egoism holds that people cannot help but act in self-interested ways or, alternatively, that self-interest is the ultimate source of morality. As a result, we cannot reasonably expect people to abide by the moral rules unless it is in their interests to do so.

For most of us, morality and self-interest fit neatly together. In normal circumstances, it serves our interests to follow the moral rules precisely because society cleverly harnesses self-interest to control our behavior. All kinds of bad things can happen to us when we behave immorally. We expose ourselves to the disappointment of our parents and religious leaders, we might lose our jobs or get kicked out of school, and – in the worst cases – we risk a prison sentence aimed at separating us from the rest of society.

By abiding by the moral rules – for example, by telling the truth and keeping our word – we develop a reputation for trustworthiness and demonstrate that we possess those characteristics that make us fit for social cooperation. Given that we depend upon these partnerships with others, it is actually in our interests to play by the moral rules. Although each of us might be better off still if we could simply ignore these constraints and think only about ourselves, rough equality of power guarantees that – as individuals – we cannot be free from the moral rules unless others are free as well. And each of us would certainly be much worse off outside a system of moral rules, where unbridled pursuit of self-interest would be possible for all others.[8]

---

[7] Gretchen Morgenson, "The boss actually said this: pay me less," *New York Times* (December 18, 2005).

[8] See Chapter 5 for a discussion of Thomas Hobbes's version of this view.

This picture of moral motivation is complicated by the power associated with leadership. In virtue of their positions, leaders are able to do things, both good and bad, that other people are typically unable to do. For example, military leaders can send people to the front line or send them home, executives can fire or promote employees, and politicians can bring resources to a neglected area or simply let crime flourish. It is probably an exaggeration to say that power changes everything, but – at the very least – it dramatically affects the incentive structures that push morality and self-interest together.

With enough power, leaders can get away with breaking moral rules that govern the behavior of ordinary people. Does this kind of power give leaders a special justification for rule-breaking behavior? First, if people cannot help but act in self-interested ways, and a leader's power gives him new ways to pursue his self-interest, is it morally acceptable for him to claim that he breaks the moral rules "because he can?" More strongly, if self-interest ultimately grounds morality, is breaking the rules in this situation exactly what he *should* do?

## THE INTERESTS OF THE STRONGER

Plato's *Republic* is often understood as a defense of a particularly inegalitarian form of leadership, albeit one that serves the interests of all members of society.[9] Generally considered to be Plato's most important dialogue, the *Republic* depicts the just state in terms of a strict division of labor. Philosopher kings make up the ruling class, while others do their part as members of the guardian or producer classes. The nature of justice is straightforward: No part of the state is to meddle in the business of the other parts. As Plato puts it, some individuals "are fitted by nature both to engage in philosophy and to rule in a city, while the rest are naturally fitted to leave philosophy alone and follow their leader."[10]

However, Plato's most compelling discussion of the nature of leadership occurs much earlier in this work. Here, Socrates, who is Plato's

---

[9] Plato, *Republic*, trans. G. M. A. Grube (Indianapolis: Hackett Publishing Company, 1992).

[10] Plato, *Republic*, 149 [474b-c]. It is far from clear that this is actually the Platonic view of leadership. For one thing, the *Republic*'s treatment of the state is metaphorical. Socrates turns to a discussion of justice in the state – "justice writ large" (43 [368c-e]) – to understand justice *in the individual*.

teacher and the protagonist of the dialogues, confronts a central challenge to morality – namely, that its demands reflect nothing more
than the interests of those in power. According to this view, morality
is essentially a dressed-up version of control and domination. If this
challenge is correct, questions about whether ethics allows exception
making by leaders blind us to the real moral problem: Leaders are the
people who get to determine what constitutes ethical behavior.

In the *Republic*, this radical challenge to leadership ethics gets its
expression in the words of Thrasymachus, one of Socrates' interlocutors. Thrasymachus claims that rulers make

laws to [their] own advantage ... And they declare what they have made –
what is to their own advantage – to be just for their subjects, and they punish
anyone who goes against this as lawless and unjust. This, then, is what I say
justice is, the same in all cities, the advantage of the established rule. Since the
established rule is surely stronger, anyone who reasons correctly will conclude
that the just is the same everywhere, namely, the advantage of the stronger.[11]

Socrates quickly dismisses this view of justice by showing that – at
least in its current form – the view is contradictory. On the one hand,
it implies that subjects must act in the interests of their rulers. On
the other hand, it implies that subjects must obey the law. Because
rulers are fallible, there will be cases in which they make laws that
are not to their own advantage. In these cases, subjects will have to
choose between obeying the law and acting in the interests of their
rulers. Socrates tells Thrasymachus, "[A]ccording to your account, it
is just to do not only what is to the advantage of the stronger, but
also the opposite, what is not to their advantage."[12] Any view that is
contradictory must be false.

Thrasymachus responds that he really "mean[s] the ruler in the
most precise sense."[13] As such, the leader he has in mind "never
makes errors and unerringly decrees what is best for himself, and this
his subject must do."[14] This qualification eliminates the contradiction
by settling on the *objective*, as opposed to the *subjective*, understanding
of the leader's interest. It also exposes Thrasymachus's view to a different objection from Socrates. According to Socrates, a craft such as

[11] Plato, *Republic*, 15 [338e].
[12] Plato, *Republic*, 15 [330d].
[13] Plato, *Republic*, 17 [341b].
[14] Plato, *Republic*, 17 [341a].

leadership is a kind of knowledge, and "[n]o kind of knowledge seeks or orders what is advantageous to itself... but what is advantageous to the weaker, which is subject to it."[15] For, given its nature as a craft, leadership is "complete or perfect,"[16] not deficient in any way.

Socrates claims that even the shepherd, insofar as he is exercising the craft of shepherding, looks out for the good of his flock. When the shepherd's attention turns to fattening the sheep for slaughter or sale, he is better described as "a guest about to be entertained at a feast" or "a money-maker," not a shepherd.[17] Socrates' thesis is that all forms of leadership are similar to shepherding in this respect. Leadership, like shepherding, is not beneficial in itself for the person who exercises the craft. For this reason, there must be other incentives to lead – either rewards or punishments. Bad people exercise leadership for money and honor, whereas good people do it to avoid the gravest kind of punishment: "to be ruled by someone worse than oneself."[18]

One problem with the Socratic response to Thrasymachus's account of justice is that it mistakes, or ignores, the main point of the account – namely, that what we take to be morality is nothing but a sham. To use Kantian language to make a very un-Kantian point, morality can be reduced to hypothetical imperatives that have as their ends the advancement of the interests of the stronger. In this respect, Thrasymachus's argument anticipates Jean-Jacques Rousseau's complaint against the institution of property. Rousseau charges that property rules were put in place to protect the interests of those who had the most to lose. Instead of opposing these rules, individuals without property "ran headlong into their chains."[19]

Thrasymachus's account of justice is similarly *descriptive*. He need not be understood as saying that we really ought – in a moral sense – to do what leaders command that we do, any more than Rousseau is saying that oppressive property rules really ought to be respected. But Thrasymachus's reductionism does imply that, in actuality, there are no real moral reasons. In this respect, Thrasymachus's account can

---

[15] Plato, *Republic*, 19 [342d].
[16] Plato, *Republic*, 18 [341e].
[17] Plato, *Republic*, 21 [345d].
[18] Plato, *Republic*, 23 [347c].
[19] Rousseau, *A Discourse on the Origin of Inequality*, in *The Social Contract and Discourses*, trans. G. D. H. Cole (London: J. M. Dent Ltd., 1973), 99.

be read as closer to the nineteenth-century argument of Karl Marx (1818–1883) than to the eighteenth-century argument of Rousseau.[20] Marx contends that there would be no need for morality in a socialist society, whereas Rousseau aims to replace the current, deficient morality with the authentic morality captured by his version of the social contract.[21] For both Thrasymachus and Marx, moral rules embody nothing more than class interests.

Understood as a purely descriptive analysis of morality, Thrasymachus's view raises the following question: How can we use moral language to criticize our leaders? On Thrasymachus's view, we could appeal to morality to condemn social and political arrangements that do not serve the interests of the stronger. For example, a critic might say, "That constitution is immoral because it does not advance the interests of our leaders." But surely our moral language is much more versatile and normatively potent than this. For one thing, we can and do use it to assess social and political arrangements that are in the interests of those who perpetuate them. Although monarchy is in the interests of monarchs, and slavery is in the interests of slaveholders, their opponents criticize these institutions on moral grounds. This kind of criticism would be impossible if the requirements of morality merely track whatever serves the interests of those in power.

To this argument, one might reply that monarchy and slavery make everyone – including monarchs and slaveholders – worse off, in which case, the dissolution of monarchy and the eradication of slavery are really in the interests of monarchs and slaveholders after all. Whatever the promise of this suggestion, it fails to vindicate Thrasymachus's descriptive analysis of morality. Monarchy and slavery are hardly subject to moral critique *because* they threaten the interests of the stronger. Rather it is precisely because these institutions threaten the interests of the weaker that they deserve criticism from a moral point of view.

As we have seen, Socrates recasts Thrasymachus's view as a *normative* analysis of morality. He thus takes Thrasymachus to be saying that leaders morally ought to pursue their own interests, not that what we

---

[20] Marx, *Economic and Philosophic Manuscripts* in *Selected Writings*, ed. Lawrence H. Simon (Indianapolis: Hackett Publishing Company, 1994), 90–91.

[21] Jean-Jacques Rousseau, *The Social Contract*, in *The Social Contract and Discourses*, trans. G. D. H. Cole (London: J. M. Dent Ltd., 1973).

think of as morality is in fact thin cover for the pursuit of self-interest by leaders. In many ways, the normative analysis that Socrates attributes to Thrasymachus is a more problematic challenge for leadership ethics. Proof of its intractability is in the fact that thinkers from Socrates to contemporary leadership scholars tend to opt for a definitional response to this challenge. Socrates makes concern for the interests of others part of the definition of the "true ruler," and both Aristotle and Niccolò Machiavelli use it to distinguish kings from tyrants.[22]

James MacGregor Burns's theory of transforming leadership, easily the most influential normative account of leadership in the twentieth century, also takes this approach:

> I *define* leadership as leaders inducing followers to act for certain goals that represent the values and the motivations – the wants and needs, the aspirations and expectations – *of both leaders and followers*...Leadership, unlike naked power-wielding, is thus inseparable from followers' needs and goals. The essence of the leader-follower relation is the interaction of persons with different levels of motivations and of power potential, including skill, in pursuit of a common or at least joint purpose.[23]

According to Burns, leadership is one thing, and power wielding is another. Power wielders, unlike leaders, are motivated to achieve their own purposes, "*whether or not these are also the goals of the respondents.*"[24]

The definitional approach to leadership ethics ultimately fails because it assumes away the problem it is meant to solve.[25] Instead of addressing the point at issue – whether leaders ought to act in their

---

[22] Plato, *Republic*, 21 [345d-e]; Aristotle, *The Politics*, trans. T. A. Sinclair (New York: Penguin Books, 1981), 189–190 [1279a28–1279a30]; and Machiavelli, *Discourses on the First Ten Books of Titius Livius*, in *Classics of Moral and Political Theory*, ed. Michael L. Morgan, 3rd ed. (Indianapolis: Hackett Publishing Company, 2001), 472. See Terry L. Price, "Philosophical Approaches to Leadership," in *Leadership: The Key Concepts*, eds. Antonio Marturano and Jonathan Gosling (London: Routledge, 2008), 126.

[23] James MacGregor Burns, *Leadership* (New York: Harper and Row Publishers, 1978), 19 (first emphasis added). See Chapter 8 for my extended discussion of transforming and transformational leadership.

[24] Burns, *Leadership*, 18. See Price, "Philosophical Approaches to Leadership," 126–127.

[25] See Terry L. Price, "Transforming Leadership," in *Leadership: The Key Concepts*, eds. Antonio Marturano and Jonathan Gosling (London: Routledge, 2008), 173. For discussions of definitional approaches to leadership ethics, see Joanne B. Ciulla, "Leadership Ethics: Mapping the Territory," *Business Ethics Quarterly* 5 (1995): 5–24; and Barbara Kellerman, *Bad Leadership: What It Is, How It Happens, Why It Matters* (Boston: Harvard Business School Press, 2004), 11–14.

self-interest – this approach simply assumes that people who advance their own interests are not exercising leadership. We are left with the very question we wanted to answer: are *these individuals*, no matter what we call them, justified in their self-interested, rule-breaking behavior? These individuals present the same moral problems even if we say that they are not leaders in the truest sense or that they are mere tyrants or power wielders.

Definitional strategies of this kind simply rename ethical and unethical versions of leadership, which does nothing to eradicate real ethical problems.[26] The refusal of Socrates and contemporary leadership scholars to think about self-interested behavior in terms of leadership is tantamount to ignoring the fact that people ostensibly in leadership roles regularly behave in self-interested ways. So our discussion of the nature of leadership has left us with all of our original questions about the connection between leadership and self-interest. Does the power that leaders have in their positions of leadership give them special justification to act on self-interest? Does having this kind of power mean that leaders are justified in pursuing their self-interest because they can? More importantly, can self-interest ground a moral justification for rule-breaking behavior by leaders?

## MUST LEADERS ACT IN SELF-INTEREST?

One argument for the claim that leaders are justified in acting on self-interest holds that people are necessarily selfish by nature. *Psychological egoism* is the view that people always act in ways that they think will advance their self-interest. As such, it is a descriptive view of human psychology and behavior: agents are motivated exclusively by what they take to be their self-interest.

The subjective qualifiers – "in ways they think" and "what they take" – are necessary if psychological egoism is to be at all plausible as a descriptive view of motivation. Given that people often do not know what would be in their objective self-interest, this view cannot

---

[26] See Price, *Understanding Ethical Failures in Leadership*, ch. 5, for the argument that there are also reasons to worry about the morality of "ethical" versions such as "authentic transformational leadership" (Bernard M. Bass and Paul Steidlmeier, "Ethics, Character, and Authentic Transformational Leadership Behavior," *Leadership Quarterly* 10 [1999]: 181–217).

hold that they are always motivated by it. For example, the leader who is assassinated at a rally can hardly be said to have been motivated to attend the rally by the fact that doing so would actually advance his self-interest. He may have thought it was in his self-interest, but clearly it was not.

The claim that people always act in their subjective self-interest nonetheless has very important implications for leadership ethics, and for morality more generally. If it is a psychological fact about moral agents that they cannot help but act in ways that they think will advance their self-interest, then we are in no position to expect them to do otherwise. A central principle of morality is "ought implies can." It must be possible for an agent to do what he morally ought to do.[27] According to the doctrine of psychological egoism, agents are motivated exclusively by self-interest and therefore cannot be expected to have altered their behavior in the past or to act differently in the present. Moreover, they have no control over this feature of their psychology. So we cannot hold them responsible for their incapacity or the behavior that results from it.

By some accounts, Abraham Lincoln was an advocate of psychological egoism:

Mr. Lincoln once remarked to a fellow-passenger on an old-time mud-coach that all men were prompted by selfishness in doing good. His fellow-passenger was antagonizing this position when they were passing over a corduroy bridge that spanned a slough. As they crossed this bridge they espied an old razor-backed sow on the bank making a terrible noise because her pigs had got into the slough and were in danger of drowning. As the old coach began to climb the hill, Mr. Lincoln called out, "Driver, can't you stop just a moment?" Then Mr. Lincoln jumped out, ran back and lifted the little pigs out of the mud and water and placed them on the bank. When he returned, his companion remarked: "Now Abe, where does selfishness come in on this little episode?" "Why, bless your soul Ed, that was the very essence of selfishness. I should have

---

[27] One exception to this principle is that we sometimes say that an agent ought to do something, even though he is incapable of doing it at the time, because – at some earlier point in time – he acted in ways to put himself in this position of incapacity. In other words, he ought to have behaved differently in the past, and his failure to do so allows us to hold him accountable for not doing what he ought in his current situation – despite the fact that he cannot now do it.

had no peace of mind all day had I gone on and left that suffering old sow worrying over those pigs. I did it to get peace of mind, don't you see?"[28]

Lincoln professes that his concern for the pigs ultimately derives from self-interest. In the absence of negative effects on his own mental state, he would have let the pigs drown in the mud, or so Lincoln would have us believe.

Joel Feinberg doubts that causation can work in this direction as part of an explanation of benevolent behavior. According to Feinberg, "If Lincoln had cared not a whit for the welfare of the little pigs and their 'suffering' mother, but only for his own 'peace of mind,' it would be difficult to explain how he could have derived pleasure from helping them. The very fact that he did feel satisfaction as a result of helping the pigs presupposes that he had a preexisting desire for something other than his own happiness."[29] There must be some psychological connection between the plight of the pigs and the pleasure Lincoln derives from helping them; otherwise, we cannot explain why his beneficence causes him to experience pleasure.

But it is not quite correct to say that Lincoln "*could not have* achieved peace of mind from rescuing the pigs, had he not had a prior concern – on which his peace of mind depended – for the welfare of the pigs for its own sake."[30] Lincoln's natural constitution, his upbringing, or some particular event in his life might also explain why he reacted as he did to the suffering of the pigs. One test for whether Lincoln really cared about the welfare of the pigs for their own sake would be to ask whether he would have wanted to be told that the pigs were drowning had he not been able to hear the squeals of their mother. Because an answer from Lincoln along the lines of "No, then I would have felt the need to save them" makes sense to us, we cannot assume that his psychological connection to the plight of the pigs ends with a concern for their welfare.

---

[28] Quoted in Joel Feinberg, "Psychological Egoism," in *Reason and Responsibility: Readings in Some Basic Problems of Philosophy*, eds. Joel Feinberg and Russ Shafer-Landau, 10th ed. (Belmont, CA: Wadsworth Publishing, 1999), 497.

[29] Feinberg, "Psychological Egoism," 497.

[30] Feinberg, "Psychological Egoism," 497 (emphasis added).

Lincoln's "disinterested benevolence"[31] would make particular sense to us if we learn that he was born with unnaturally burdensome sensibilities for animals, that his upbringing caused him to have strong feelings of guilt in situations of this kind, or even something as simple as that the mother's cry for her young reminded Lincoln of his own mother's cry. If some such story were true of Lincoln, then his psychological connection to the plight of the pigs might end not in a concern for the welfare of the pigs for their own sake, but rather in a concern for his own happiness. His detached benevolence would make him a psychological egoist after all.

Notice, however, that explanations of this kind make the motivation for Lincoln's behavior akin to an irrational obsession.[32] In these cases, he does not endorse benevolence toward the pigs because he finds their welfare intrinsically valuable; indeed, he engages in the behavior despite his own conflicting views about value. Being made aware of their plight, he is overcome with an oppressive form of sympathy, a socialized guilt response, or transferred feelings that would be rationally directed only toward his own mother. This is why – as the psychological egoist's explanation must assume – Lincoln can say that he would rather not know about the suffering of the pigs in the first place.

Fortunately, the critique of psychological egoism does not have to show that Lincoln – or anyone else for that matter – gets pleasure from benevolent actions only because "he has previously desired the good of some person, or animal, or mankind at large."[33] All the critique has to show is that behavior is *sometimes* motivated by something other than an agent's self-interest. An alternative way to examine the thesis of psychological egoism, then, is to see it as "a matter for a psychologist (not for a philosopher) to decide; and the psychologist himself can only decide *empirically*, i.e., by making ... observations."[34]

Experimenters in social psychology have done exactly this. In fact, they have found support for something stronger than the claim that behavior is *sometimes* grounded in motivations other than self-interest. For example, Dale T. Miller and Rebecca K. Ratner have demonstrated

---

[31] Feinberg, "Psychological Egoism," 496.
[32] See Price, *Understanding Ethical Failures in Leadership*, 34–35.
[33] Feinberg, "Psychological Egoism," 497.
[34] Feinberg, "Psychological Egoism," 502.

in a series of studies that "people's belief in the power of self-interest leads them to overestimate its impact on the attitudes and behavior of others."[35] Subjects overestimate the effect that financial incentives will have on people's willingness to give blood; the effect that gender will have on people's attitudes with respect to abortion policy; the effect that class year will have on student views of a campus alcohol policy aimed at underage drinking; and the effect that smoking preferences will have on people's views on cigarette taxes, advertising bans, and public-smoking bans.[36] Miller and Ratner's work thus suggests that self-interest is not a good predictor of human behavior. In fact, it was only in the smoking study that Miller and Ratner found any self-interest effect at all, and even here – as in the other studies – subjects overestimated the impact that self-interest would have on the attitudes of respondents.[37]

The fact that the self-interest effect was confirmed only in the smoking study is interesting for two reasons. First, among all the self-interested motivations that Miller and Ratner consider, the desire to smoke is the one most easily identified as an irrational obsession. Because of the strongly addictive nature of nicotine, many people continue to smoke despite their own views about the overall value of the activity. There is a sense in which people *want* a cigarette when they smoke. However, as Harry Frankfurt would put it, smokers are afflicted with a lower-order desire that conflicts with their higher-order desire not to want the cigarette.[38]

This feature of the focal behavior in the smoking study leads to a second interesting distinction. Smoking, like many other obsessions and addictions, is clearly not a self-interested behavior! So, as it turns out, Miller and Ratner get a self-interest effect with respect to attitudes toward policies that are *not* in the objective interest of smokers, and there is no self-interest effect when it comes to attitudes toward policies that *are* in people's interests, such as healthcare plans that cover abortion costs for women.

---

35 D. T. Miller and R. K. Ratner, "Disparity Between the Actual and Assumed Power of Self-Interest," *Journal of Personality and Social Psychology* 74 (1998): 53.
36 Miller and Ratner, "Assumed Power of Self-Interest," 53–62.
37 Miller and Ratner, "Assumed Power of Self-Interest," 58.
38 Harry Frankfurt, "Freedom of the Will and the Concept of a Person," *Journal of Philosophy* 68 (1971): 5–20.

This set of findings raises an important question about what counts as self-interested behavior. Miller and Ratner deal with this question in this way:

> On what authority, a skeptic might ask, can it be claimed that it is more in the interest of women than men for there to be the implementation of a health plan that provides for abortion coverage? Could it not be argued that men have as great, and perhaps even greater, stake in this policy than women? Possibly, but we did not rely on our own judgment in deciding who was more vested. Instead, we asked the respondents themselves. The overwhelming opinion of the respondents was that women would be more personally affected by the policy than would men. It was on the basis of this subjective classification, then, and not on an objective classification, that we deemed women to be more vested than men. Moreover, this seems the most appropriate strategy because presumably it is perceived, not objectively defined, self-interest that theorists have in mind when they speak of the power of self-interest.[39]

Like the advocate of psychological egoism, then, Miller and Ratner understand self-interest in terms of what people *think* will advance their interests.

Our theories of self-interest are actually more subjective than these authors propose. Considering that smoking behavior does not lend itself to either an objective or a subjective classification of *self-interest* – smoking really is bad for smokers, *and* they know it – the explanatory theory people must have in mind when they appeal to the "self-interested" behavior of smokers is rather that people are inclined to act in ways that satisfy their desires. The subjectivity in question, then, is the subjectivity of desire, not the subjectivity of perceived self-interest.

Once we isolate the central assumption of the psychological egoist, it is easier to locate the main weakness of the view. To a large extent, the appeal of psychological egoism rests on confusion about what it means to say that people always act on their desires.[40] Whenever I act,

---

[39] Miller and Ratner, "Assumed Power of Self-Interest," 60. Admittedly, one might suggest that abortion is not in the interest of women either. But this is not the standard line of objection to abortion. According to the standard line, abortion is wrong because it harms an innocent human being, and the mother who resorts to having an abortion is being "selfish."

[40] See Feinberg, "Psychological Egoism," 495–496, 503–504; and Patricia H. Werhane, *Moral Imagination and Management Decision-Making* (New York: Oxford University Press, 1999), 18–19.

I act on my own desires; otherwise, it would not be considered action. Mere bodily motion, for instance, is not sufficient for genuine human agency. If my body moves in a way unconnected to my desires – say, because I am in the grips of a seizure – it is not right to talk about how I was *acting*.

So what follows from the fact that all action is based on our desires? Certainly not that all action is based on *selfish* desires – that is, that all action has the actor's pleasure or satisfaction as its purpose. If I believe that justice is a good thing or that group goals ought to be achieved, then I am likely to have desires that correspond to my beliefs and commitments. Moreover, these desires will clearly be *my* desires. However, to infer from this that behavior in the service of justice or group goals is self-regarding, much less selfish – both straightforward implications of psychological egoism – would be to stretch the language of self-interest beyond recognition and, as a consequence, blur morally important motivational and behavioral distinctions.[41]

In leadership ethics, psychological egoism takes a more plausible form. This variation holds not that *ordinary people* always act on desires for pleasure or satisfaction but that *leaders* are particularly inclined to do so. For most of us, the consequences of immorality significantly constrain our ability to act on selfish desires. But given power differentials between leaders and followers, leaders are sometimes immune – or believe they are immune – to the consequences of immorality. The possibility of getting away with rule-breaking behavior thus makes

---

[41] Psychological findings that support these distinctions suggest that "people often care more about the fairness of the procedures they are subjected to than about the material outcomes these procedures yield, that they often care more about their group's collective outcomes than about their personal outcomes, and that their attitudes toward public policies are often shaped more by their values and ideologies than by the impact these policies have on their material well-being" (Miller and Ratner, "Assumed Power of Self-Interest, 53). Miller and Ratner cite T. R. Tyler, "Justice, Self-Interest, and the Legitimacy of Legal and Political Authority," in *Beyond Self-Interest*, ed. J. J. Mansbridge (Chicago: Chicago University Press, 1990), 171–179; R. M. Dawes, A. J. C. van de Kragt, and J. M. Orbell, "Not Me or Thee but We: The Importance of Group Identity in Eliciting Cooperation in Dilemma Situations: Experimental Manipulations," *Acta Psychologica* 68 (1988): 83–97; D. O. Sears and C. L. Funk, "Self-Interest in Americans' Political Opinions," in *Beyond Self-Interest*, 147–170; and D. O. Sears and C. L. Funk, "The Role of Self-Interest in Social and Political Attitudes," in *Advances in Experimental Social Psychology*, ed. M. P. Zanna, Vol. 24 (New York: Academic Press, 1991), 2–91.

the satisfaction of selfish desires seem significantly more compatible with self-interest.

Dean Ludwig and Clinton Longenecker convincingly develop this line of argument, suggesting that success itself serves to undermine a leader's motivational ties to morality.[42] According to these authors, the "by-products of success" include "loss of strategic focus, privileged access [to information, people, or objects], [unconstrained] control of resources, and inflated belief in ability to manipulate outcomes."[43] In short, success encourages leaders to act on their selfish desires simply "because they can." Bill Clinton explains his affair with intern Monica Lewinsky in these terms: "I think I did something for the worst possible reason – just because I could."[44] Once successful, leaders such as Clinton are no longer bound by the same rules that bind the rest of us.

To make their case, Ludwig and Longenecker apply an egoistic behavioral analysis to a biblical story about King David.[45] In the story, David takes sexual advantage of Bathsheba, and Bathsheba becomes pregnant with David's child. As part of a cover-up, David calls Uriah, Bathsheba's husband, home from battle in the hope that Uriah will have sexual relations with Bathsheba and later draw the conclusion that Bathsheba's child is his own. But the cover-up fails because Uriah refuses to go to bed with Bathsheba out of loyalty to the soldiers still in battle. In response to the failed cover-up, David sends Uriah to the front of the battle where he is killed.

David is ultimately found out when "the prophet Nathan (who was in this case the equivalent of a modern day whistle-blower) ... led David to realize that his cover-up had been a failure."[46] David's central mistake was to believe that satisfaction of his selfish desires would be in his self-interest. Ludwig and Longenecker conclude that today's leaders similarly assume that they will not get caught satisfying their selfish desires. As a result, leaders mistakenly believe that it is in their self-interest to break the moral rules.

[42] Dean C. Ludwig and Clinton O. Longenecker, "The Bathsheba Syndrome: The Ethical Failure of Successful Leaders," *Journal of Business Ethics* 12 (1993): 265–273.

[43] Ludwig and Longenecker, "Bathsheba Syndrome," 269.

[44] Howard Kurtz, "Bill Clinton's very personal reflections: In '60 Minutes' interview, ex-president calls affair 'terrible moral error,'" *Washington Post* (June 17, 2004).

[45] Ludwig and Longenecker, "Bathsheba Syndrome," 268–269.

[46] Ludwig and Longenecker, "Bathsheba Syndrome," 271.

According to this version of psychological egoism, solutions to immoral leadership must reinforce the idea that a leader's self-interest really is aligned with the moral rules, not with rule-breaking behavior aimed at satisfying selfish desires. Perhaps this is what Clinton had not learned as the governor of Arkansas and, unfortunately, had to learn the hard way through congressional impeachment proceedings. It would also explain why he failed to predict the impact that the affair with Lewinsky and its aftermath would have on his own self-interest – both personal and political self-interest. Some would say that his presidential legacy suffers – and will continue to suffer – as a result of the indiscretion and his efforts to cover it up.

Does this explanation justify Clinton's behavior? No. There is clearly an important difference between saying that Clinton had the affair and lied about it because *he could* and saying that he behaved as he did because *he had to.* Descriptive theses about human behavior have implications for an assessment of leadership ethics only if their truth makes it impossible or unreasonably difficult to expect leaders to do what morality requires – that is, only if the behavior in question is the necessary result of psychological facts about the way leaders are motivated. Clinton's behavior does not meet this threshold. He himself admits that power constitutes "just about the most morally indefensible reason that anybody could have for doing anything."[47] Clinton's words imply that *he should* have done otherwise and therefore that *he could* have done otherwise. In other words, he was not psychologically compelled to do what he did.

SHOULD LEADERS ACT IN SELF-INTEREST?

If egoism is to justify rule-breaking behavior by leaders, then this approach to morality must move beyond psychological explanations of human motivation and behavior. Specifically, the egoist must appeal to the *moral* importance of self-interest and substantiate the claim that it justifies rule-breaking behavior. What the advocate of egoism needs is *ethical egoism*: the view that we morally ought to act in our self-interest. This thesis is normative or prescriptive, not descriptive. Ethical egoism tells us what we should do, not what we actually do. As such, it is to be

47 Kurtz, "Bill Clinton's Very Personal Reflections."

distinguished from the thesis of psychological egoism, which offers an empirical account of human motivation.

In fact, ethical egoism assumes the falsity of psychological egoism. If it were a psychological fact that people always act in ways they think will advance their self-interest, there would be no need for the claim that they morally ought to do so. First of all, psychological egoism is a deterministic view of human action. So it hardly leaves room for people to alter their behavior to conform to morality. Normative theories – at least if they are to be action guiding – must assume the possibility of our doing otherwise. Second, self-interest already serves as the source of motivation for psychological egoism. Why advocate a moral doctrine that requires people to be motivated by what motivates them naturally? Psychological egoism thus makes ethical egoism both impractical and unnecessary.

Ethical egoism draws a clearer distinction than does psychological egoism between acting in self-interest and acting on selfish desires. Highlighting the importance of this difference for morality, Ayn Rand (1905–1982), the most famous defender of the doctrine of ethical egoism, draws a sharp distinction between mere desire for pleasure or satisfaction and the advancement of self-interest:

> Man's life . . . is not the life of a mindless brute, of a looting thug or a mooching mystic, but the life of a thinking being – not life by means of force or fraud, but life by means of achievement . . . [N]either life nor happiness can be achieved by the pursuit of irrational whims . . . [H]e is free to seek his happiness in any mindless fraud, but the torture of frustration is all he will find, unless he seeks the happiness proper to man.[48]

Edwin Locke, a contemporary advocate of egoistic leadership, similarly denies that self-interest "consists simply of doing whatever one *feels* like

---

[48] Rand, "Why Self-Interest is Best," in *The Ethics of Leadership*, ed. Joanne B. Ciulla (Belmont, CA: Wadsworth/Thomson Learning, 2003), 47 (reprinted from Ayn Rand, *Atlas Shrugged* [New York: Random House, 1959]). In a 1957 letter to the *New York Times*, Alan Greenspan, who would later become chairman of the Federal Reserve, defended Rand's philosophy this way: "Creative individuals and undeviating purpose and rationality achieve joy and fulfillment. Parasites who persistently avoid either purpose or reason perish as they should" (quoted in Harriet Rubin, "Ayn Rand's literature of capitalism," *New York Times* [September 15, 2007]).

doing at the time ... Just because one 'wants' to do something does not mean it is in one's actual self-interest."[49]

So, according to the ethical egoist, we should not understand egoism as condoning the behavior of the leader who engages in rule-breaking behavior simply to satisfy his selfish desires. Behavior of this kind tends to bring about social consequences that are severely detrimental to a leader's self-interest. Just ask Eliot Spitzer, who was forced to resign as governor of New York when – in March 2008 – his involvement with prostitutes was uncovered. People who are controlled by their selfish desires often find that they have trouble getting others to cooperate with them, let alone getting others to follow.[50]

This articulation of the doctrine of ethical egoism implies that rule breaking by leaders is justified only if it really does advance the leader's self-interest. Rule breaking must make – or be expected to make – an all-things-considered contribution to self-interest. Indeed, the strictest version of ethical egoism holds that morality requires that leadership behavior *maximally* contribute to the leader's self-interest. According to this version of the thesis, leaders morally ought to do the action that would *best* advance self-interest. Gains from the action must outweigh losses in terms of self-interest, *and* net gains must be greater for this action than for all alternative actions.

Whatever version of ethical egoism we consider, the radical nature of this view of morality is best reflected in the fact that it does not hold that self-interested behavior is merely *permissible*. Ethical egoism *requires* that we act in our self-interest. Not only is a leader in the right when she behaves self-interestedly, but she actually does a moral wrong – to herself – when she fails to do so. Ethical egoism would thus seem to imply that leaders are sometimes justified in breaking the rules to secure their own interests.

Yet Edwin Locke denies that egoistic leaders should put their own interests ahead of the interests of others. Given what it is to have an interest, he claims, there can be no real "conflicts of interests

---

49  Bruce J. Avolio and Edwin A. Locke, "Contrasting Different Philosophies of Leader Motivation: Altruism versus Egoism," *Leadership Quarterly* 13 (2002): 171.
50  In contrast, true ethical egoists often prove to be exceedingly dependable colleagues and co-workers, in part because they are cognizant of powerful incentives to maintain bonds of trust and reciprocity.

among rational men."[51] And without these conflicts, there is no need for leaders to break the rules to advance their self-interest. His first argument goes this way:

> For a rational person, desires are not the starting point in deciding how to act or what is good. One first has to identify and validate a proper code of morality... It is not rational to hold a wish based on an invalid premise, e.g., one that is wrong because it contradicts reality, such as wanting something you have no right to.[52]

The egoistic leader therefore pursues only that to which he has a right. Other desires are irrational.

In this argument, Locke's appeal to *desires* serves as something of a distraction. Properly understood, ethical egoism raises concerns not about conflicts between desires and interests, which – as the ethical egoist makes perfectly clear – can be relevantly different, but about conflicts between the interests of leaders and the interests of others. To appeal to rationality to address conflicts of *interests*, Locke would have to say that a leader cannot have an interest in something to which he has no right, and that what a leader has a right to is determined by the proper code of morality.

But ethical egoism supposedly is the proper code! So Locke cannot – without circularity – use the notion of self-interest to tell us what morality requires, only then to turn around and use the notion of morality to tell us what really constitutes self-interest. Either egoism is the correct moral theory, in which case self-interest can conflict with the interests of others, or Locke must appeal to some moral theory other than ethical egoism to identify the interests that leaders have a right to pursue.

Locke's second attempt to explain away conflicts of interests between leaders and others makes an empirical claim about what rationality demands, not a logical claim about the nature of rationality. According to Locke, "[A] rational person does not desire ends divorced from means. In a free society, the proper means of getting what you want is voluntary trade."[53] Because self-interest ultimately constitutes what is "proper" for the ethical egoist, we can read Locke

[51] Avolio and Locke, "Contrasting Different Philosophies of Leader Motivation," 179.
[52] Avolio and Locke, "Contrasting Different Philosophies of Leader Motivation," 179.
[53] Avolio and Locke, "Contrasting Different Philosophies of Leader Motivation," 179.

to mean that in a free society, self-interest always demands voluntary interactions between individuals.[54] Theft, for example, "may be tempting ... but such an act leads not to happiness but to jail."[55]

Other rule-breaking behaviors, such as lying and promise breaking, are also wrong because they undermine consent in human interactions. Ethical egoism accordingly prohibits consumer fraud and breech of contract. It similarly restricts the behavior of leaders toward followers. For example, "A manager knows that to make the business succeed, he must make the organization an enjoyable place for the employees to work."[56] In essence, Locke is making what Marvin Brown calls "the business case"[57] for ethical leadership in organizations, which takes as its main premise the old saw, "Good ethics is good business."

It is probably correct that when rule-breaking behaviors such as lying and promise breaking rise to the level of fraud and breach of contract, they are not justified on a theory of ethical egoism. This argument is especially compelling for everyday leaders. Even if there are real-world cases in which illegal activity is the only means for a business leader to advance his self-interest, it would surely be a mistake to take these cases as exemplars in an egoistic theory of everyday leadership ethics. We can assume that the situations in which it is in the interests of everyday leaders to engage in illegal activity are few and far between.

However, the business case has a much harder time precluding lesser forms of moral rule breaking in everyday life; as a consequence, its advocates are susceptible to the charge that they do not pay sufficient attention to potential conflicts of interests between people. The perception of business is often that, short of breaking the law, everything is permitted in market contexts. In fact, some people go so far as to say that the market rewards particular forms of morally questionable behavior. For example, successful marketing advances the interests of business leaders regardless of whether – and sometimes

54 Here, "proper" cannot mean some other sense of "morally proper" for the reasons I gave in the previous paragraph.
55 Avolio and Locke, "Contrasting Different Philosophies of Leader Motivation," 179.
56 Avolio and Locke, "Contrasting Different Philosophies of Leader Motivation," 180.
57 Marvin T. Brown, *Corporate Integrity: Rethinking Organizational Ethics and Leadership* (Cambridge: Cambridge University Press, 2005), 27.

*especially when* – it gets consumers to buy products that do not advance their own interests and, in the case of products such as tobacco, actually make consumers worse off.

We should also question the general truth of Locke's claim that successful businesses provide enjoyable workplaces for employees – if, that is, Locke is referring simply to *financial* success in business.[58] Businesses can be financially successful precisely because many people are willing to work in less than enjoyable conditions. Other things being equal, keeping labor costs low is one way to increase profits. As long as labor is plentiful, self-interest does not always dictate that employers make working conditions more enjoyable. This reality does not mean that the state should do more to make the workplace enjoyable, in addition to safe and healthy, any more than it should interfere with the market to resolve conflicts of interests between sellers and buyers – say, by prohibiting the sale of products that do not make people better off, or even products that make them worse off. What it does mean, however, is that we cannot naively expect that market mechanisms alone will keep people from acting immorally to resolve conflicts of interests in their own favor.

No wonder conflicts of interests can give rise to rule-breaking behavior by egoistic leaders. After all, the demands of ethical egoism are ultimately grounded in a view of moral importance that allows leaders to see their interests as exceptional. We could hardly expect an alternative resolution to conflicts of interests from a theory that holds, as Rand puts it, that "your highest moral purpose is the achievement of your own happiness,"[59] where happiness "proceeds from the achievement of [your] values."[60] The real question, then, is whether self-interest can justify a leader in breaking the rules to put his interests ahead of the interests of others.

The strongest argument Rand gives for answering this question in the affirmative is that an accurate conception of self-worth for an agent depends on his acting to advance his own values, not the values of

---

[58] Avolio and Locke, "Contrasting Different Philosophies of Leader Motivation," 181.

[59] Rand, "The Ethics of Emergencies," in *Reason and Responsibility: Readings in Some Basic Problems of Philosophy*, eds. Joel Feinberg and Russ Shafer-Landau, 10th ed. (Belmont, CA: Wadsworth Publishing, 1999), 534.

[60] Rand, "Why Self-Interest is Best," 47.

others.[61] The leader who sacrifices his own values gives the impression that he cares so little about himself and his values that he is willing to set them aside for the values of someone he does not care about at all, and perhaps does not even know. This kind of behavior violates the "rational principle of conduct... [A]lways act in accordance with the hierarchy of your values, and never sacrifice a greater value to a lesser one."[62] In making this kind of sacrifice, the leader fails to respect himself as a rational agent with his own values, his own goals, and his own life to live. To Rand, only a person with low self-esteem would do such a thing.

The egoist's insight is exactly what popular normative theories of leadership such as *servant leadership* might be said to miss. For example, Robert Greenleaf, the original proponent of this view, proposes "the fusing of the servant and the leader" so that the "natural servant [should] become a leader."[63] Greenleaf tells us,

The servant-leader *is* servant first... It begins with the natural feeling that one wants to serve, to serve *first*. Then conscious choice brings one to aspire to lead. That person is sharply different from one who is *leader* first, perhaps because of the need to assuage an unusual power drive or to acquire material possessions. For such it will be a later choice to serve – after leadership is established. The leader-first and the servant-first are two extreme types. Between them there are shadings and blends that are part of the infinite variety of human nature.[64]

Does this servant–leader have a proper sense of self-esteem?

A potentially serious ethical problem with this theory of leadership is that it risks encouraging a kind of servility.[65] If we understand Greenleaf's motivational continuum as moving from the leader-first, who wants to lead to accomplish his own ends, to the servant-first, who is motivated only by a concern for others and their ends, we are left

---

[61] Rand, "Why Self-Interest is Best," 49.
[62] Rand, "The Ethics of Emergencies," 534.
[63] Robert K. Greenleaf, *Servant Leadership: A Journey into the Nature of Legitimate Power* (New York: Paulist Press, 1977), 12.
[64] Greenleaf, *Servant Leadership*, 13.
[65] See Bowie, "A Kantian Theory of Leadership," *Leadership and Organizational Development Journal: Special Issue on Ethics and Leadership* 21 (2000): 185–193; and Price, *Understanding Ethical Failures in Leadership*, 56–57. For the original Kantian critique of servility, see Thomas E. Hill Jr., "Servility and Self-Respect," in *Autonomy and Self-Respect* (Cambridge: Cambridge University Press, 1991), 4–18. I discuss Hill's argument in Chapter 5.

with the picture of the ideal leader as someone who has no real goals and projects of her own. The servant–leader – at least in the extreme form that Greenleaf explicitly recommends – is hardly a rational agent at all. She is instead much closer to someone who sacrifices her agency to the agency of others. In keeping with the idea of what it is to be a servant, she lives in service of goals and projects that belong to someone else. Making service the defining ethical attitude of leadership therefore fails to respect the worth of leaders as rational agents.[66]

Rand is correct, then, that morality demands that rational agents, including leaders, treat themselves with respect. They should not simply abandon their goals and projects and adopt an attitude of "selfless service" toward others and their ends.[67] But, precisely stated, the main objection to servant leadership is that this theory condones active subordination of leaders to followers, not that it accords equal moral status to leaders and followers. The most that Rand's argument establishes, then, is that leaders should not act in ways that undermine their conception of self-worth as the moral equals of other rational agents. This is a far cry from showing that leaders are justified in breaking the rules to advance their self-interest as the moral superiors of followers.

A leader's worth as a rational agent justifies him in having his own projects and goals to pursue. Without such ends, he is in no position to exercise his rational agency. Yet the moral importance of having ends to pursue does not justify rule-breaking behavior in the pursuit of these ends. To the leader who seeks to make an exception of himself, the appropriate question is, "Exactly what justifies the exception?" The leader cannot simply respond, "These are *my* goals and projects." For we already know that it is for the sake of his own ends that he seeks to break the rules. This reply is hardly more convincing than saying, "My behavior is justified because it is my behavior." The fact that the ends and the behavior are his own is irrelevant to a justification. It

---

[66] John Stuart Mill similarly suggests that Christian ethics can promote "a low, abject, servile type of character" (*On Liberty*, ed. Elizabeth Rapaport [Indianapolis: Hackett Publishing Company, 1978], 49). The association between servant leadership and Christianity also brings to mind Nietzsche's famous discussion of "slave morality" (Friedrich Nietzsche, *Beyond Good and Evil: Prelude to a Philosophy of the Future*, trans. Walter Kaufmann [New York: Random House, 1966], 207–208.

[67] See Patty Devlin, "Valuing Servants' Ends: A New Theory of Ethical Service," Senior Honors Thesis, Jepson School of Leadership Studies, University of Richmond, 2004.

is precisely the exceptional nature of rule breaking that calls for a justification in the first place. A leader's appeal to self-interest as a justification for rule breaking is therefore no justification at all.

## SELF-INTEREST WITHIN THE BOUNDS OF MORALITY

The fact that a leader's ends are *his own* cannot justify the leader's commitment to his goals and projects, let alone rule-breaking behavior in pursuit of these goals and projects. Leaders, no more or less than anyone else, pursue goals and projects simply because the goals and projects are *their own*. Justification of the pursuit of particular ends must appeal to the reasons for having those ends. So the real issue for justification – both *rational* and *moral* justification – is what values ground the goals and projects that leaders have in the first place.

A complete answer cannot be that these goals and projects are the ones that advance self-interest. Although Rand sees individual happiness as the aim of morality, she ultimately appeals to more than the state of happiness to explain why leaders pursue their particular ends. Rand's egoistic answer is that leaders are committed to certain goals and projects because they see these ends as valuable.[68] This answer explains why, given the worth of rational agents, there is something morally problematic about a leader who simply abandons her goals and projects to serve the ends of others. She gives up valuing altogether and becomes an instrument for pursuing what other people value.

Commitments to the value of particular ends also explain why leaders pursue some ends and not others. In effect, leaders see their particular goals and projects as having more value than alternative goals and projects to which they might be committed. Of course, leaders need not see all their goals and projects as *intrinsically* valuable – that is, as valuable in and of themselves. But even if leaders are pursuing some goals and projects for merely *instrumental* reasons, there must be some other end or ends that they see as valuable, something for the sake of which they are pursuing these particular goals and projects.

Would we not therefore expect leaders to see themselves as justified in treating their own ends as being more valuable than the ends of

[68] Rand, "Why Self-Interest is Best," 47.

others? Put another way, if leaders believe that their own goals and projects really have more value than other goals and projects they might have chosen instead, does it not stand to reason that leaders would treat their own goals and projects as having more than equal weight in their decisions about how they should act?

In one sense, it is perfectly reasonable for leaders to act as though their own ends are more valuable than the ends of others. Moral theory generally accommodates this insight by making room – what we might call "moral space" – for people to pursue the particular goals and projects to which they are committed. For example, Kant recommends that "everyone endeavours...so far as lies in him, to further the ends of others" and that their ends "be also, as far as possible, [*our*] ends."[69] But notice the qualifiers "so far as lies in him" and "as far as possible." Because the duty to help others is derived from the fact that we ourselves must will that others help us with our goals and projects, this duty cannot be so demanding that it precludes the pursuit of our own ends. In other words, a strong duty to help others would undermine the foundation of Kant's argument. Accordingly, "so far as lies in him" and "as far as possible" cannot mean "to the extent that leaders are in a position to do something to forward the ends of others." It must instead mean "to the extent leaders can do so while keeping in mind that they have their own lives to live and their own goals and projects to pursue." Any stronger understanding of our duties to help others would threaten our ability to pursue our own goals and projects.

There is a second sense, however, in which morality does not allow leaders to act as though their own ends are more valuable than the ends of others. The leader's "egotism which thinks self and its concerns more important than everything else"[70] must be constrained by the fact that pursuit of his goals and projects occurs in the context of social relationships with others. Most obviously, followers also have goals and projects that they find valuable. In some cases, the goals and projects of leaders and followers will fit together easily. However, commitments to value are almost always subject to disagreement. In

[69] Immanuel Kant, *Groundwork of the Metaphysic of Morals*, trans. H. J. Paton (New York: Harper and Row Publishers, 1964) 98.
[70] Mill, *On Liberty*, 76.

these cases, leaders and followers owe each other rational justifications for why particular goals and projects ought to be collectively pursued. They must work through disagreement in order for leadership to take place.[71] An ethical path to common purpose requires that no parties simply assume that their personal ends are more worthy of pursuit than the ends of the other parties.

Within the context of justification, all personal goals and projects must be put on equal footing. In keeping with Kantian ethics, rational justification requires background conditions of universal honesty and honoring one's word. Stated differently, rational justification requires an attitude of respect for the rational faculties of those to whom the justification is given. These conditions for justification give leaders very strong duties not to use behaviors such as lying and promise breaking to get followers to help leaders forward their own personal ends. In other words, leaders will not be justified in breaking the rules to advance their own "pet projects."

A leader's decision to live by the standard conditions of rational justification reflects his acceptance of his equal status as a moral agent. He is no different from others in morally relevant respects, and he is in no position simply to assume that his goals and projects are more valuable than the goals and projects of others. As a consequence, his efforts to pursue his ends, like the efforts of everyone else, must be constrained by proper respect for the rationality of all moral agents – including his own.

Do leaders really have to accept this kind of equality? After all, we often hear that leaders are different from followers, that they break the rules for followers – not for themselves – and that their goals and projects really are more important than the goals and projects of other people. If any of these lines of reasoning were convincing, leaders would not need to use the fact that their goals and projects are their own to justify rule-breaking behavior. Instead, they could point to the fact that they really are special, that followers permit them to break the rules, or that their collective ends really are of exceptional importance.

---

[71] In fact, James MacGregor Burns and Ronald Heifetz would say this is part of what leadership is. See Burns, *Leadership*, and Heifetz, *Leadership Without Easy Answers* (Cambridge, MA: Belknap Press of Harvard University Press, 1994).

We must therefore consider these three justifications for rule-breaking behavior by leaders. Chapter 4 examines the claim that leaders are different from followers, and Chapter 5 considers the argument that followers, as evidenced by the nature of the leadership relation, ultimately consent to rule-breaking behavior by leaders. Chapter 6 looks at leaders' beliefs about the importance of group goals and projects.

# 4

## Traits and Virtues

As we have seen, Kant's ethics holds that our duties are determined by an attempt to universalize our actions. Because it is impossible to conceive of a world in which everyone lies and breaks his promises in order to get what he wants, there is a duty not to engage in actions such as lying and promise breaking. In such a world, no one would be willing to accept the word of anyone else. Indeed, no one would have an incentive to give his word to others in the first place. Appeals to truth and fidelity would be laughed off for what they really are in such a world – very thinly veiled attempts by actors to get what they want.

Although it is impossible for us to conceive of a world in which everyone lies and breaks promises, we can conceive of a world in which only some individuals tell lies or break promises. If an individual gives a careful description of the action to be universalized, then she seemingly avoids the contradiction. For example, can Martha Stewart imagine a world in which everyone named "Martha Stewart" engages in exception-making behavior? Of course she can! Yet it is clearly not in the spirit of Kant's categorical imperative for Martha Stewart to consider a world in which only *she* (and maybe a few others who share her name) tells lies and break promises to get her (their) way. It is beside the point that she can imagine such a world just for herself. Or, rather, this is exactly Kant's point. Kant has a reply to the individual who attempts to index the description of her proposed action to herself: "What is so special about you? Why are you justified in doing what the rest of us cannot do? Why should we see you as exceptional?"

Can we conceive of a world in which many special people resort to lying and promise breaking to achieve their ends? This world is clearly easier to imagine than a world in which everyone lies and breaks his promises. In the former world, most people do not engage in lying and promise breaking, and their contributions to this social good are probably sufficient to maintain a backdrop of truth and fidelity. Moreover, people are not all the same. So why should the same rules apply to everyone? Justification of this kind of rule-breaking behavior might thus be understood as proper moral discrimination, not blatant rationalization. To be sure, this justification will be compelling only if there is indeed something special about the individuals who seek to break the rules. But this argument is not hard to fashion, especially when it comes to a discussion of leaders.

Historically, the view that leaders are special has been a dominant feature of our understanding of leadership. Neither kings and priests nor presidents and CEOs are simply part of the crowd. The view that leaders are special also has a good intellectual pedigree. It gets its most famous expression in Plato's *Republic,* in which Socrates tells us that leaders are "fitted by nature both to engage in philosophy and to rule in a city, while the rest are naturally fitted to leave philosophy alone and follow their leader."[1] The conception of the state articulated in the *Republic* rests on the claim that leaders are different from followers. According to Socrates' account, these differences justify the exercise of power of some individuals over others and, among other things, the perpetuation of a "noble falsehood," which is necessary to maintain the strict class divisions in the ideal state.[2]

In the early nineteenth century, G. W. F. Hegel similarly suggested that "world-historical individuals...who grasp...a higher universal" are not bound by

acknowledged duties, laws, and rights... [but by] those possibilities which are adverse to this system, violate it, and even destroy its foundations and

---

[1] Plato, *Republic,* trans. G. M. A. Grube (Indianapolis: Hackett Publishing Company, 1992), 149 [474c].
[2] Plato, *Republic,* 91 [414c].

existence . . . They see the very truth of their age and their world . . . The world-historical persons, the heroes of their age, must therefore be recognized as its seers – their words and deeds are the best of the age . . . For it is they who knew best and from whom the others eventually learned and with whom they agreed or, at least, complied . . . For this reason their fellow men follow these soul-leaders.[3]

The essential idea behind such historical views is that the special characteristics of leaders justify differential behavior. If a leader can show that she is different from others, then there is no contradiction in her claiming that she is justified in engaging in behaviors that are prohibited in society more generally. What we must consider, then, is whether the everyday leader is justified in breaking the rules "because she is special."

The intellectual descendents of the view that leaders are special by nature are the *trait views of leadership*. Here, "[t]he term *trait* refers to a variety of individual attributes, including aspects of personality, temperament, needs, motives, and values. Personality traits are relatively stable dispositions to behave in a particular way."[4] In the early twentieth century, the view that leaders differ from followers on these dimensions not only boasted the support of our common, historical understanding of leadership, but also served as the standard assumption of organizational theory. Support for the trait view of leadership declined, however, after the appearance of a 1948 review of the literature by Ralph Stogdill.[5] Stogdill's most surprising conclusion was that "[a] person does not become a leader by virtue of the possession of some combination of traits, but the pattern of personal characteristics of the leader must bear some relevant relationship to the characteristics, activities, and goals of the followers."[6]

Such findings ultimately led to the ascendancy of *contingency* or *situational* approaches to leadership.[7] As we might expect, however,

---

3 Adapted from Georg Wilhelm Friedrich Hegel, *Reason in History: A General Introduction to the Philosophy of History*, trans. Robert S. Hartman (New York: The Liberal Arts Press, 1953), 39–41. George Williamson pointed out the relevance of Hegel for my work.

4 Gary Yukl, *Leadership in Organizations*, 6th ed. (Upper Saddle River, NJ: Prentice Hall, 2006), 180–181.

5 Ralph Stogdill, "Personal Factors Associated with Leadership: A Survey of the Literature," *The Journal of Psychology* 25 (1948): 35–71.

6 Stogdill, "Personal Factors Associated With Leadership," 64.

7 See Chapter 6.

interest in the personal characteristics of leaders has hardly died out. Recent research on leadership traits takes a practical approach and focuses less on what makes someone a leader than on what makes someone an *effective* leader. The question for the present chapter, then, is twofold: (1) what traits are associated with effective leadership, and (2) do these traits justify rule-breaking behavior by leaders?

LEADER EFFECTIVENESS

Gary Yukl's review of trait research identifies several characteristics of leaders that are associated with managerial effectiveness.[8] Drawing on the work of other leadership theorists, Yukl concludes that effective leaders differ from followers – and from ineffective leaders – in terms of:

1. Energy level and stress tolerance
2. Self-confidence
3. Locus of control
4. Power motivation
5. Achievement orientation
6. Need for affiliation
7. Emotional stability and maturity
8. Personal integrity[9]

Effective leaders have *higher* energy levels and a *higher* tolerance for stress than followers do.[10] These leaders are also *more* self-confident, and they draw on a strong *internal* locus of control, which means that they see themselves, rather than external forces, as controlling outcomes.[11] Yukl also suggests, following David McClelland, that on measures of managerial motivation, effective leaders generally have *high* power needs, *moderately high* achievement needs, and *low* affiliation needs.[12] Finally, effective leaders have *greater* emotional stability and maturity, as well as *greater* personal integrity.[13] Can these particular

[8] Yukl, *Leadership in Organizations*, ch. 7.
[9] Yukl, *Leadership in Organizations*, 189–196.
[10] Yukl, *Leadership in Organizations*, 189.
[11] Yukl, *Leadership in Organizations*, 190–191.
[12] Yukl, *Leadership in Organizations*, 184, 193–196.
[13] Yukl, *Leadership in Organizations*, 191–193.

trait differentials justify rule-breaking behavior by effective leaders? Let us examine each trait in turn.

It is difficult to see how either high energy levels or high tolerance for stress might ground a general justification for rule-breaking behavior. High energy levels and high stress tolerance may be relevant to a justification for putting someone in a leadership position and, moreover, for an explanation of his success once he is in it. As Yukl points out, "High energy level and stress tolerance help managers cope with the hectic pace, long hours, and unrelenting demands of most managerial jobs."[14] But these characteristics are relevant to moral justification only insofar as they contribute to an ability to do something that others are unable to do. For example, a leader might be justified in coming to a meeting on little or no sleep, whereas others would not be similarly justified because they – unlike he – would be unable to do their part in the meeting. In this case, having a higher than normal energy level makes the leader different from others in relevant respects, and this difference justifies his making an exception of himself.

Notice, however, that this line of argument does not lend itself to a justification for rule-breaking behaviors such as lying and promise breaking. Although high energy levels may make a leader better able to devise a successful cover-up of his deception, and high stress tolerance may make him better able to deal with any stress associated with deceiving others, these characteristics do not come to bear on a moral justification of these behaviors. At most, they are part of a rationalization for breaking the rules.

This general argument also applies to a moral justification that appeals to the trait of self-confidence. Leaders probably need a certain amount of self-confidence to be effective in their positions, and having self-confidence can be necessary for justifying an action that would not be successful without self-confidence. Self-confidence is a sign that the leader has the ability to carry out the action or, at the very least, that she will not fail out of fear or panic. In most cases, leaders who lack confidence in their abilities to be successful ought to delegate the task to someone in whom they have more confidence – assuming, of course, the chosen person has sufficient confidence in herself. But,

---

[14] Yukl, *Leadership in Organizations*, 189.

like high energy levels and high stress tolerance, self-confidence is unlikely to get us very far in a justification of rule breaking by leaders.

In fact, self-confidence can be morally dangerous. The moral danger is in the fact that "[l]eaders with high self-confidence are more likely to attempt difficult tasks and to set challenging objectives for themselves . . . These leaders are more persistent in pursuit of difficult objectives, despite initial problems and setbacks."[15] Sometimes morality presents "problems and setbacks" to the achievement of "challenging objectives." Self-confidence can encourage leaders to break the rules even though they are not morally justified in doing so.

Self-confidence is dangerous because it is a matter of belief, not knowledge.[16] This belief does not perfectly track what one is able to do or what one is justified in doing. People can feel confident that, in fact, they can do something that they are unable to do. They can also be mistaken as to whether an action is justified, despite their being confident that they have sufficient justification for their behavior. Self-confidence is simply a measure of the degree to which one believes that one is able to do something or the degree to which one believes that one is justified in doing it. As a consequence, effective leaders may be more likely to break the rules because their self-confidence makes them prone to believe that they are justified in doing so, even though they are actually no more likely than others to be justified.

For similar reasons, a strong internal locus of control can promote rule-breaking behavior by leaders. *Internals*, as they are called, "are more flexible, adaptive, and innovative in their response to a problem and in their management strategies."[17] Sometimes particular problems can be solved only if leaders are willing to bend the rules or come up with rules of their own. In these circumstances, *moral* flexibility and innovation give leaders more control over outcomes.

But, here again, the trait itself cannot justify these exceptions. The issue of whether leaders believe they are in control of outcomes, like the issue of whether leaders have self-confidence, is relevant to moral

[15] Yukl, *Leadership in Organizations*, 190.
[16] David M. Messick and Max H. Bazerman note research supporting the claim that people who are 75 percent confident in their beliefs are right only 60 percent of the time ("Ethical Leadership and the Psychology of Decision Making," *Sloan Management Review* 37, 2 [1996]: 19).
[17] Yukl, *Leadership in Organizations*, 191.

justification only if the absence of the relevant beliefs and attitudes would make them unjustified in engaging in the behavior in question. At most, then, internal locus of control is a necessary condition for justification in particular circumstances. Some other condition (or conditions) must be met for a full justification of leaders' behavior. Bending the rules or coming up with rules of one's own would have to be morally desirable *before* considerations of locus of control become relevant. Considerations of control would then be part of a determination of whether a particular leader is the right person to do what ought to be done.

Another moral concern about internals is that leaders with this locus of control can make exceptions of themselves *at their own expense.* For example, one feature of internals is that "they take more responsibility for their own actions and for the performance of their organization."[18] It is generally a good thing for leaders to take responsibility for what they and their organizations do. Yet even this characteristic can be morally problematic. Public relations aside, taking responsibility is a good thing only insofar as one really is responsible for what was done. When a leader sincerely blames himself for circumstances and consequences that were actually *external* to his control, this way of thinking constitutes a view of self-worth that reflects something less than moral equality.[19] Because people can be much too hard on themselves, leaders with an internal locus of control are at moral risk of taking too much responsibility for their own actions or the performance of their organizations.

Does the argument that differences between leaders and followers justify rule-breaking behavior get more help from what Yukl, in his review of the literature, identifies as the motivational needs of effective leaders?[20] For example, with respect to power motivation, McClelland distinguishes between "personalized power" and "socialized power."[21] The former need is typically associated with leaders who are motivated to exercise power for egoistic reasons, and the latter with leaders who do so for altruistic reasons.

[18] Yukl, *Leadership in Organizations*, 190.
[19] See my critique of *servant leadership* in Chapter 3.
[20] Yukl, *Leadership in Organizations*, 184.
[21] David C. McClelland, *Power: The Inner Experience* (New York: Irvington Publishers, 1975), 257.

As we saw in the last chapter, egoism does not justify rule-breaking behavior by leaders. One might suggest, however, that altruism, or a need for socialized power, does. After all, leaders motivated in this fashion would break the rules only for the good of others. Indeed, the motivation of socialized power, not personalized power, characterizes effective leadership.[22] But notice that this trait of effective leaders is not sufficient for morality. A leader can be mistaken in thinking that she is justified in breaking the rules even in cases in which her behavior is for the good of others. Doing good for others does not give leaders a moral *carte blanche.* What justifies the exception, then, cannot be the fact that the leader was motivated by altruism – the good of some others. If the rule breaking is justified, it must have something to do with a higher good – perhaps the good of all – that the leader aims to achieve.[23]

High needs for achievement and low needs for affiliation, like many of the other characteristics that distinguish effective leaders from followers – and from ineffective leaders – can also do more to encourage unjustified rule breaking than to give us reasons to think that rule breaking is justified. When moral rules stand in the way of success, high needs for achievement make it that much harder for a leader to do what she morally ought to do. Fortunately, as Yukl notes, "[T]he relationship of achievement motivation to managerial effectiveness [may be] curvilinear rather than linear. In other words, managers with a moderately high amount of achievement motivation are more effective than managers with low achievement motivation, or managers with very high achievement motivation."[24] This finding suggests that the moral risks of the high achievement needs of effective leaders are not as great as they might otherwise be. Still, there is no reason to think that moderately high achievement needs would be relevant to the justification of a leader's rule-breaking behavior.

The moral risks of low affiliation needs for effective leaders may also be less worrisome than some of the alternatives. Leaders with high affiliation needs "show favoritism to personal friends in making assignments and allowing exceptions to rules."[25] But low and high

---

[22] Yukl, *Leadership in Organizations*, 193.
[23] See Chapter 8.
[24] Yukl, *Leadership in Organizations*, 194.
[25] Yukl, *Leadership in Organizations*, 196.

affiliation needs are not the only alternatives. Having moderate needs for affiliation makes it more likely that a leader would care about the moral judgments that others make of her behavior. There is some value in having a "[concern for] being liked and accepted and ... [being] sensitive to cues indicating rejection or hostility from others."[26] So, for moral purposes, although the effective leader's low needs for affiliation are preferable to high needs for affiliation, moderate needs for affiliation would be preferable to either high or low needs for affiliation.

In summary, none of the standard traits that distinguish effective leaders from others – leaving aside for the moment emotional stability and maturity and personal integrity – justifies rule-breaking behavior by leaders. In most cases, these traits are not even relevant to moral justification. When they are relevant, their presence is more likely to compete with justification than to support it. Traits such as high self-confidence, internal locus of control, and low needs for affiliation can encourage the *belief* that one is justified in breaking the rules. However, the traits themselves cannot ground a justification.

The problem is that the trait differentials thus far discussed simply point to *descriptive* differences between people. If these differences are to justify rule-breaking behavior by leaders, then the justification must appeal to *normative* differences between effective leaders and followers – and ineffective leaders. In other words, the justification needs to show not that effective leaders are set apart from the rest of us in terms of non-moral qualities such as self-confidence but, rather, in terms of moral qualities such as *virtue*. The question, then, is whether effective leaders are *morally* different and, if so, whether these differences can justify their rule-breaking behavior.

## MORAL TRAITS

Are effective leaders *morally* special? To answer this question, we need to look at a particular kind of trait – namely, *virtues*. Virtues are personal dispositions to respond in morally appropriate ways. The previous section introduced, but did not discuss, what might be understood as two general virtues associated with effective leadership:

---

[26] Yukl, *Leadership in Organizations*, 184.

(1) emotional stability and maturity, and (2) personal integrity.[27] Unlike the traits already discussed, both of these characteristics have clear moral dimensions. First, virtue theorists such as Aristotle (384– 22 BCE) suggest that morality involves not just appropriate action but appropriate feeling, and we might expect that emotionally developed leaders are more likely to feel the right way in response to the various situations they face.[28]

Second, morality is an explicit component of personal integrity. Trait theory understands integrity to mean "that a person's behavior is consistent with espoused values, and the person is honest, ethical, and trustworthy."[29] This conception of integrity combines personal authenticity with correct moral values. It does not suffice for an attribution of integrity to say that a leader acts on his values. Hitler's behavior may have been consistent with his values, but we would hardly say that he had integrity. At most, he showed personal authenticity. To have integrity in this complete sense, a leader must also act on the *right* values. Using Aristotle's language, we can say that the leader with integrity is neither "incontinent" (weak-willed in his behavior) nor "base" (committed to wrong morality).[30] In other words, an attribution of integrity to a leader implies that he is not only consistent but also ethical.

What follows from the claim that effective leaders are more likely to have morally appropriate feelings and to engage in morally appropriate behaviors? Initially at least, we might think that effective leaders would refrain from rule-breaking behaviors such as lying and promise breaking. According to Yukl, "One important indicator of integrity is the extent to which one is honest and truthful rather than deceptive... Another indicator of integrity is keeping promises."[31]

But this initial reaction to the association between effective leadership and morally appropriate feelings or behaviors makes an unfounded assumption about what morality really requires. It assumes that morality demands that leaders simply follow the rules. If we begin instead with the virtue ethicist's assumption that virtue determines

---

[27] Yukl, *Leadership in Organizations*, 191–193.

[28] Aristotle, *Nicomachean Ethics*, trans. Terence Irwin (Indianapolis: Hackett Publishing Company, 1985), 44 [1106b21–23].

[29] Yukl, *Leadership in Organizations*, 192.

[30] Aristotle, *Nicomachean Ethics*, 197 [1152a20–1152a24].

[31] Yukl, *Leadership in Organizations*, 192–193.

right action, and we combine this assumption with the claim that effective leaders are distinguished from others in terms of virtue, then the implication is not that effective leaders will never break the rules, but rather that they will recognize when rule breaking is appropriate and when it is not.

Perhaps what follows, then, is that the best way to determine whether rule breaking is justified is to see how effective leaders respond in various situations. We could simply rely on the fact that effective leaders are more likely to have morally appropriate feelings and to engage in morally appropriate actions. This proposal draws not only on the connection that virtue ethics makes between morality and effectiveness, but also on this theory's method of identifying right action. According to this theory, ethics does not lend itself to a neat list of rules. Julia Annas calls the idea that ethics can be specified in this way "the technical manual model" of ethics.[32] Rather, according to the virtue theorist, ethics is determined by the exercise of practical wisdom in particular situations.

Aristotle defines virtue "by reference to reason, i.e., to the reason by reference to which the intelligent person would define it."[33] This way of understanding virtue allows us to move from the premise that effective leaders are virtuous to the conclusion that what they do is justified. We do not look to some set of rules to determine whether their actions are ethical. Again, a central assumption of virtue ethics is that there is no set of rules that specifies what ethics requires. As Annas puts it, "If we define right action as what the virtuous person would do, but it turns out that the virtuous person is even in part defined in turn by the doing of right action ... we have a circle, and so no [alternative explanation of ethics]."[34] According to virtue theory, "An action is right if and only if it is what a virtuous person would do, adding '*reliably* (or *characteristically*)' or the like since virtue is a matter of character."[35]

If this approach to leadership ethics is to be successful, it must fend off a serious attack aimed at virtue ethicists' preoccupation with character traits and their seeming unawareness of how people actually

---

[32] Julia Annas, "Being Virtuous and Doing the Right Thing," *Proceedings and Addresses of the American Philosophical Association* 78, 2 (November 2004): 63.

[33] Adapted from Aristotle, *Nicomachean Ethics*, 44 [1107a1–2].

[34] Annas, "Being Virtuous and Doing the Right Thing," 67.

[35] Annas, "Being Virtuous and Doing the Right Thing," 67.

behave. Philosophical critics such as John Doris and Gilbert Harman draw on empirical research in social psychology to argue that behavior is determined not by virtues, habits, or dispositions but rather by the demands of the situation.[36] This view – referred to as *situationism* – is the orthodoxy in social psychology, and it gets its primary support from studies such as the infamous Milgram obedience experiments.[37]

In these studies, subjects were instructed to administer electric shocks to "learners" who gave incorrect answers on a word-pairing test. The shock was increased when the learner gave a wrong answer. Fortunately, the learners were confederates, and their horrifying responses to the "shocks" were feigned. Subjects were given only non-coercive instructions (for example, "The experiment requires that you continue"), yet very few people refused to give the shocks even when the intensity was characterized as "Strong Shock," "Very Strong Shock," or "Intense Shock."[38] Indeed, in some of these experiments, roughly two-thirds of the subjects were willing to administer shocks to the maximum level of 450 volts – at the shock level, "XXX," which was greater than the level marked "Danger: Severe Shock."[39] Doris gives us good reason to believe that these results cannot be explained away by the suggestion that the subjects actually were aware of the deception. In a 1972 study by Sheridan and King, more than three-quarters of subjects were willing to administer *real* shocks at the highest level to a live puppy.[40]

If the subject pool in the Milgram experiments – drawn from Yale University's New Haven community – was made up of decent, ordinary

[36] See John Doris, *Lack of Character: Personality and Moral Behavior* (Cambridge: Cambridge University Press, 2002); Gilbert Harman, "Moral Philosophy Meets Social Psychology: Virtue Ethics and the Fundamental Attribution Error," *Proceedings of the Aristotelian Society* 99 (1999): 315–331; and Gilbert Harman, "No Character or Personality," *Business Ethics Quarterly* 13 (2003): 87–94.

[37] Stanley Milgram, *Obedience to Authority: An Experimental View* (New York: Harper and Row Publishers, 1974). The treatment of the subjects in Milgram's experiments, as well as in other experiments in this tradition, itself raises important questions about the justification of rule-breaking behavior. Are psychologists justified in bypassing the rationality of participants – say, lying to them – to achieve their research goals?

[38] Milgram, *Obedience to Authority*, 20–21, 35.

[39] Milgram, *Obedience to Authority*, 61.

[40] Doris, *Lack of Character*, 45. The original study is C. L. Sheridan and R. G. King, "Obedience to Authority with an Authentic Victim," *Proceedings of the American Psychological Association* 2 (1972): 165–166.

people, then why were they willing to engage in this kind of behavior? Outside of this experimental context, it is unlikely that these individuals would strike us as having the vices of submissiveness and cruelty or that they would see themselves in this way. Should we infer that the participants were bad people? Social psychologists call this tendency to explain behavior in terms of personal characteristics of actors the *fundamental attribution error*.[41]

An alternative explanation for the behavior in the Milgram studies is to see it not as a result of the fact that the subjects were bad people – we can assume they were no worse than the average person – but as a function of situational pressures.[42] Zimbardo's Stanford Prison Experiments similarly support this explanation of some immoral behavior.[43] Philip Zimbardo and colleagues randomly assigned subjects as "prisoners" and "guards" to reproduce the conditions of a prison. Subjects quickly adopted behaviors associated with their roles. For example, "guards" devised "creative sadisms" to punish, humiliate, and control "prisoners."[44] As Doris puts it, "Once again, it appears that persons are swamped by situations."[45] Situations can also swamp persons outside of experimental contexts. Here, we need only think about the behavior of many ordinary Germans in World War II and some U.S. soldiers in Vietnam – or in Iraq, for that matter.[46]

One objection to this critique of virtue theory is that the problems it raises do not apply to everyday leadership ethics. It does not follow from the fact that we cannot rely on character traits in extraordinary circumstances, that we cannot rely on them in everyday life. After all, most of us do not face the contrived conditions that characterized the experiments of Milgram and Zimbardo. Nor are we likely to live under a regime such as Hitler's or to be ordered to participate in a massacre, as were the U.S. soldiers in My Lai. According to this objection,

---

[41] See Richard Nisbett and Lee Ross, *Human Inference: Strategies and Shortcomings of Social Judgment* (Englewood Cliffs, NJ: Prentice-Hall, 1980), 31.

[42] Doris, *Lack of Character*, 42; Owen Flanagan, *Varieties of Moral Personality: Ethics and Psychological Realism* (Cambridge, MA: Harvard University Press, 1991), 296–298.

[43] Doris, *Lack of Character*, 51–53. For the original experiment, see Craig Haney, Curtis Banks, and Philip Zimbardo, "Interpersonal Dynamics in a Simulated Prison," *International Journal of Criminology and Penology* 1 (1973): 69–97.

[44] Doris, *Lack of Character*, 51.

[45] Doris, *Lack of Character*, 52.

[46] See, for example, Doris, *Lack of Character*, 53–58.

"[W]hat the Milgram experiment shows – and what subsequent events in Vietnam made all too painfully obvious – was that despite our high moral opinions of ourselves and our conformist chorus singing about what independent individuals we all are, Americans, like Germans before them, are capable of beastly behavior in circumstances where their *practiced* virtues are forced to confront an unusual situation in which unpracticed efforts are required."47

Maybe, then, we can rely on the virtues of effective leaders – general traits such as personal integrity and emotional development – in "usual" situations where these virtues are practiced. Unfortunately, other work in social psychology suggests that situationism can be extended to explain less extreme, morally problematic behavior in everyday life.48

Social psychologists Darley and Batson come to this conclusion in their famous study of helping behavior of seminarians, based on the parable of the Good Samaritan.49 In this parable,

A man was going down from Jerusalem to Jericho, and fell into the hands of robbers, who stripped him, beat him, and went away, leaving him half dead. Now by chance a priest was going down that road; and when he saw him, he passed by on the other side. So likewise a Levite, when he came to the place and saw him, passed by on the other side. But a Samaritan while traveling came near him; and when he saw him, he was moved with pity. He went to him and bandaged his wounds, having poured oil and wine on them. Then he put him on his own animal, brought him to an inn, and took care of him. The next day he took out two denarii, gave them to the innkeeper, and said, "Take care of him; and when I come back, I will repay you whatever more you spend."50

Translating this parable into an experimental context, Darley and Batson presented seminarians on their way to lectures with a "victim" in

47 Solomon, "Victim of Circumstances? A Defense of Virtue Ethics in Business," *Business Ethics Quarterly* 13 (2003): 53.
48 Doris, *Lack of Character*, 31–32.
49 John M. Darley and C. Daniel Batson, "'From Jerusalem to Jericho': A Study of Situational and Dispositional Variables in Helping Behavior," *Journal of Personality and Social Psychology* 27 (1973): 100–108. See the discussion by Doris, *Lack of Character*, 33–34.
50 *The New Oxford Annotated Bible: New Revised Standard Version*, ed. Michael D. Coogan, 3rd ed. (Oxford: Oxford University Press, 2001), Luke 10:30b-35.

need. Darley and Batson's findings ultimately support the situation-ist explanation. Contrary to what trait and theorists would suggest, personality variables such as religiosity did not predict whether seminarians on their way to give lectures – some on the parable of the Good Samaritan itself – would stop to help the "victim."[51]

What Darley and Batson found instead was that a single situational variable predicted the behavior of the seminarians. Whether seminarians stopped to help depended only on the degree to which they were in a hurry![52] Some seminarians had been told that they were late, and others had been told they had plenty of time to get to the lecture. Hurried seminarians went so far as to step right over the person who needed their help.[53] In this respect, the inclination of these individuals was to respond like the priest and the Levite. Cleverly describing the behavior of the religious leaders in the parable, Darley and Batson write, "One can imagine the priest and Levite, prominent public figures, hurrying along with little black books full of meetings and appointments, glancing furtively at their sundials."[54]

The situationist explanation is also supported by other helping studies. Something as simple as whether a person finds a dime in a phone booth can predict whether the subject will help a "victim" who has dropped her belongings.[55] Experiments of this kind thus require something well short of "heroic" behavior.[56] Running into someone who needs our help is pretty much an everyday occurrence.

Of course, we could say that it is not completely clear what one morally ought to do in everyday cases in which others could use our help. Annas seems to have this objection in mind when she suggests that "a virtue is a disposition to act *for reasons*, and claims about frequency of action are irrelevant to this, until some plausible connection is established with the agent's reasons, something none

---

[51] Darley and Batson, "'From Jerusalem to Jericho,'" 102.
[52] Darley and Batson, "'From Jerusalem to Jericho,'" 107–108.
[53] Darley and Batson, "'From Jerusalem to Jericho,'" 107.
[54] Darley and Batson, "'From Jerusalem to Jericho,'" 101.
[55] See Doris, *Lack of Character*, 30–32, for a description of this experiment and others on the effect of mood on helping behavior. The original experiment is A. M. Isen and P. F. Levin, "Effect of Feeling Good on Helping: Cookies and Kindness," *Journal of Personality and Social Psychology* 21 (1972): 384–388.
[56] Doris, *Lack of Character*, 31.

of the situationists have done."[57] To be sure, the social psychological studies do not establish a connection between agents' reasons and the morally recommended behavior in question – say, helping a victim in need. However, these experiments do establish that people's behavior is determined by considerations that *cannot* constitute good reasons for action – for instance, something as morally irrelevant as whether they find a dime in a phone booth. Accordingly, it does not make sense to explain the behavior of individuals who fail to engage in helping behavior by suggesting that they may have had good reasons to behave as they did. These individuals readily altered their behavior when morally irrelevant situational factors were introduced.

A better response to the situationist critique of virtue theory holds that the experiments in social psychology do not show that the virtues fail to predict behavior. What they show is that fewer people than we might imagine have the relevant virtues, even in everyday situations. So, to the charge "We cannot count on the virtuous person to do the right thing," the virtue ethicist responds that people who do the wrong thing are not virtuous after all. For example, Annas rejects the case "where there would be agreement on what was the right thing to do, but this is patently not what the virtuous person would (reliably or characteristically) do."[58] Annas claims that "the virtuous person wouldn't have behaved badly in the first place."[59]

Even in the Milgram studies, some people managed to resist the pressures of the situation. As Owen Flanagan notes, "It is important to keep in mind that a significant minority – fully one-third of the participants – did refuse to obey."[60] Jonathan Glover similarly describes a Princeton follow-up to the Milgram studies:

Eighty per cent of his subjects were fully obedient. The widespread tendency to obey was confirmed, but it was not universal. The kind of person someone is can make a difference. There is something satisfying about the fact that

---

[57] Annas, "Virtue Ethics," in *Oxford Handbook of Ethical Theory*, ed. David Copp (Oxford: Oxford University Press, 2006), 519.

[58] Annas, "Being Virtuous and Doing the Right Thing," 67.

[59] Annas, "Being Virtuous and Doing the Right Thing," 67.

[60] Flanagan, *Varieties of Moral Personality*, 295. He goes on to say that this should not make the trait theorist hopeful.

Ronald Ridenhour, who later blew the whistle on the massacre at My Lai, refused to give even the first shock.[61]

Does the fact that individuals such as Ridenhour overcame the situation, instead of being overcome by it, vindicate virtue ethics?

This response is only *partial* vindication. Vindication is in the fact that some people may indeed be able to rely on their traits to do what is morally right. The response is only partially vindicating, however, because it leads to a new concern. If almost everyone would fail to do what is right when circumstances are manipulated in morally irrelevant ways, then we can no longer be sure we know who the virtuous people really are. Inability to identify the virtues in ourselves and in others would mean that we cannot look to the virtuous people for a determination of morality and, in particular, for a determination of cases in which rule breaking would be justified for effective leaders.

## UNIQUENESS

We can trust leaders to engage in justified rule breaking only if we can predict when they have the virtues in question. As it turns out, we are very bad at predicting whether people will be virtuous in particular situations. For example,

When asked to predict how far a diverse group of Americans would go [in the Milgram experiments], [thirty-nine Yale] psychiatrists predicted, on average, that fewer than 50 percent would still be obedient at the tenth level (150 volts), fewer than four in a hundred would reach the twentieth level, and fewer than one in a thousand would administer the maximum shock. It is remarkable that psychiatrists, who are trained to perceive subtle force fields in the social environment, and who are also well aware of dark, seamy, and destructive urges, could be so far off the mark here.[62]

Worse still is our ability to make predictions about our own behavior. These same psychiatrists, along with a group of college students and middle-class adults, made even more inaccurate predictions about the strength of their own virtues: "Everyone was sure he or she would break

---

[61] Jonathan Glover, *Humanity: A Moral History of the Twentieth Century* (New Haven, CT: Yale University Press, 2000), 333.

[62] Flanagan, *Varieties of Moral Personality*, 295.

off very early."[63] Insofar as effective leaders are like the rest of us in this respect, the general tendency to inflate one's own virtuousness will make it unlikely that effective leaders will be able to predict their own prospects for moral success.

Social psychologists call the differential between our expectations of others and our expectations of ourselves the *uniqueness bias*.[64] This phenomenon has been confirmed for both non-moral and moral qualities. As George Goethals, David Messick, and Scott Allison note in their survey of the research on this effect, "The uniqueness bias reflects our tendency to see ourselves as somewhat better than average, a tendency that has been observed in a wide variety of domains including vulnerability to major life events, driving ability, responses to victimization, perceptions of fairness, and goodness."[65] These studies on uniqueness caution us about relying on leaders to determine when rule-breaking behavior is justified. Because of the uniqueness bias, leaders will think that they are more effective and more virtuous than they really are.

Goethals, Messick, and Allison also refer to a study that was carried out at the University of California, Santa Barbara, in which

subjects were asked whether they and their peers would or could perform a variety of behaviors involving moral choices (termed *would* items) or academic, athletic, creative, or interpersonal skill (termed *could* items) . . . All subjects were [also] asked . . . to indicate the percentage of their peers at UCSB that could perform them . . . The results of this study show a number of things. First, as many other studies have shown, there is a strong self-serving bias, specifically, a uniqueness bias in consensus estimates. The proportion of people indicating that they would or could perform socially desirable behaviors is higher than the proportion people estimate would or could perform them. Second, this . . . study shows that would items, dealing with a variety of moral choices, produce more self-other differentiation than could items, dealing with a variety of ability-linked performances.[66]

---

[63] Flanagan, *Varieties of Moral Personality*, 295.

[64] G. R. Goethals, D. W. Messick, and S. T. Allison, "The Uniqueness Bias: Studies of Constructive Social Comparison," in *Social Comparison: Contemporary Theory and Research*, ed. J. Suls and T. A. Wills (Hillsdale, NJ: Erlbaum, 1991), 149–176.

[65] Goethals, Messick, and Allison, "The Uniqueness Bias," 149.

[66] Goethals, Messick, and Allison, "The Uniqueness Bias," 161–162. The study described is G. R. Goethals, "Social Comparison Theory: Psychology From the Lost

Goethals, Messick, and Allison explain the second finding this way: "Estimates of how much more likely one is to perform moral behaviors may be less constrained by reality than estimates of how much more likely one is to perform behaviors requiring ability."[67] In other words, there are fewer barriers to exaggerating our moral qualities than there are to exaggerating our non-moral qualities.

An appeal to the constraints of reality similarly explains why, with respect to the "could" items, "the uniqueness bias was stronger for the general items than for the specific. Indeed, for the specific [could] items there was virtually no uniqueness bias."[68] Reality constrains our behavioral predictions in two ways.[69] First, for more specific "could" items – for example, "could parallel park a car within 6 inches of the curb" – there is a greater chance that we will *know* whether we have the ability in question.[70] This is a *cognitive* constraint. Our general abilities are not self-evident, so we may not be able to answer the question of whether we are good drivers. Second, because specific items lend themselves to verification, there are greater *incentives* for giving accurate responses. If a subject says that she can park a car within six inches of the curb, she may well be asked to prove it. This is a *motivational* constraint.

Because effectiveness is a *general* trait, we can expect that it will be especially subject to the uniqueness bias. Determinations of effectiveness do not lend themselves to the cognitive and motivational constraints that apply to more specific measurements of effectiveness, measurements such as profit or productivity. According to Yukl, "Of the many different taxonomies of skills, a widely accepted approach for classifying managerial skills uses the three broadly defined skill categories" – *technical skills, interpersonal skills,* and *conceptual skills.*[71] So, even the skills that constitute "the [abilities] to do something in

---

and Found," *Personality and Social Psychology Bulletin* 12 (1986): 261–278. Coincidentally, RiskMetrics CEO Ethan Berman, whose leadership I discuss in Chapter 3, assisted in this research when he was a student at Williams College.

[67] Goethals, Messick, and Allison, "The Uniqueness Bias," 163.
[68] Goethals, Messick, and Allison, "The Uniqueness Bias," 163.
[69] The authors do not clearly separate these constraints, but they make implicit appeals to each (Goethals, Messick, and Allison, "The Uniqueness Bias," 163, 166).
[70] Goethals, Messick, and Allison, "The Uniqueness Bias," 163.
[71] Yukl, *Leadership in Organizations,* 181.

an effective manner"[72] are themselves general abilities, not specific abilities.

The nature of leadership and, more specifically, the leader-follower relationship give us additional reasons to think that leaders will be particularly susceptible to seeing their traits and virtues as unique. Some of the most important of these reasons have to do with the kind of information that is cognitively available to leaders. Behind these cognitive explanations is "the idea that we compare with other people who are salient or available, or with whom we interact often, whether we want to or not. That is, social comparison is often forced."[73]

First, leaders are generally surrounded by individuals who have relatively fewer chances to demonstrate their positive qualities. The many opportunities leaders have to behave in ways that show their skills may well cause leaders to think they are more special than they really are. In the classroom, professors get this kind of advantage from availability biases.[74] Professors choose the texts, which they have read and studied, and ask the questions, which they have thought about and are often able to answer. As a result, they come across as being even smarter than they really are.

Second, even in cases in which it is true that we can legitimately differentiate leaders from their followers based on personal characteristics, the available sample that constitutes a leader's primary point of social comparison is nevertheless biased. Simply put, the leader may not need to engage in "constructive social comparison" to "manufacture a less fortunate other."[75] In the leadership context, constructive social comparison is often unnecessary because the leader has a comparison point that is ready made to support his high opinion of himself. Because the sample normally includes only the leader and followers, many of whom – by assumption – are less talented or admired than he, it can seem to support a strong conclusion about the uniqueness of the leader's talents and virtues relative to the population at

---

[72] Yukl, *Leadership in Organizations*, 181.

[73] Goethals, Messick, and Allison, "The Uniqueness Bias," 153.

[74] Richard Nisbett and Lee Ross also discuss this kind of "role-conferred advantage" (*Human Inference: Strategies and Shortcomings of Social Judgment*, 85).

[75] Goethals, Messick, and Allison, "The Uniqueness Bias," 154–155. The second quoted phrase is from S. E. Taylor, B. P. Buunk, and L. G. Aspinwall, "Social Comparison, Stress, and Coping," *Journal of Personality and Social Psychology Bulletin* 16 (1990): 74–89.

large. Yet the stronger conclusion does not follow, because the sample that is available to the leader is not representative of the general population, which surely includes other, similarly talented and virtuous individuals.

A final reason to think that leaders will be particularly susceptible to the uniqueness bias is that the tendency to engage in constructive social comparison is "strongest when information about actual consensus is the least available or accessible."[76] Although actual consensus information would give leaders the truth about how unique or common their traits and virtues really are, "people are likely to engage in realistic social comparison [only if] they are motivated to support a positive self-appraisal, or a specific social comparison conclusion."[77] But why would leaders think they have to justify their views of themselves to others? Many leaders will see their positions of leadership as being sufficient justification for their perceptions of themselves. As John Stuart Mill puts it, "Absolute princes, or others who are accustomed to unlimited deference, usually feel ... complete confidence in their own opinions on nearly all subjects."[78]

Moreover, on the off chance that leaders are moved to offer some kind of justification of their superiority, they are unlikely to learn about the weaknesses of their reasoning from others who may have a better sense of just how ordinary these leaders actually are. Power differentials between leaders and followers, as well as the interest we all have in keeping powerful people happy, often make it difficult to "speak truth to power." Leaders are therefore relatively unlikely to get appropriate feedback about actual consensus. As in the Hans Christian Anderson story "The Emperor's New Clothes," few people are willing to point out the emperor's nakedness. This general feature of leadership – namely, its barriers to critical feedback – along with its tendencies (1) to underemphasize the positive personal characteristics of followers, and (2) to encourage comparisons only with followers, suggests that leaders are probably not as special as they are inclined to see themselves.

---

[76] Goethals, Messick, and Allison, "The Uniqueness Bias," 157.

[77] Goethals, Messick, and Allison, "The Uniqueness Bias," 155.

[78] Mill, *On Liberty*, ed. Elizabeth Rapaport (Indianapolis: Hackett Publishing Company, 1978), 17.

## THE VIRTUE THEORIST AS SITUATIONIST

Can traits and virtues justify rule breaking by effective leaders? First, leaders would have to know that they themselves are effective. Second, leaders would have to know that they have the virtues associated with effectiveness – namely, personal integrity and emotional development. The discussion of the uniqueness bias in the previous section should make us suspicious about any leader's claims to such knowledge. In fact, it is sometimes difficult to determine which comes first, a leader's belief that he is justified in his behavior or his belief that he has the virtues in question. Leaders sometimes start with the assumption that their rule-breaking behavior is justified, and infer that they must be virtuous.

The theory of *cognitive dissonance* supports this point: "Cognitive dissonance theory provides the key idea of self-justification... [A]t the heart of the theory is the idea that people generate cognitions to fit, and therefore *justify* their feelings and behavior."[79] In other words, the need for justification will often precede an attribution of the relevant virtues. When this happens, leaders do not make a determination of whether they have personal integrity and are emotionally developed *before* coming to a conclusion about whether rule-breaking behavior would be justified. Instead, as predicted by the research on cognitive dissonance, the attributions of virtue are derived *after* the formation of beliefs about justification. Even more worrisome, perhaps, is the fact that the behavior itself often precedes any attempt at moral justification.

Other aspects of social comparison theory prove equally instructive for this way of thinking about leaders' efforts to justify rule-breaking behavior. Goethals, Messick, and Allison, in their discussion of faulty consensus estimates, appeal to F. H. Allport's notion of *illusion of universality*, which holds "that people often assume that others are responding in a given situation in the same way as they and imagine that their own response is universal."[80] This may be especially true for morally questionable behaviors, as when people choose competitive

---

[79] Goethals, Messick, and Allison, "The Uniqueness Bias," 153 (emphasis added).
[80] Goethals, Messick, and Allison, "The Uniqueness Bias," 157. Their citation to the original is F. H. Allport, *Social Psychology* (Cambridge, MA: Riverside Press, 1924).

over cooperative responses.[81] In these cases, leaders who seek to justify rule-breaking behavior would not need to believe that everyone breaks the rules. To conclude that they are justified in this behavior themselves, leaders need only believe that there is consensus that anyone similarly situated has a justification for rule breaking.

Why would leaders hold this belief? One explanation is that the uniqueness bias does not apply to opinions. People believe that they are special when it comes to their positive traits and virtues, but that "their opinions are common."[82] We can therefore expect that leaders who hold the opinion that their rule-breaking behavior is justified will also believe that others share this belief. This cognitive bias generates universalization with respect to beliefs about justification. The leader can craft the description of his behavior in such a way that it can be universalized: "Anyone relevantly like me would be justified in acting as I am about to act."

For the sake of argument, let us assume that a leader who makes this claim of justification is both effective and virtuous. How would her justification for rule-breaking behavior work? All we know is that, according to virtue theory, this leader will make the right decision when she breaks the rules. But not even a virtuous leader would be justified in indiscriminately breaking the rules. How, then, does a virtuous leader decide when rule-breaking behavior is justified? The determination cannot be based simply on the fact that she is virtuous. In other words, she cannot see her being virtuous as a sufficient justification for rule breaking. If virtue were sufficient, then – because this leader is virtuous – she would always be justified in breaking the rules. On what, then, can a virtuous leader base her decision, if not the fact that she is virtuous?

Here, Aristotle's virtue ethics gives us a clue. Aristotle tells us that "intelligent young people do not seem to be found. The reason is that intelligence is concerned with particulars as well as universals, and particulars become known from experience, but a young person lacks

---

[81] Goethals, Messick, and Allison, "The Uniqueness Bias," 149.

[82] Goethals, Messick, and Allison, "The Uniqueness Bias," 156. The authors cite G. Marks, "Thinking One's Abilities are Unique and One's Opinions are Common," *Personality and Social Psychology Bulletin* 10 (1984): 203–208. See Chapter 5 of this book for a discussion of the role of agreement in the justification of leadership behavior.

experience, since some length of time is needed to produce it."[83] Practical wisdom, as exercised by the virtuous person, is knowledge applied to *particular situations*. The only way to understand a particular situation is by drawing on past experiences and ascertaining the extent to which the present circumstances are similar to, and different from, other circumstances to which one has been exposed. This means that the virtuous leader must ultimately look to the features of a situation to justify exception-making behavior. In other words, even virtue theory must appeal to the situation to explain the behavior of the virtuous leader!

The virtuous leader is distinguished from others precisely by her capacity to identify elements of the situation that determine whether an exception would be justified. With respect to both emotion and action, she is the one who responds "at the right times, about the right things, towards the right people, for the right end, and in the right way, [which] is the intermediate and best condition, and this is proper to virtue."[84] Leaders must use the situation to decide whether rule breaking would be justified.

What is it about particular situations that justifies rule-breaking behavior by leaders? Chapter 6 will consider the claim that the importance of group goals can justify rule breaking by leaders in particular situations. First, however, Chapter 5 turns to the argument that leaders are justified in breaking the rules based on the agreement of followers. As we will see, this argument also calls for an analysis of the situationist justification of rule breaking.

[83] Aristotle, *Nicomachean Ethics*, 160 [1142a15].
[84] Aristotle, *Nicomachean Ethics*, 44 [1106b21–23].

PART II

GROUP-CENTRIC APPROACHES

# 5

## Permission and Consent

ALLOWING EXCEPTIONS

The argument of the previous chapter challenged one familiar way of grounding the special moral status of leaders. Trait views of leadership, as well as virtue theories of ethics with which they are associated, ignore the tendency of leaders to exaggerate how special they are in terms of their personal characteristics. Because of these tendencies, we should be especially wary of leaders who appeal to particular traits and virtues to justify their rule-breaking behavior.

To the student of leadership, it will come as little surprise to learn that if leaders do have special moral status, then this status cannot be derived simply from the qualities of leaders themselves. Moral and political analyses of leadership long ago turned their attention to the nature of the *relationships* between leaders and followers – for example, to the ethical importance of "the consent of the governed." Leader-centric approaches to the empirical study of leadership have also gone out of favor, at least in part because of their failure to attend to the role of followers in the leadership process. Whether prescriptive or descriptive in nature, most contemporary work on leadership recognizes that leadership is a complex phenomenon, one that involves more than individual leaders and their personal characteristics.

The search for an answer to the central question of leadership ethics – *Do the distinctive features of leadership justify rule-breaking behavior?* – must therefore expand the potential grounds of justification for rule-breaking behavior by leaders and consider group-centric approaches. One such approach sees followers as the primary source of justification and holds that the special moral status of leaders rests on the permission or consent of followers. In essence, a leader is justified in breaking the rules "because we said he could."

The idea that follower consent justifies leadership behavior has a central place in the history of political theory. For example, in his *Leviathan*, Thomas Hobbes (1588–1679) famously defends absolute sovereignty as the outcome of a *social contract*.[1] According to Hobbes, pre-political conditions – what social contract theorists refer to as the *state of nature* – ultimately spawn a war "of every man, against every man."[2] Because no one has the power to resolve conflicts in the state of nature, "the life of man [is] solitary, poor, nasty, brutish, and short."[3] To escape these conditions, society must resort to an all-powerful leader who can put an end to the conflict that characterizes life in the natural state. As a present-day Hobbesian might put it, "Someone has to be the boss."[4]

One particularly relevant feature of Hobbesian leadership is that the leader himself is not subject to the rules: "Because the right of bearing the person of them all is given to him they make sovereign by covenant . . . of one to another and not of him to any of them, there can happen no breach of covenant on the part of the sovereign."[5] In other words, the parties to the social contract give the leader a blanket exception to the rules that apply more generally to followers. This is necessary for the peace and security that strong leadership brings with it.[6]

---

[1] Thomas Hobbes, *Leviathan*, ed. Richard Tuck (Cambridge: Cambridge University Press, 1991).

[2] Hobbes, *Leviathan*, 88.

[3] Adapted from Hobbes, *Leviathan*, 89.

[4] Randy Barnett identifies his grandfather's sentiment that "there's got to be a boss" with a principle of politics and law: "[T]he Single Power Principle involves a belief in the need for a *coercive monopoly of power* (Randy E. Barnett, *The Structure of Liberty: Justice and the Rule of Law* [Oxford: Oxford University Press, 1998], 240).

[5] Adapted from Hobbes, *Leviathan*, 122.

[6] When Douglas Wilder was inaugurated as mayor of Richmond, Virginia, in 2005, citizens seemed to think that a "strong" mayor was just what the city needed. Among Wilder's exercises of strength was a failed attempt to run school administrators out of City Hall in October 2007, an action that made the financial and political costs of a new city governance structure much more obvious. City Council

By making the leader exceptional, followers preempt potentially dangerous, and ultimately irresoluble, controversies over whether the leader is justified in his behavior. Whatever the sovereign does

can be no injury to any of his subjects nor ought he to be by any of them accused of an injustice. For he that does anything by authority from another, does therein no injury to him by whose authority he acts. But by this institution of a commonwealth, every particular man is author of all the sovereign does; and consequently he that complains of injury from his sovereign complains of that whereof he himself is author; and therefore ought not to accuse any man but himself; no nor himself of injury because to do injury to oneself is impossible.[7]

In short, because followers have consented, it is their will that gets exercised through the rule-breaking behavior of the leader. Followers are in no position to complain because what their leader does to them can be equally described as what they have done to themselves.

Consent plays a parallel role in more recent studies of organizational leadership. E. P. Hollander, for instance, sees it as the ultimate source of a leader's status within the group:

[A] leader denotes an individual with a status that permits him to exercise influence over certain other individuals. Specifically, our concern is directed toward leaders deriving status from followers who may accord or withdraw it, in a group context. Group consent is therefore a central feature in the leader-follower relationship.[8]

Hollander's research, as discussed in Chapter 1, suggests that leaders gain the consent of followers by showing both early competence in group tasks and conformity to group rules. Having earned "idiosyncrasy credit" in these early interactions, leaders "reach a threshold which permits deviation and innovation."[9]

---

President William J. Pantele responded to a Circuit Court ruling against Wilder: "There is no exception or excuse for not following the law, and that's what the judge ruled" (Michael Martz, "Judge faults Wilder on eviction; ruling lets school board sue over aborted move, validates City Hall lease," *Richmond Times-Dispatch* [November 6, 2007]).

[7] Adapted from Hobbes, *Leviathan*, 124.

[8] Hollander, *Leaders, Groups, and Influence* (New York: Oxford University Press, 1964), 16.

[9] Hollander, *Leaders, Groups, and Influence*, 167, 159.

According to Hollander, "[T]his formulation serves to explain the seeming paradox that the leader both conforms to group norms and yet operates to alter group norms."[10] Once a group member has sufficient status to become a leader, his rule-breaking behavior receives "rubber stamping" by the group and goes "unhindered."[11] Yet followers refuse to allow rule-breaking behavior by individuals who have not emerged as leaders in the group. In effect, followers consent to the exceptions leaders make of themselves, but withhold consent from other group members who seek to engage in similar behavior.[12]

If followers consent to rule-breaking behavior by leaders, then – initially at least – it is hard to see how even a Kantian can object. First, properly described, the behavior in question would seem to be universalizable. The leader who is about to resort to deceptive behavior would imagine a world in which people engage in deception only when they have the consent of other individuals who are subject to the rules of morality. This world is importantly different from the one in which people engage in deception without the consent of others. A world of universal deception is self-undermining because deception works only in a world generally characterized by veracity. It is for this reason that deception serves as the Kantian paradigm of immorality. But in a world in which leaders engage in deception only when they have the consent of followers, consent strictly limits the extent to which people can permissibly engage in rule breaking. The resulting scheme, in which only leaders are allowed to break the rules, seems to preserve the backdrop of general rule-following behavior.

Second, this way of differentiating leaders from followers does not assume that there are fundamental differences in moral status between leaders and followers. When leaders are permitted to break the rules, it is not because of the alleged moral superiority of leaders but rather because followers rationally decide that these rules should not apply to leaders in the same way that they apply to followers. In other words, the consent-based justification for rule breaking by leaders does not necessarily imply that leaders who break the rules treat followers as mere means. Leaders respect the rationality of followers by subjecting

[10] Hollander, *Leaders, Groups, and Influence*, 159.
[11] Hollander, *Leaders, Groups, and Influence*, 203.
[12] Hollander, *Leaders, Groups, and Influence*, 203.

their rule-breaking behavior to the follower consent. The consent-based justification thus appears to be consistent with the idea that followers are ends in themselves – that they are rational agents capable of deciding what rules they and others ought to live by.

## THE SCOPE OF CONTRACTARIAN MORALITY

*Contractarian* ethical theories see morality as the result of agreement. Parties to the agreement consent to moral rules because doing so serves their rational self-interest. Why is it rational for the contractors to accept the rules of morality? Ultimately they are motivated by a desire to constrain the self-interested behavior of the other members of society. The rules of morality provide protection to all parties in exchange for their willingness to comply with these rules.

From the perspective of naked self-interest, the best possible situation for any rational agent would be one in which other members of society comply with moral rules but the agent himself is allowed to break these rules. However, being rational, this agent recognizes that each of the other members has similar desires and that if everyone were to act on unrestrained self-interest, people would wind up in the worst possible situation – a world that looks a lot like Hobbes's state of nature. So, according to the basic contractarian line of argument, rational agents willingly opt for a "second-best solution." As Glaucon in Plato's *Republic* puts it, people conform to the rules of morality only because they have to.[13] Rational agents willingly accept some sacrifices in terms of self-interest in exchange for the relatively greater gains associated with the protections of morality.

One striking feature of contractarian ethical theories is that the moral rules they generate are quite limited in scope: the *protections* of morality extend only to members of the society in question.[14] Because "outsiders" – by definition – are not party to the contract, they do not fall within the scope of the rules that derive from it. As a result, contractarianism is necessarily silent on the treatment of outsiders. The treatment of outsiders is a critical moral issue for leadership, one to which we will return in Chapters 7 and 8. For now, suffice it to

[13] Plato, *Republic*, trans. G. M. A. Grube (Indianapolis: Hackett Publishing Company, 1992), 35 [359c].
[14] See Chapter 1 for a discussion of the scope of morality.

say that even if consent is morally relevant to a justification of what would otherwise be mistreatment of society's members, the consent of these individuals is morally irrelevant to a justification of the mistreatment of people outside their society. Follower consent to a leader's mistreatment of outsiders would do nothing more than make followers complicit in the leader's wrongdoing. So leaders cannot cloak themselves in follower consent to justify potentially immoral behavior toward people who are not members of their own society.

Contractarianism also refuses to extend the protections of morality to some people within the contracting society. Individuals that we typically consider to be "insiders" will not be accorded the protections of morality when, as Allen Buchanan puts it, they lack "the capacity to contribute and the capacity to harm."[15] The potential to help and the potential to harm constitute "*strategic* capacities insofar as an individual can use them to influence the behavior of other rational, purely self-interested agents."[16] Here, Buchanan has foremost in mind the exclusion of severely impaired group members.[17] He refers to the basic contractarian sentiment behind their exclusion from the scope of morality's protections as "justice as reciprocity."[18]

For example, the purely physical limitations of some fully rational individuals can effectively mean that they have no strategic capacities. This is not to say that such individuals have nothing to offer society by virtue of their cognitive capacities. But it is safe to assume that whatever contribution some disabled individuals might be able to make will be outweighed by the costs of responding to their physical needs, especially when these costs are combined with the expense of significantly adapting the social environment to make any such contributions possible.[19] In other words, because of physical disabilities alone, these individuals will not be in a position to make a *net* contribution to the self-interest of other members of society. As a consequence,

---

[15] Buchanan, "Justice as Reciprocity versus Subject-Centered Justice," *Philosophy and Public Affairs* 19 (1990): 228.

[16] Buchanan, "Justice as Reciprocity," 228.

[17] Buchanan, "Justice as Reciprocity," 230–232.

[18] Buchanan, "Justice as Reciprocity," 227.

[19] See Allen Buchanan, Dan W. Brock, Norman Daniels, and Daniel Wickler, *From Chance to Choice: Genetics and Justice* (Cambridge: Cambridge University Press, 2000), ch. 7.

contractarianism will not extend the basic protections of morality to them, regardless of how rational such agents might be.

By itself, then, the capacity for rational agreement does not serve as a strategic capacity in moral theories committed to the idea of justice as reciprocity. Contractarianism values only those capacities that have an instrumental payoff within the contingent circumstances of the contracting situation. Because rationality alone has no such payoff, but must be combined with other capacities, the basic value of rationality is reduced to what it can achieve for agents simply as a vehicle for negotiation. One way to put this contractarian point is to say that rationality is the price of admission to the contracting situation. Once admitted to this situation, each contractor uses the goods he has to offer, as well as the harm he can threaten, to drive the outcome of the contract. In this sense, the capacity for rational agreement is necessary for the protection of morality, but it is by no means sufficient.

Even agents who have strategic capacities, and thereby qualify for the protections of morality, are not guaranteed the *full* protection of the moral rules. This vulnerability is another result of the fact that what the contracting parties get from the agreement ultimately depends on what they bring to it. The least capable members of group will be in the worst bargaining position and, as a consequence, may be able to negotiate only minimal protections of morality.

We see this kind of inequality in moral status, for instance, in situations in which the least powerful members of an organization are protected by rules against physical abuse and dangerous working conditions, but not by rules against deception and promise breaking. For instance, some workers will be the last to know that they are about to lose their jobs as a result of downsizing or restructuring, perhaps because they have been explicitly told otherwise. Because these individuals are perceived to have little to offer the company, and few means of defending themselves against mistreatment, they are unable to negotiate better terms from the other parties to the agreement – in this case, their employers.[20]

---

[20] Douglas Hicks discusses voluntariness and coercion to defend strong protections for employees (Douglas A. Hicks, *Religion and the Workplace: Pluralism, Spirituality, Leadership* [Cambridge: Cambridge University Press, 2003], 168–173).

Contractarian ethical theories also have their own answer to a second set of questions regarding the scope of morality. These questions ask who is *bound* – and to what extent – by the moral rules. Like questions about who is *protected* by the moral rules, these scope questions ask how morality should be applied to particular individuals. But here the issue of application is not about whether morality's protections extend to outsiders or to the most vulnerable members of society. Instead the issue is whether the most capable members of society must follow the same rules that others are required to follow. The basic contractarian answer is that the contract itself establishes how morality binds particular individuals. Whether the most capable members of society are justified in breaking the rules depends on the details of the contract they are able to negotiate.

This answer is particularly relevant to a determination of whether rule-breaking behavior is justified for particular group members. As we might expect, the most capable members of the group will be in the best bargaining position and, as a consequence, better able to negotiate permission to break rules that other group members are expected to follow. Because the most capable group members have the greatest capacity to help or harm other members of the group, they are in a solid position to claim that they are owed something more in virtue of their participation in the collective enterprise. Who will these individuals be? We would be foolish not to expect that they will often be the potential leaders of their group, organization, or society.

An appeal to the greater bargaining power of leaders does not assume that leaders will always have greater strategic capacities. As we have seen, they will often be inclined to exaggerate the value of their strategic capacities.[21] Nor does this appeal ignore the fact that followers will sometimes mistakenly inflate the amount of control leaders have over the situation.[22] In fact, barriers to knowledge fuel the negotiating power of leaders. According to the contractarian approach, *perception* is what matters. Followers are therefore left to judge the

---

[21] See the discussion of uniqueness in Chapter 4.
[22] Gary Yukl, *Leadership in Organizations*, 6th ed. (Upper Saddle River, NJ: Prentice Hall, 2006), 129.

capacities of potential leaders from their own perspectives and, based on these judgments, to decide whether to give some individuals leeway to break the rules.

Why might followers consent to rule breaking by leaders? The answer that best fits with the contractarian framework is that followers think that it is in their self-interest to allow leaders to break the rules. For one thing, the fewer restraints there are on leaders, the more likely leaders will be to cooperate with followers. In this respect, contractarianism gives some weight to follower interests. When followers consent to rule breaking, leaders can assert that they are advancing something more than their own self-interest. Even the interests of followers, they might tell us, support the conclusion that leaders should be less than fully bound by morality.

Does follower self-interest support this conclusion? As it turns out, what a follower stands to gain from social cooperation has only a partial effect on the outcome of the contract. What a follower gets is a result not only of *his* needs and wants but also of what others are willing to offer him given *their* needs and wants. The terms of the contract for any particular individual are therefore a function of his self-interest *and* his bargaining power. Although the interests of followers play a role, the leader can still get better terms simply "because he can."

As we saw in Chapter 3, an appeal to the fact that someone can get away with breaking the rules to advance his self-interest does not count as a moral justification. It is nothing more than the exercise of power. A person is justified in doing what he can in service of his interests only on the assumption that his behavior conforms to a set of rules that appropriately limits his exercise of power and reasonably adjudicates between his interests and the interests of others. For example, a landlord is within his rights to charge what the market will bear "because he can" only within a justified property scheme.

The contractarian argument makes no such assumption about a background set of rules that constrain the contracting parties. The rules themselves, as well as their application, are determined by the contract itself. Outcomes will therefore reflect extreme power disparities in the contracting situation. Follower self-interest determines the outcome of the contract only insofar as it is coupled with the *power* to get contractual terms that serve the needs and wants of followers. In

other words, contractarianism gives at least as great a justificatory role
to unconstrained power as it does to follower self-interest.

## CONTRACTUALISM AND FAIRNESS

Concerns of this kind lead to a variant of contractarianism sometimes referred to as *contractualism*. Contractualism, as articulated by
John Rawls (1921–2002) in *A Theory of Justice*, grounds morality not in
*actual* agreement but rather in *hypothetical* agreement.[23] Rawls develops "a conception of justice which generalizes and carries to a higher
level of abstraction the familiar theory of the social contract found,
say, in Locke, Rousseau, and Kant... [T]he guiding idea is that the
principles of justice... are the principles that free and rational persons concerned to further their own interests *would* accept in an initial
position of equality as defining the fundamental terms of their association."[24] A defining feature of contractualist theories, then, is that
they control for strategic capacities that result from "natural chance
or the contingency of social circumstances."[25]

Although contractualism is much closer to what Buchanan calls
"subject-centered conceptions of justice,"[26] some interpretations of
this view will not be exactly generous in the extension of morality's
protections. For example, Peter Carruthers, in his articulation of the
contractualist position, claims that rights do not extend to non-human
animals.[27] Carruthers's argument highlights the moral necessity of the
capacity for rationality, not the capacity to help or harm.[28] Non-human
animals are clearly capable of helping and harming – for example, as
rescue animals during disasters or as police dogs in paramilitary units.
However, what non-human animals do not have, and what Carruthers
believes they must have, is sufficient rationality for sophisticated rule-
making and rule-following behavior: "[N]o animals appear capable
of conceptualizing (let alone acting under) generally socially agreed

---

[23] Rawls, *A Theory of Justice* (Cambridge, MA: Belknap Press of Harvard University Press,
     1971).
[24] Rawls, *A Theory of Justice*, 11 (emphasis added).
[25] Rawls, *A Theory of Justice*, 12.
[26] See Buchanan, "Justice as Reciprocity," 230n6.
[27] Peter Carruthers, *The Animals Issue* (Cambridge: Cambridge University Press, 1992).
[28] Carruthers, *The Animals Issue*, ch. 5.

rules."[29] Morality's protections extend only to agents who can think of themselves and others as being *bound* by morality.[30]

Contractualism is nonetheless a great moral improvement on standard contractarian theories, at least when it comes to questions about the membership of rational agents in the moral community. Standard contractarian theories allow bargaining power, as determined by strategic capacity, to affect the outcome of the contract. In contrast, contractualist theories work from *fair bargaining conditions* that preclude stronger or wealthier parties from using their power and resources to force an agreement that offers minimal protection to some rational agents while allowing the strong and wealthy to be only minimally bound by the rules.

To this end, contractualism appeals to a hypothetical contract designed to equalize the disparities in power that plague actual contracts:

In justice as fairness the original position of equality corresponds to the state of nature in the traditional theory of the social contract. This original position is not, of course, thought of as an actual historical state of affairs, much less as a primitive condition of culture. It is understood as a purely hypothetical situation characterized so as to lead to a certain conception of justice. Among the essential features of this situation is that no one knows his place in society, his class position or social status, nor does any one know his fortune in the distribution of natural assets and abilities, his intelligence, strength, and the like ... The principles of justice are chosen behind a veil of ignorance ... Since all are similarly situated and no one is able to design principles to favor his particular condition, the principles of justice are the result of a fair agreement or bargain. For given the circumstances of the original position, the symmetry of everyone's relations to each other, this initial situation is fair between individuals as moral persons, that is, as rational beings with their own ends and capable, I shall assume, of a sense of justice. The original position is, one might say, the appropriate initial status quo, and thus the fundamental agreements reached in it are fair. This explains the propriety of the name "justice as fairness": it conveys the idea that the principles of justice are agreed to in an initial situation that is fair.[31]

---

[29] Carruthers, *The Animals Issue,* 145.

[30] Carruthers does suggest that contracting agents would assign moral rights to all humans for practical reasons – namely, to avoid a "slippery slope" and for reasons of "social stability" (*The Animals Issue,* 114–118).

[31] Rawls, *A Theory of Justice,* 12.

No individuals represented in the original position will wind up with fewer protections just because they do not have the capacity to help or harm, and no one will escape the binding nature of the rules simply because he can threaten to withhold help or to impose harm on others.

Do fair bargaining conditions, by abstracting away from power inequalities, necessarily produce a set of rules that fully protect and equally bind all rational agents? Admittedly, on the Rawlsian scheme, contractors are prevented from instituting rules designed to serve their *particular advantage*. The requirement that they choose principles of justice behind a veil of ignorance guarantees that they will be limited precisely in this way. Yet might not the contractors accept moral rules that vary in application on the grounds that doing so would be to their *general* advantage, not to the particular advantage of any of the contractors? In other words, does limiting the use of strategic capacities for personal advantage also guarantee that the contractors will not adopt a set of rules that differentially protect or bind rational agents for the *collective good*?

For example, although none of the contractors is in a position to advance his own interests by advocating a system of slavery, granting less than full moral *protection* to all members of society may be to the general advantage of the contractors.[32] Rawls anticipates this line of questioning, replying that it

hardly seems likely persons who would view themselves as equals, entitled to press their claims upon one another, would agree to a principle which may require lesser life prospects for some simply for the sake of a greater sum of advantages enjoyed by others. Since each desires to protect his interests, his capacity to advance his conception of the good, no one has reason to acquiesce in enduring loss for himself in order to bring about a greater net balance of satisfaction.[33]

In effect, this particular justification for a variable application of moral rules sacrifices some individuals for the greater good of the group.[34] Because the outcome is not to the advantage of *each* and *every* rational agent, contractors would reject it. No one would be willing to accept a system of slavery for fear that he himself might turn out to be a slave.

---

[32] For Rawls's discussion of the "slaveholder's argument," see *A Theory of Justice*, 167ff.
[33] Rawls, *A Theory of Justice*, 62.
[34] See Chapter 8.

It is significantly more plausible to suggest, however, that the contractors would permit some individuals to be less than equally *bound* by the moral rules. According to this suggestion, although contractualism rules out principles of justice that institutionalize less than full moral protection for some parties to the contract – for example, by permitting institutions such as slavery – it may well make room for a kind of moral elitism on the grounds that doing so is to the individual advantage of all of the contracting parties. In this case, the inequality in moral status would be to any particular contractor's advantage, not simply to the advantage of society as a whole. As a result, each contractor might come to the conclusion that it would be in his best interest to agree to a set of rules that do not bind *leaders* in the same way that these rules bind other members of the group.

One argument for this conclusion appeals directly to Rawls's characterization of the original position. The veil of ignorance does not make the contractors completely ignorant. For instance, "[T]hey know the general facts about human society. They understand political affairs and the principles of economic theory; they know the basis of social organization and the laws of human psychology."[35] Among the general facts about human society that the contractors can be expected to know are facts about the nature of leadership and its function in society. First, leadership – at least as it is commonly understood – is hardly an egalitarian social phenomenon. As we have seen, inequality in the application of rules appears to be a defining feature of the circumstances of leadership.[36] Second, we depend on leadership for our ability to work in groups and engage in cooperative behavior.

If the contractors couple the circumstances of leadership with an understanding of the necessary role that leadership plays in social life, they will have some reason to accept the variable application of the principles that derive from the contract. "The general facts of human society" seem to demand a social relationship in which the rules do not equally bind all members of society. These facts seem to demand, that is, that leaders be allowed to break the rules.

---

35 Rawls, *A Theory of Justice*, 137.
36 See Chapter 1. See also Terry L. Price and Douglas A. Hicks, "A Framework for a General Theory of Leadership," in *The Quest for a General Theory of Leadership*, eds. George R. Goethals and Georgia L. J. Sorenson (Cheltenham, UK: Edward Elgar, 2006), 123–151.

## THE MORAL CONSTRAINTS OF SELF-RESPECT

According to Rawls, the parties to the hypothetical contract would reject a system of justice according to which some agents are not bound by the rules – or not bound to the same extent – as are other agents. The first order of business in the original position would be the adoption of a principle of equal liberty: "Each person is to have an equal right to the most extensive total system of equal basic liberties compatible with a similar system of liberty for all."[37] Rawls understands liberty in terms of "the agents who are free, the restrictions or limitations which they are free from, and what it is that they are free to do or not to do."[38] Equal liberty therefore implies that all rational agents are equally bound by the rules generated by agreement.

Why would the contractors accept a principle of equal liberty? The principles of justice govern the distribution of what Rawls refers to as "primary goods, that is, things that every rational man is presumed to want...whatever [his] rational plan of life."[39] Chief among the primary goods is the Kantian notion of *self-respect*, the morally appropriate attitude a rational agent should have toward himself as a member of social and political life.[40] Allowing leaders to have greater liberty is at odds with a just distribution of this primary good.

According to Rawls, everyone must have "a similar and secure status when they meet to conduct the common affairs of the wider society."[41] Any alternative organization "would have the effect of publicly establishing their inferiority as defined by the basic structure of society. This subordinate ranking in the public forum experienced in the attempt to take part in political and economic life, and felt in dealing with those who have a greater liberty, would indeed be humiliating and destructive of self-esteem."[42] Given the importance of self-respect, rational agents would refuse to trade it away in exchange for other primary goods. In keeping with the first principle of justice, even leaders must be equally subject to the rules.

[37] Rawls, *A Theory of Justice*, 302. It is worth noting that Rawls's theory is designed to be applied to the basic structure of society, not all of its moral rules.
[38] Rawls, *A Theory of Justice*, 202.
[39] Rawls, *A Theory of Justice*, 62.
[40] Rawls, *A Theory of Justice*, 440.
[41] Rawls, *A Theory of Justice*, 544.
[42] Rawls, *A Theory of Justice*, 545.

Thomas Hill also makes the argument that we can treat ourselves, or allow ourselves to be treated, in ways that significantly threaten our self-respect.[43] For example, Hill points to Kant's "now unfashionable view that each person has duties to himself as well as to others."[44] Kant's own commitment to this view is evident in his defense of a strict duty not to commit suicide and a broad duty to develop one's talents.[45] Hill draws the similar conclusion that "[t]o avoid servility to the extent that one can is not simply a right but a duty, not simply a duty to others but a duty to oneself."[46] To make this argument, Hill relies on the notion of self-respect to "isolate the defect of servility," a defect that defines stock characters such as the *Uncle Tom*, the *Self-Deprecator*, and *the Deferential Wife*.[47] The servile characters in Hill's examples all "have a certain attitude concerning [their] rightful place in a moral community."[48]

Notice, however, that the servile behavior that Hill objects to is different from the behavior of someone who has her own reasons for not asserting her rights. According to Hill,

[The Uncle Tom] is not the shrewdly prudent calculator, who knows how to make the best of a bad lot and mocks his masters behind their backs . . . A black . . . is not necessarily servile because he does not demand a just wage; for, seeing that such a demand would result in his being fired, he might forbear for the sake of his children . . . [The Self-Deprecator] is not simply playing a masochist's game of winning sympathy by disparaging himself . . . A woman need not be servile whenever she works to make her husband happy and prosperous; for she might freely and knowingly choose to do so from love or from a desire to share the rewards of his success.[49]

Someone who has her own reasons not to assert her rights differs from the servile person in two respects. First, such an individual is

---

43 Thomas E. Hill Jr., "Servility and Self-Respect," in his *Autonomy and Self-Respect* (Cambridge: Cambridge University Press, 1991), 4–18. See my discussion of self-esteem and servant leadership in Chapter 3.

44 Hill, "Servility and Self-Respect," 4. Rawls also traces his notion of self-respect to Kant (*A Theory of Justice*, 256).

45 Immanuel Kant, *Groundwork of the Metaphysic of Morals*, trans. H. J. Paton (New York: Harper and Row Publishers, 1964), 89–91, 96–98. See my discussion in Chapter 2 of the distinction between strict and broad duties.

46 Hill, "Servility and Self-Respect," 4.

47 Hill, "Servility and Self-Respect," 4–5.

48 Hill, "Servility and Self-Respect," 6.

49 Hill, "Servility and Self-Respect," 6. Hill correctly notes that there may remain "grounds for objecting to the attitudes in these cases."

well aware that she has a "rightful place in a moral community" and, consequently, that she deserves the full protection of morality. Second, her behavior can be part of a plan of action that expresses her "nature as a free and equal rational agent."[50] Because she is pursuing her own projects as an end in herself, she – unlike the servile person – does not allow herself to be treated as a mere means.

Can followers who are similarly aware of their moral status likewise consent to their leaders' being less than fully bound by the moral rules? Doing so would make it very difficult for followers to discharge their Kantian duties of self-respect. Rational agents should both have the sense of self-respect associated with rational agency and act in ways that are consistent with a corresponding understanding of their place in the moral community. Even if followers recognize that they ultimately deserve better treatment, there remains a sense in which they are not living up to their Kantian duties to themselves when they act as though their leaders are in a position of moral superiority.

There can also be something wrong with contributing to an individual's view that he is morally superior to others. In a system in which some people are unequally bound by the moral rules, a leader can see himself as having "a higher status than he is [actually] entitled to."[51] This kind of leader does not believe that he deserves less than other moral agents. Instead, he believes he deserves more. To be sure, the leader's attitude of superiority is opposed to the attitude of servility. But it is no less problematic on the Kantian account for that. Thinking about oneself in this way denies one's true moral status as a rational agent and, moreover, jeopardizes the equal moral status of other rational agents. By allowing leaders to act as though they are not bound by the rules of morality, followers encourage a morally unacceptable view of status, regardless of whether they actually buy into this view themselves.

Here we can draw upon yet another formulation of Kant's Categorical Imperative. In addition to defining our duties in terms of universalization and the value of humanity – as conveyed by the first and second versions of the Categorical Imperative, respectively – Kant characterizes morality by means of an analogy to a *kingdom of ends*.[52]

---

[50] Rawls, *A Theory of Justice*, 276.
[51] Hill, "Servility and Self-Respect," 12.
[52] Kant, *Groundwork*, 100–102.

According to the third version of the Categorical Imperative, we are to think of ourselves as part of

a systematic union of different rational beings under common laws. Now since laws determine ends as regards their universal validity, we shall be able – if we abstract from the personal differences between rational beings, and also from all the content of their private ends – to conceive a whole of all ends in systematic conjunction... Since these laws are directed precisely to the relation of such beings to one another as ends and means, this kingdom can be called a kingdom of ends (which is admittedly only an Ideal) ... Thus morality consists in the relation of all action to the making of laws whereby alone a kingdom of ends is possible... [D]uty appl[ies] to every member and to all members in equal measure.[53]

We are all moral lawmakers and, at the same time, equal subjects of the moral law.

What does the argument from the kingdom of ends tell us? Our behavior, and our expectations on the behavior of others, ought to promote this ideal by encouraging the kind of relations between rational beings that make it possible. Even if we assume that allowing leaders to be less subject to the moral law would be to the benefit of each and every contractor, it would not constitute a sufficient justification for unequal application of the moral rules. Followers cannot exempt leaders from morality.

## PAY AND PERKS

The contractualist argument does not require strict equality in all areas of social life. For example, Rawls's second principle of justice allows "[s]ocial and economic inequalities" so long as they are "to the greatest advantage of the least advantaged."[54] Known as the "difference principle," this component of Rawls's second principle justifies disparities in income and wealth when such inequalities maximally benefit the least well-off members of society.

---

53 Kant, *Groundwork*, 100–101.
54 Rawls, *A Theory of Justice*, 302. For sake of simplicity, my statement of Rawls's second principle ignores what he refers to as "fair equality of opportunity." Rawls's notion of fair equality of opportunity, which is also relevant to leadership ethics, holds that "positions are to be not only open in a formal sense, but that all should have a fair chance to attain them ... [T]hose with similar abilities and skills should have similar life chances" (73).

As Rawls puts it:

The basis for self-esteem in a just society is not then one's income share but the publicly affirmed distribution of fundamental rights and liberties. And this distribution being equal, everyone has a similar and secure status when they meet to conduct the common affairs of the wider society...But an equal division of all primary goods is irrational in view of the possibility of bettering everyone's circumstances by accepting certain inequalities. Thus the best solution is to support the primary good of self-respect as far as possible in the assignment of the basic liberties that can indeed be made equal, defining the same status for all.[55]

So, for example, the contractors might allow leaders to be paid significantly more than followers. If compensating leaders at the same level as everyone else would make the least advantaged members of society worse off, then rationality requires an unequal distribution of this primary good. Financial incentives are justified to the extent that they contribute to the improvement of the least well-off followers.

This general way of thinking about economic inequality has important implications for executive compensation. Are current levels of executive compensation really in the best interest of the least well-off followers? According to the *Wall Street Journal*, the average CEO makes 39 times what the average worker makes.[56] For CEOs of Standard & Poor companies, the ratio is 212 to 1.[57]

Dana Hermanson gives three reasons to doubt whether "CEOs [really are] creating that much more value than rank-and-file employees."[58] First, executive compensation is sometimes relatively unconnected to company performance. CEOs often fare just as well in failing companies. Second, citing a study by Bebchuk and Grinstein, Hermanson notes that "top executives' pay grew from 5 percent of earnings in 1993–1995 to 10 percent of earnings in 2001–2003."[59] So, at least in

---

[55] Rawls, *A Theory of Justice*, 544–546.
[56] "Hot topic: Are CEOs worth their weight in gold," *Wall Street Journal* (January 21, 2006).
[57] "Hot topic."
[58] Dana Hermanson, "Executive Compensation and Corporate Governance," *Internal Auditing* 21, 2 (2006): 36–37.
[59] Hermanson, "Executive Compensation and Corporate Governance," 26. The study cited is L. Bebchuk and Y. Grinstein, "The Growth of Executive Pay," *Oxford Review of Economic Policy* 21 (2005): 285–303.

terms of proportions, financial gains by CEOs are outpacing the gains in earnings to which CEO compensation is supposed to be the means. Third, in some cases, executive compensation can be explained simply in terms of poor corporate governance.

Jay Conger explains that CEOs typically exercise inordinate power over their boards of directors and, furthermore, that boards are often made up of other CEOs, many of whom have an interest in reciprocal generosity.[60] Conger also points out that compensation committees rely heavily on compensation consultants who – because of their work in "executive recruiting, auditing, pension advice, and [other] consulting services" – have a financial interest in pleasing CEOs.[61]

Current levels of executive compensation not only have the potential to neglect follower interests but also can lead the CEO to think he has "a higher status than he [actually] is entitled to."[62] We can trace this attitude to a phenomenon Conger refers to as "the romance of leadership."[63] According to Conger, despite the complexity of modern-day organizations, we often assume that corporate success or failure rests exclusively in the hands of CEOs. This assumption "is particularly apparent in the press, business books, and in the financial community where there is a singular focus on the statements and actions of CEOs to explain the successful performance of companies."[64] Given widespread commitment to these naive assumptions about control and responsibility, it is no wonder that followers willingly give leaders whatever they want or need, including significant leeway to break the rules.

---

[60] Jay A. Conger, "Oh Lord, Won't You Buy Me a Mercedes-Benz: How Compensation Practices Are Undermining the Credibility of Leaders," in *The Quest for Moral Leaders: Essays in Leadership Ethics*, eds. Joanne B. Ciulla, Terry L. Price, and Susan E. Murphy (Cheltenham, UK: Edward Elgar, 2005), 83–84.

[61] Conger, "Oh Lord, Won't You Buy Me a Mercedes-Benz," 84–85. Questions about the connection between compensation and the interests of followers also extend to educational leadership. The faculty senate at Indiana State University approved a vote of no confidence in university president Lloyd Benjamin after Benjamin accepted a $25,000 raise during a serious financial crisis at the university (Paul Fain, "Faculty Group Votes No Confidence in President of Indiana State U.," *Chronicle of Higher Education* [May 5, 2006]).

[62] Hill, "Servility and Self-Respect," 12.

[63] Conger, "Oh Lord, Won't You Buy Me a Mercedes-Benz," 85–86.

[64] Conger, "Oh Lord, Won't You Buy Me a Mercedes-Benz," 86.

Conger refers to the resulting characteristics in terms of "executive narcissism and entitlement:"[65]

These qualities reveal themselves in executive compensation. For example, it is not uncommon to hear executives rationalize their pay packages by comparing them to those of sports figures or entertainment celebrities who receive multi-million dollar pay contracts. They argue that their own contributions as business leaders overseeing organizations that are providing essential goods and services for the public are far more important than those of celebrities. Therefore they deserve comparable if not higher rewards. As highly competitive individuals, executives often rationalize their pay and perks using the "equity theory" of compensation, which is most evident in the benchmarking of peer groups.[66]

These kinds of comparisons, perhaps as much as the benefits themselves, contribute to the view that executives are a breed apart.

Nor is it any wonder that some leaders come to "believe their own press" – in other words, become convinced that they really are special and deserve special treatment. When an executive receives extravagant compensation and special privileges, it must be difficult indeed for her to resist the conclusion that she is a lot more important than other people, including individuals in the organization. A *New York Times* article gives us some insight into the relationship between perks and the attitudes of superiority:

The perks puff [the executive] up. "Not only do these things make you feel special, it's the prestige . . . [Y]ou tell your friends you've got these free tickets, and they go, 'Wow, that's really cool.' People are the way they are. They like to top other people. I am certainly a person who loves perks."[67]

This executive's attitude is plainly contrary to Kant's idea of how one should view oneself in relation to other rational beings. Excessive compensation and perks, not unlike the willingness of followers to allow leaders to break the moral rules, threaten the idea that we are all equally protected and equally bound members of the moral community.

---

[65] Conger, "Oh Lord, Won't You Buy Me a Mercedes-Benz," 87.
[66] Conger, "Oh Lord, Won't You Buy Me a Mercedes-Benz," 87.
[67] N. R. Kleinfield, "Life, liberty and the pursuit of free box seats: One man's perks anger many, but to New Yorkers, corporate goodies are a right," *New York Times* (September 22, 2002).

## UNIVERSALIZING DISCRETION

There is one additional reason to question whether the contractarian argument can justify rule breaking by leaders. Consider behavior such as the use of deception. The Kantian argument tells us that for deception to work, there must be a general backdrop of veracity. In a society in which no one trusts anyone else to tell the truth, leaders – like everyone else – will be unsuccessful in their attempts to deceive followers. But successful deception also requires that people generally trust *the would-be deceiver* to tell the truth. Habitual liars develop a reputation for infidelity, and, as a result, they eventually find that deception is no longer a successful strategy for them to use. So, even if leaders have followers' consent to use deception, they cannot use deception indiscriminately and expect it to continue to work.

Deceptive leaders must therefore establish a general backdrop of veracity *for themselves* and deviate from this backdrop only when necessary. Putting this in Kantian language, we might say that leaders who consider engaging in deception cannot universalize rule-breaking behavior even for themselves, regardless of whether they have the consent of followers. Leaders who always or often engage in deception undermine their reputation for veracity. A reputation for truth telling is necessary to make any particular act of deception successful. In effect, this kind of rule breaking must be exceptional even for leaders.

Particularly prudent leaders might be skilled enough at choosing when to tell the truth and when to use deception. But deceptive leadership behavior, if it is to have any semblance of treating followers as rational agents who are ends in themselves, must rely on more than the prudential calculations of leaders. The most straightforward way to engage the rational agency of followers would be for the leader to ask followers directly whether he would be justified in deceiving them. However, followers cannot consent to being deceived in particular instances! Follower knowledge of the deception would defeat the purpose of the leader's strategy.

A contractarian justification of deception must therefore be indexed more generally to a leader's behavior. Because follower consent cannot be so general that the leader is justified in deceiving followers at every whim and fancy, a sensible way of focusing follower consent would be to see it as limiting a leader's leeway to precisely those cases in which using strategies such as deception is *necessary* to advance group goals. Justified deception by a leader must have some connection to the goals to which his followers are committed as rational agents.

John Locke (1632–1704), another representative of the social contract tradition, resorts to the notion of leader discretion, what he refers to as *prerogative*.

> This power to act according to discretion, for the public good, without the prescription of the law, and sometimes even against it, is that which is called prerogative. For since in some governments the law-making power is not always in being, and is usually too numerous, and so too slow, for the dispatch requisite to execution: and because also it is impossible to foresee, and so by laws to provide for, all accidents and necessities, that may concern the public, or to make such laws as will do no harm, if they are executed with an inflexible rigor, on all occasions, and upon all persons, that may come in their way, therefore there is a latitude left to the executive power, to do many things of choice, which the laws do not prescribe.[68]

Locke's defense of the place of prerogative should add to our suspicions about the consent-based justification of rule-breaking behavior by leaders. Leaders who have the general consent of followers must nevertheless decide when the rules apply or, better put, when the "public good" allows leaders to break the rules. Consent gets us only so far in the contractarian account.

Locke's retreat to the public good shows that contractarian theory needs an additional source of justification. David Hume (1711–1776) identifies this need in his "Of the Original Contract."[69] Consider Rawls's summary of Hume's criticism:

> Hume maintains that the principle of fidelity and allegiance both have the same foundation in utility, and therefore that nothing is gained from basing political obligation on an original contract. Locke's doctrine represents, for Hume, an unnecessary shuffle: one might as well appeal directly to . . . the general interests and necessities of society.[70]

---

[68] Adapted from John Locke, *Two Treatises of Government*, ed. Peter Laslett (Cambridge: Cambridge University Press, 1988), 375.

[69] David Hume, "Of the Original Contract," in *Essays: Moral, Political, and Literary*, ed. Eugene F. Miller (Indianapolis, IN: Liberty Fund, 1987), 465–487.

[70] Rawls, *A Theory of Justice*, 32.

The Humean point is that a contractarian promise cannot be what makes promises generally binding. The contract itself is supposed to generate moral rules such as the requirement that we keep our promises! Some value such as the good of the group must be in the background of the argument.

Even if contractarian theory can explain the moral force of contracts without resorting to an alternative source of justification – for example, the good of the group – advocates of contractarianism will be hard pressed to justify rule-breaking behavior by leaders without appealing to something such as the "necessities of society."[71] The notion of necessity returns us to the question with which we were left at the end of Chapter 4: What is it about particular situations that justifies rule-breaking behavior by leaders? Chapter 6 now turns to the suggestion that rule breaking by leaders is *necessary* given the importance of group goals.

---

[71] See Chapter 8 for a discussion of the claim that "the general interests of society" justify rule breaking.

# 6

## Situations and Circumstances

### MORAL SITUATIONISM

*Moral situationism* refers to the view that what ought to be done is determined not by a rule or principle of action, but rather by particular features of the situation. For example, according to this general class of moral theories, whether a leader ought to lie depends on the necessity of the circumstances in which he finds himself. In some circumstances, lying can be the right thing to do because of facts about the situation. However, in circumstances with different facts, it would be wrong to tell a lie. So the moral situationist has a complicated answer to questions about whether leaders are justified in breaking the rules. Leaders, like everyone else, are confronted with exceptional circumstances in everyday life, and the moral challenge is to determine what actions are necessary.

Although this approach to ethics is sometimes derided as "mere situationism," it must be distinguished from the view that "[e]very situation has only its particularity."[1] The complexity of moral situationism can make it attractive to think "it all depends," especially to students of leadership. Given the variety of circumstances leaders face, it is often tempting to think that leaders must approach each situation anew and decide what to do, as though there are no generalizations about morality. The temptation is to conclude that

---

[1] Joseph Fletcher, *Situation Ethics: The New Morality* (Philadelphia: Westminster Press, 1966), 24.

nothing about morality carries over from one set of circumstances to the next.

However, if leaders are to draw on moral situationism as a guide to justified rule breaking, the theory's use of the moral language of "right" and "wrong" must lend itself to consistent application across similar circumstances. Without a commitment to common features of situations that determine the morality of actions, it would be meaningless to say that two behaviors share the common feature of "being right" or "being wrong." As a result, moral situationism would give leaders no direction whatsoever about how to act.

On what grounds does the moral situationist decide how to act in particular situations? Because moral situationism forsakes the absolutism of rules or principles, its recommendations for action must rely on overriding values. Ultimately, what a leader ought to do in a given situation will depend on the values of the particular situationist theory to which she is committed. Candidate values include social stability, survival, and the achievement of organizational goals.

One influential example of this approach is Joseph Fletcher's *Situation Ethics*. In his version of moral situationism, Fletcher gives pride of place to the value of love, "the *agapē* of the summary commandment to love God and the neighbor."[2] Although rules and principles have an advisory role to play, the situationist must be "prepared in any situation to compromise them or set them aside *in the situation* if love seems better served by doing so."[3] To put this in Kantian language, the situationist sees moral rules as "hypothetical, not categorical. Only the commandment to love is categorically good."[4] For instance, "We are only 'obliged' to tell the truth . . . if the situation calls for it; if a murderer asks us his victim's whereabouts, our duty might be to lie."[5] Actions are right or wrong across situations, then, depending on their consistency or inconsistency with the overriding value of love.

Fletcher presents situation ethics as "the new morality," not as a theory of leadership ethics. Yet it is worth emphasizing that he traces

[2] Fletcher, *Situation Ethics*, 30.
[3] Fletcher, *Situation Ethics*, 25.
[4] Fletcher, *Situation Ethics*, 26.
[5] Fletcher, *Situation Ethics*, 27. For Kant's opposing view, see his "On the supposed right to lie from philanthropy," in *Practical Philosophy*, trans. Mary J. Gregor (Cambridge: Cambridge University Press, 1996), 605–615.

its roots to the religious leadership of Jesus and Paul. Fletcher points out that Jesus's and Paul's leadership was directed at the legalism of the Pharisees, as their laws were represented by the requirements of the Torah.[6]

> Christian situation ethics reduces law from a statutory system of rules to the love canon alone. For this reason, Jesus was ready without hesitation to ignore the obligations of Sabbath observance, to do forbidden work on the seventh day. 'The Sabbath was made for man' (Mark 2:27–28). In exactly the same way Paul could eat his food kosher or not, simply depending on whether in any situation it is edifying (upbuilding) for others (1 Cor. 10:23–26).[7]

According to Fletcher, the behavior of Jesus and Paul rejects the morality of rules and principles, thereby instituting a new morality. In other words, the actions of these religious leaders were not simply cases of *rule breaking*; they were also cases of *rule making*.

Jesus's authority to make new rules is evident in the verse immediately following the passage Fletcher cites in the Gospel of Mark. Jesus says, "[T]he Son of Man is lord even of the sabbath."[8] Holding Jesus and his disciples to the old laws would thus be like using new cloth to darn "an old cloak" or putting "new wine into old wine skins."[9]

In these examples, and for moral situationists more generally, right action is *necessitated* by the situation. For example, Fletcher notes that Jesus appeals to necessity to justify the rule-breaking behavior of King David.[10] In Jesus's defense of his own disciples, who were being criticized for picking grain on the Sabbath, he asks:

> Have you never read what David did when he and his companions were hungry and in *need* of food? He entered the house of God, when Abiathar was high priest, and ate the bread of the Presence, which is not lawful for any but the priests to eat, and he gave some to his companions.[11]

---

[6] Fletcher, *Situation Ethics*, 45–46.
[7] Fletcher, *Situation Ethics*, 69.
[8] *The New Oxford Annotated Bible: New Revised Standard Version*, ed. Michael D. Coogan, 3rd ed. (Oxford: Oxford University Press, 2001), Mark 2:28.
[9] *New Oxford Annotated Bible*, Mark 2:21–22.
[10] Fletcher, *Situation Ethics*, 85–86. I discuss a different case of rule breaking by David in Chapter 3. See also Terry L. Price, *Understanding Ethical Failures in Leadership* (New York: Cambridge University Press, 2006), ch. 1.
[11] *New Oxford Annotated Bible*, Mark 2:25–26 (emphasis added).

David eats the forbidden bread and allows group members to do so as well because of their physical state of need.

Other leaders similarly contend that their behavior was necessary in the situations they faced. But a leader's recourse to necessity does not always assume that conforming to the rule or principle would have put her life at risk, as David's life might have been put at risk. Still less does the claim of necessity imply the leader had no choice in the sense that she could not have done otherwise. The claim is not that features of the situation make it *impossible* for her to refrain from engaging in the prohibited behavior. What, then, does it mean to say that the leader broke the moral rules "because she had to?"

An analysis of the situationist justification for exception making by leaders must therefore consider the notion of *necessity*. The leader who claims that she had to break the rules faces the following question: What makes the exception necessary?

## MACHIAVELLIAN NECESSITY

The most famous defense of moral situationism for leaders is Niccolò Machiavelli's (1469–1527) *The Prince*.[12] In this work, Machiavelli challenges the standard view that morality applies to leaders in the same way that it applies to followers, calling this view a "fantas[y] about rulers," not "what happens in fact."[13] According to Machiavelli:

I know that everyone will acknowledge that it would be most praiseworthy for a ruler to have all the ... qualities that are held to be good. But because it is not possible to have all of them, and because circumstances do not permit living a completely virtuous life, one must be sufficiently prudent to know how to avoid becoming notorious for those vices that would destroy one's power ... Yet one should not be troubled about becoming notorious for those vices without which it is difficult to preserve one's power, because if one considers everything carefully, doing some things that seem virtuous may result in one's ruin, whereas doing other things that seem vicious may strengthen one's position and cause one to flourish.[14]

[12] Niccolò Machiavelli, *The Prince*, eds. Quentin Skinner and Russell Price (Cambridge: Cambridge University Press, 1988).
[13] Machiavelli, *The Prince*, 55.
[14] Machiavelli, *The Prince*, 55.

We have to give up our idealism about leadership because a ruler "must be prepared to vary his conduct as the winds of fortune and changing circumstances constrain him and . . . be capable of entering upon the path of wrongdoing when this becomes *necessary*."[15] In short, he "must be prepared to act immorally."[16] Otherwise he is blind to the relevant features of his situation.

In this respect, Machiavelli's views in *The Prince* can be seen as an intellectual precursor to contingency theories of leadership.[17] These theories were developed in the twentieth century as a social scientific response to trait views of leadership. As discussed in Chapter 4, trait views hold that particular qualities or characteristics prove effective across leadership situations. Like Machiavelli, advocates of contingency theories reject this kind of universalism, insisting that leaders must adjust their styles in response to the particulars of the situation.

In *The Prince*, Machiavelli frames his advice about leadership style in terms of a stark contrast between law and force.[18] Like Kant, he identifies the former with behavior befitting humans: law constitutes a "properly human means" because it both engages the rationality of the ruler who conforms his behavior to law and respects the rationality of the subjects who are protected by the law.[19] In contrast, force bypasses rationality, especially the rationality of those against whom it is exercised.

Despite the fact that Machiavelli readily associates force with animal life, he recommends that leaders be prepared to use it. Machiavelli is not urging that leaders treat followers as badly as animals are sometimes treated, though this could be seen as one implication of his advice. Rather, the ruler himself "must know how to act like a beast."[20] Machiavelli even has particular animals in mind: the leader "should

---

[15] Machiavelli, *The Prince*, 62 (emphasis added).
[16] Machiavelli, *The Prince*, 55.
[17] See Terry L. Price, "Philosophy," in *Encyclopedia of Leadership*, Vol. 3, eds. George R. Goethals, Georgia Sorenson, and James MacGregor Burns (Thousand Oaks, CA: Sage Publications, 2004), 1195–1199.
[18] Machiavelli, *The Prince*, 61.
[19] Here, I do not mean to identify the law of the state with the law of reason. I have in mind the more general Kantian idea of acting on a law.
[20] Machiavelli, *The Prince*, 61.

imitate both the fox and the lion."[21] Force thus includes not only the physical force represented by "a lion's strength" but also the fox's capacity for deception.[22] We can again use Kantian language to make sense of this pairing. Deception, no less than force, is inimical to the rationality that distinguishes human beings from animals.[23]

Although Machiavelli's justification for rule-breaking behavior by leaders bears some resemblance to the arguments from power and self-interest discussed in Chapter 3, a close reading shows that Machiavellian necessity is not simply, or even primarily, egoistic. The consequences of Machiavelli's political realism are straightforward: leaders sometimes have to be mean instead of generous, cruel instead of merciful, and faithless instead of faithful.[24] But this is not for self-interest alone. For example, in Machiavelli's defense of meanness, he claims that the profligate ruler will ultimately have to pay for his behavior by imposing heavy taxes on his subjects.[25] The ruler's generosity will thus have "harmed many people and benefited few."[26] In contrast, the leader who refuses to be extravagant is not mean in any morally important sense. This ruler is actually generous according to all-things-considered judgments of this virtue. For "he will be acting generously towards the vast majority, whose property he does not touch, and will be acting meanly towards the few to whom he gives nothing."[27]

The ruler's refusal to take from some in order to be "generous" to others also respects a rule to which Machiavelli suggests there are no exceptions:

[A]bove all, he must not touch the property of others... [T]here will always be pretexts for seizing property; and someone who begins to live rapaciously will always find pretexts for taking the property of others. On

---

[21] Machiavelli, *The Prince*, 61. James MacGregor Burns's biography of Franklin Delano Roosevelt is entitled *Roosevelt: The Lion and the Fox* (New York: Harcourt Brace, 1956).

[22] Machiavelli, *The Prince*, 61.

[23] The capacity for deception is now used as an indicator of higher cognitive powers associated with personhood. See Steven M. Wise, *Rattling the Cage: Towards Legal Rights for Animals* (Cambridge, MA: Perseus Books, 2000), ch. 10.

[24] Machiavelli, *The Prince*, chs. 16–18.

[25] Machiavelli, *The Prince*, 56.

[26] Machiavelli, *The Prince*, 56.

[27] Machiavelli, *The Prince*, 56.

the other hand, reasons or pretexts for taking life are rarer and more fleeting.[28]

Even Machiavelli recognizes, then, that some rules have no exceptions. It is not enough that a ruler has "a proper justification and obvious reason," because allowing this kind of justification would open the door to limitless rule breaking by the ruler.[29]

Machiavelli similarly contends that leaders must sometimes be "cruel to be kind." Here, again, it is for the good of the whole, not simply the leader's self-interest, that he deviates from ordinary morality. Machiavelli puts it this way:

if a ruler can keep his subjects united and loyal, he should not worry about incurring a reputation for cruelty; for by punishing a very few he will really be more merciful than those who over-indulgently permit disorders to develop, with resultant killings and plunderings. For the latter usually harm a whole community, whereas the executions ordered by a ruler harm only specific individuals.[30]

Machiavelli's focus on the good of the whole thus gives us reason to doubt whether power and self-interest are the complete story. Power has a significantly broader meaning – not, that is, as it relates to mere self-interest but rather as it relates to the maintenance of the community.[31] Ultimately, according to Machiavelli, leaders must do what is necessary to maintain the community over which their power is exercised.

This interpretation of Machiavellian necessity might cause us to question whether he really is committed to moral situationism. Properly understood, so the objection goes, the behavior Machiavelli recommends really is generous and kind and therefore in accord with the virtues of generosity and kindness. Stinginess with taxpayer money and cruelty to particular individuals simply reflects a more enlightened approach to these virtues.

---

[28] Machiavelli, *The Prince*, 59–60. Machiavelli also warns leaders against taking "the womenfolk" of subjects.

[29] Machiavelli, *The Prince*, 59.

[30] Machiavelli, *The Prince*, 58.

[31] Quinton Skinner and Russell Price's translation supports this reading. They note that *stato* in the phrase *mantenere lo stato* can be translated as "power" or "government," but that it also "signifies 'political community'" (Machiavelli, *The Prince*, 63nb). See also 62nb.

But the Machiavellian point is situationist in this sense: we cannot expect leaders to be generous and kind in the way that we continue to expect others to display these qualities. Leaders are responsible for the group as a whole, and this responsibility generates demands that transcend the everyday expectations on the way subjects or citizens treat each other. So there remains a strong sense in which leaders must act as moral situationists and deviate from these everyday expectations. Leaders must sometimes break the rules as a matter of necessity. The claim is not that rulers have tapped into a higher morality that would be appropriate for followers to adopt. Instead, there are two different moralities. Leaders are expected to be generous and kind in a sense not captured by the rules of everyday ethics. For leaders, behaviors recommended by the rules only "seem virtuous," and rule-breaking behaviors only "seem vicious."[32]

The idea of alternative moralities for leaders is especially evident in a different argument Machiavelli makes for the permissibility of promise breaking. According to Machiavelli:

[A] prudent ruler cannot keep his word, nor should he, when such fidelity would damage him, and when the reasons that made him promise are no longer relevant. This advice would not be sound if all men were upright; but because they are treacherous and would not keep their promises to you, you should not consider yourself bound to keep your promises to them.

Leaders are justified in breaking the moral rules precisely because others are not behaving morally.[33]

Michael Walzer echoes this argument, pointing out that "[e]ven if [our representatives] would like to act differently, they probably can not: for other men are all too ready to hustle and lie for power and glory, and it is the others who set the terms of the competition."[34] This Machiavellian reality of leadership is part of what Walzer refers to as "the problem of dirty hands":

They can do no good themselves unless they win the struggle, which they are unlikely to do unless they are willing and able to use the necessary means . . . No

---

[32] Machiavelli, *The Prince*, 55.

[33] Norman Gillespie, "The Business of Ethics," *University of Michigan Business Review* 27 (1975): 3.

[34] Michael Walzer, "Political Action: The Problem of Dirty Hands," *Philosophy and Public Affairs* 2 (1973): 163.

one succeeds in politics without getting his hands dirty... But one's hands get dirty from doing what it is wrong to do.[35]

Once again, the reality of leadership – at least in political contexts – is that a leader cannot accomplish the goals of his group if he plays by ordinary moral rules. Because these are not the rules that others play by, it would put the leader – and, more importantly, the group – at a significant disadvantage were he alone to behave morally.

Walzer gives two examples of the kinds of cases in which rule breaking by leaders is justified by the situation. In one case, Walzer describes a leader who "is asked to authorize the torture of a captured rebel leader who knows or probably knows the location of a number of bombs hidden in apartment buildings around the city, set to go off within the next twenty-four hours."[36] If the leader does what he is asked to do, while at the same time feeling appropriately guilty about it, then that is proof "both that he is not too good for politics and that he is good enough. Here is the moral politician: it is by his dirty hands that we know him."[37]

In a second case, "[i]n order to win the election the candidate must make a deal with a dishonest ward boss, involving the granting of contracts for school construction over the next four years."[38] Whether he ought to make the deal, Walzer thinks, depends on "what is at stake in the election" and the fact that "[h]is decision to run was a commitment (to all of us who think the election important) to try to win, that is, to do within rational limits whatever is necessary to win."[39]

Justification of rule-breaking behavior in the first example – the terrorism case – points to important political values such as safety and security. Alan Wolfe's research in *Moral Freedom* suggests that Americans are quite comfortable with this kind of justification:

Some lies... are justifiable, perhaps even required... A number of our older respondents recall that Franklin Roosevelt insisted on his isolationism even as he prepared to lead the country into World War II, that the Allies intentionally confused the Germans about the location of their invasion of Europe, and

---

[35] Walzer, "Political Action," 164.
[36] Walzer, "Political Action," 167.
[37] Walzer, "Political Action," 167–168.
[38] Walzer, "Political Action," 165.
[39] Walzer, "Political Action," 165.

that Harry Truman kept secret the use of the atomic bomb that ended that same war. These, they believe, were fully justified actions ... [M]atters of state require very different kinds of actions ... So long as national security is really at stake ... politicians would be justified in lying.[40]

According to this sentiment, overriding values necessitate rule breaking.

Wolfe's research ultimately gives us reason to think that Americans are even more forgiving of immorality in leadership than the previous quotation would suggest. In their mind, national security is sufficient to justify rule-breaking behavior by politicians, but it is hardly necessary:

> Some of them believe that because politics is a different realm than ordinary life, the rules of ordinary life do not, and perhaps ought not, apply ... 'I guess if they have their eye on the right star and on the right goal that is a laudable goal ... I could overlook a few things along the way' ... It is not that ... the end always justifies the means ... But ... if politicians might have to bend a few rules here and there, nothing is really wrong if they do so in pursuit of worthwhile causes ... [There is] nothing wrong if a politician lies – so long as she does so for the purpose of doing good.[41]

This line of justification is closer to the reasoning attributed to the leader in Walzer's second example – the corruption case. The politician who partners with the ward boss dirties his hands in order that he might work toward the goals of his supporters, not so that he can do something as grand as protecting the nation from a terrorist threat.

To evaluate the necessity-based justification, we must separate these two kinds of arguments for rule breaking. Only then will we be able to determine the relative strength and frequency of each in the everyday lives of leaders.[42]

TWO KINDS OF NECESSITY

Bowen H. McCoy's "The Parable of the Sadhu," a standard reading in business ethics anthologies, tells the story of an ethical dilemma McCoy

---

[40] Alan Wolfe, *Moral Freedom* (New York: W. W. Norton and Company, 2001), 112. See my discussion of Wolfe's research in Chapter 1.

[41] Wolfe, *Moral Freedom*, p. 113.

[42] See Chapter 8 for a discussion of necessity in "ticking time bomb" cases.

and fellow climbers faced during their trek through the Himalayas.[43]
The dilemma occurred at a critical point in their journey, which McCoy
had joined as part of his sabbatical from work as an investment banker
at Morgan Stanley. McCoy and his group were approaching what was –
in more than one sense – a "high point," an 18,000-foot pass to the village of Muklinath, when they came upon an individual who obviously
needed their help.[44] In McCoy's words:

Just after daybreak, while we rested at 15,500 feet, one of the New Zealanders,
who had gone ahead, came staggering down toward us with a body slung
across his shoulders. He dumped the almost naked, barefoot body of an
Indian holy man – a sadhu – at my feet. He had found the pilgrim lying on
the ice, shivering and suffering from hypothermia. I cradled the sadhu's head
and laid him out on the rocks... I took a carotid pulse and found that the
sadhu was still alive. We figured he had probably visited the holy shrines at
Muklinath and was on his way home... Stephen [an anthropologist] and the
four Swiss began stripping off outer clothing and opening their packs. The
sadhu was soon clothed from head to foot. He was not able to walk, but he was
very much alive. I looked down the mountain and spotted below the Japanese
climbers marching up with a horse. Without a great deal of thought, I told
Stephen and Pasang [their sherpa] that I was concerned about withstanding
the heights to come and wanted to get over the pass. I took off after several
of our porters who had gone ahead... Stephen arrived at the summit an
hour after I did. Still exhilarated by victory, I ran down the snow slope to
congratulate him... Stephen glared at me and said: "How do you feel about
contributing to the death of a fellow man?"[45]

Was McCoy justified in deviating from the moral requirement that
we help others in need on the grounds that breaking the rule was
necessary in the circumstances?

McCoy's assessment of his own behavior is equivocal. On the one
hand, he "felt and continue[s] to feel guilt."[46] On the other hand,
McCoy's description of the circumstances, especially in the response
he ultimately gives to Stephen's challenge, seems to suggest that the

---

[43] Bowen H. McCoy, "The Parable of the Sadhu," in *Ethical Issues in Business: A Philosophical Approach,* eds. Thomas Donaldson, Patricia H. Werhane, and Margaret Cording
(Upper Saddle River, NJ: Prentice Hall, 2002), 262–268.
[44] McCoy, "The Parable of the Sadhu," 263.
[45] McCoy, "The Parable of the Sadhu," 263–264. McCoy was unable to confirm whether
the sadhu survived.
[46] McCoy, "The Parable of the Sadhu," 265.

necessity of the situation may have given him a justification for leaving the sadhu to die. McCoy's first appeal to necessity precedes the sadhu's appearance in the story. He tells us, "Six years earlier I had suffered pulmonary edema, an acute form of altitude sickness, at 16,500 feet in the vicinity of Everest base camp, so we were understandably concerned about what would happen at 18,000 feet."[47] Later, in his response to Stephen, McCoy says, "Where, in your opinion... is the limit of our responsibility in a situation like this? We had our own well-being to worry about."[48]

The mother of a recent Mt. Everest casualty similarly emphasized the necessity of such situations.[49] Her son, David Sharp, had been climbing Everest alone when he encountered difficulties. As many as forty climbers marched by as he froze to death.[50] Even she defended the behavior of the other climbers: "Your responsibility is to save yourself – not to try to save anybody else."[51] Less than two weeks after Sharp's death, Australian climber Lincoln Hall was likewise abandoned on the mountain.[52] Although "he was pronounced dead by the sherpa guides... at 28,500 feet," Hall survived long enough on his own to be found the next day by American climber Dan Mazur.[53] He was ultimately rescued and taken to a camp at 23,000 feet.

This necessity argument rests on the assumption that struggling climbers cannot be saved without putting the lives of other climbers at great risk. Because morality does not require people to do what is physically impossible, or even what is unreasonably difficult, climbers in real danger are justified in looking out for themselves. But notice that we can accept this limit on morality and still refuse to admit that the situations faced by particular climbers are characterized by this kind of necessity. For example, Hall's rescue raises "the question of what might have happened to the Briton, David Sharp, if he had been

---

47 McCoy, "The Parable of the Sadhu," 263.
48 McCoy, "The Parable of the Sadhu," 265.
49 Alan Cowell, "Adventures change. Danger does not." *New York Times* (June 4, 2006).
50 The fact that Sharp was not a member of any climbing group made it less likely that he would be protected by the agreements or relationships among other climbers. See Chapters 5 and 7.
51 Cowell, "Adventures change" (originally quoted in the *London Sunday Times*).
52 Cowell, "'Dead' climber's survival impugns Mount Everest ethics," *New York Times* (May 28, 2006).
53 Cowell, "'Dead' climber's survival impugns Mount Everest ethics."

helped."[54] It was neither impossible nor unreasonably difficult to get Hall down the mountain, and the same may well have been true for Sharp.

McCoy considers the parallel possibility in his own case, albeit well after the fact: "What would have happened had Stephen and I carried the sadhu for two days back to the village and become involved with the villagers in his care?"[55] Even at the time the sadhu was abandoned, the climbers in McCoy's party recognized that they could use the Japanese's horse or have their own porters carry the sadhu down the mountain.[56] Yet McCoy later asks, "What more could we do?"[57] Because McCoy could have done more without risking his life or the life of others, he cannot use these considerations to justify his behavior.

If matters of life and death really are the issue for potential rescuers, then dangerous climbs in the Himalayas are not a good model for thinking about everyday leadership ethics. This kind of necessity would make the expeditions a better model for what philosophers sometimes refer to as "lifeboat ethics." Lifeboat ethics asks questions about what people owe one another in emergencies in which there are not enough supplies or equipment to save everyone. Who should have access to the lifeboat when there is not enough room for all passengers of the sinking ship?

In everyday life, leaders rarely face life-and-death situations. In fact, the absence of personal emergency – at least for the leaders themselves – can be understood as a defining feature of everyday leadership ethics. However, there is another kind of necessity at play in the cases of the sadhu, David Sharp, and Lincoln Hall, and this kind of necessity *is* a familiar part of everyday life, especially for leaders. In each of the climbing cases, the parties involved had good reason to believe that abandoning another human being was necessary to achieve goals that they viewed as being critically important. Leaving the needy individual behind to die was necessary not for the potential rescuers' own survival but rather for the achievement of their goals.

Bowen McCoy underscores the importance of his journey when he sets up his article, noting that "[i]f we failed to cross the pass, I feared

---

[54] Cowell, "'Dead' climber's survival impugns Mount Everest ethics."
[55] McCoy, "The Parable of the Sadhu," 268.
[56] McCoy, "The Parable of the Sadhu," 264.
[57] McCoy, "The Parable of the Sadhu," 265.

that the last half of our 'once in a lifetime' trip would be ruined."[58]
McCoy also asks Stephen, "What right does an almost naked pilgrim
who chooses the wrong trail have to disrupt our lives? . . . Are you really
saying that, no matter what the implications, we should, at the drop
of a hat, have changed our entire plan?"[59] Here, the necessity that
McCoy has in mind is clearly of the weaker variety. His goal, not his
life, is in jeopardy.

Writing about the climbers who did not help David Sharp on Everest, journalist Alan Cowell surmises that it may be the commercial
nature of such expeditions that makes a successful climb seem so
important.[60] Experienced climbers such as Sir Chris Bonington contend that this shift represents an unjustifiable "change of morality."[61]
In Bonington's view, nothing can be "more important" than providing
help to a fellow climber in distress, given the brutal conditions on the
mountain.[62] Sir Edmund Hillary, the first climber to reach the summit
of Everest, agrees. The decision of whether to rescue another human
being reflects the climbers' views of what really matters: "[P]eople
have completely lost sight of what is *important*. . . In our expedition,
there was never any likelihood whatsoever if one member of the party
was incapacitated that we would just leave him to die."[63]

This weaker kind of necessity – where breaking the rule is necessary to achieve one's ends – is commonplace in leadership. But so are
claims of the stronger kind of necessity. We see both, for example,
in the justifications leaders give for using the company jet for private purposes: "Taking the corporate jet is variously described as . . . a
security precaution" or as "a necessity for time-pressed executives and
politicians."[64] The second description refers to simple ends-based reasoning associated with *weak necessity*, whereas the first description aims
to establish the *strong necessity* associated with matters of life and death.

---

[58] McCoy, "The Parable of the Sadhu," 263.
[59] McCoy, "The Parable of the Sadhu," 265.
[60] Cowell, "Adventures change."
[61] Cowell, "Adventures change."
[62] Cowell, "Adventures change."
[63] Cowell, "'Dead' climber's survival impugns Mount Everest Ethics" (emphasis added).
Notice that Hillary imagines a member of his *own* party in need. See Chapters 5 and
7 for discussions of moral theories that privilege group members.
[64] Geraldine Fabrikant, Patrick McGeehan, and David Cay Johnston, "Executives Take
Company Planes As If Their Own," *New York Times* (May 10, 2006).

David Yermack of New York University's Stern School of Business suggests that strong necessity is often meant to provide cover for what is really weak necessity:

> It is like telling the C.E.O.: "We insist that you eat at a five-star restaurant for your own nutrition, and we insist that you drink $800 Champagne for your health"...I could see it if they were the chief executives in Afghanistan or Colombia. But it seems so preposterous in our country.[65]

Proving that actual executive behavior is sometimes stranger than fiction, Jay Conger came across a CEO who, in developing both kinds of necessity justification, could have been the subject of Yermack's hypothetical example:

> One CEO argued that she required a personal chef as an essential perk. She explained that she did not have time to go down to the cafeteria on the first floor of the building given the demands on her time. Her use of a personal chef would ensure that her day was spent more efficiently. Moreover, as the CEO, she was so valuable that any chance of food poisoning needed to be minimized. By having a chef she could control the quality of her food as well as control her diet and therefore her health.[66]

This CEO draws our attention both to what is necessary for her to achieve her ends and, rather unconvincingly, to what is necessary for her well-being and survival more generally.

Rejecting the strong version of necessity for everyday leaders still leaves us with the weaker ends-based understanding of necessity. Can neglecting people in dire need or otherwise breaking the moral rules be justified because it is necessary for a leader to achieve his group's goals? The Himalayan cases, as well as executive justifications of perks, suggest that an affirmative, situationist answer to this question is also unconvincing. These cases leave us wondering less about whether the behavior in question is justified than about why people in these situations act as though they have a justification for their behavior.

---

[65] Quoted in Fabrikant, McGeehan, and Johnston, "Executives Take Company Planes As If Their Own."

[66] Jay A. Conger, "Oh Lord, Won't You Buy Me a Mercedes-Benz: How Compensation Practices are Undermining the Credibility of Leaders," in *The Quest for Moral Leaders: Essays in Leadership Ethics*, eds. Joanne B. Ciulla, Terry L. Price, and Susan E. Murphy (Cheltenham, UK: Edward Elgar, 2005), 87.

One explanation of the behavior of McCoy's party, proffered by McCoy's companion Stephen, is that their failure to help the sadhu can be attributed to group biases grounded in stereotypes about class, race, or nationality.[67] Stephen quizzes McCoy, "I wonder what the Sherpas would have done if the sadhu had been a well-dressed Nepali, or what the Japanese would have done if the sadhu had been a well-dressed Asian, or what you would have done, Buzz, if the sadhu had been a well-dressed Western woman?"[68] These biases may be part of the story. But the treatment of the Western climbers Sharp and Hall by other Westerners shows that they are not the whole story. Stephen and McCoy are on better explanatory footing when they point to group commitments to "a superordinate goal."[69]

McCoy's "Parable of the Sadhu" is an effective teaching tool precisely because it takes the reader out of her own group and away from her life projects, showing her how badly people can behave when they are committed to goals that they find to be especially important. By putting us in the unfamiliar context of a Himalayan climb, McCoy's case takes us away from our own relationships, preoccupations, and pursuits so that we might get a clearer view of what morality requires.

Yet, if we are to prevent the virtue of McCoy's case from becoming its vice, we must do more than sustain an outward gaze. The ultimate goal of the exercise, McCoy suggests, is to apply the insight of the parable to our own behavior:

For each of us the sadhu lives. Should we stop what we are doing and comfort him; or should we keep trudging up toward the high pass? Should I pause to help the derelict I pass on the street each night as I walk by the Yale club en route to Grand Central Station?[70]

Once we recognize that the relevant kind of necessity in the "Parable of the Sadhu" is not the necessity that characterizes life-and-death situations for the leader, it becomes clear that leaders face similar moral challenges in everyday life. Sometimes, what is necessary to achieve group goals will conflict with the rules of morality, and morality may require the sacrifice of group goals.

---

67 McCoy, "The Parable of the Sadhu," 265.
68 McCoy, "The Parable of the Sadhu," 265.
69 McCoy, "The Parable of the Sadhu," 265–266.
70 McCoy, "The Parable of the Sadhu," 268.

As we will see in the next section, appropriately resolving these conflicts requires a better understanding of the importance of group goals and, especially, of our tendency to attribute greater importance to these goals than they deserve.

## THE MORE-IMPORTANT-THAN-AVERAGE EFFECT

The *better-than-average effect* refers to the inclination of people to see their personal qualities and their own actions as being uncommonly positive. Mark Alicke and Olesya Govorun call this effect "one of social psychology's chestnuts" and "one of the most robust of all self-enhancement phenomena," noting that it has been established "in numerous studies, with diverse populations, on multiple dimensions, and with various measurement techniques."[71] Very few people are willing to believe that they are just average in terms of how good-looking or athletic they are or in terms of how competently or morally they will behave. Still less are they willing to believe that they are *below* average on these and other positive dimensions.[72] But someone has to be average, and many people have to be below average. Somebody has to be wrong about his traits and behavior. Indeed, many people stand to be corrected!

Because the better-than-average effect is indexed to particular traits and behaviors, its connection to leadership is often straightforward. For example, some studies of the effect look specifically at students' beliefs about their leadership ability. Alicke and Govorun cite results associated with the 1976 College Board Exams, which show that "70 [percent] placed themselves above the median in leadership ability."[73] More recently, *The American Freshman National Norms for Fall 2005* finds that 61.3 percent of all student respondents (64.5 percent of the men and 58.7 percent of the women) rated themselves as "above

---

[71] Mark D. Alicke and Olesya Govorun, "The Better-Than-Average Effect," in *The Self in Social Judgment*, eds. Mark D. Alicke, David A. Dunning, and Joachim I. Krueger (New York: Psychology Press, 2005), 85.

[72] Individuals with low self-esteem or depression are regularly cited as showing reduced susceptibility to this effect (Alicke and Govorun, "The Better-Than-Average Effect," 92–93.)

[73] Alicke and Govorun, "The Better-Than-Average Effect," 87.

average" or as the "highest 10 percent" in leadership ability.[74] Still, champions of the better-than-average effect have not fully explored the leadership implications of this phenomenon and related psychological tendencies. What additional beliefs associated with leadership suffer distortion from this bias? Do leaders tend to think that their *goals* are *more important than average?*

The philosopher can make the conceptual point that people must see their goals as being especially important; otherwise, people would not have the goals that they have. Beliefs about importance are part of an explanation of why people do not abandon their particular goals to pursue other, more attractive alternatives. But we can also test this conceptual point by gathering data. In an effort to see if there is a "more-important-than-average effect," my colleagues and I surveyed student leaders and non-leaders at the University of Richmond.[75] These students were members of Greek organizations, student government, honor and judicial councils, political organizations, religious organizations, and other interest groups.

The survey asked subjects a series of questions about the importance of their group goals and personal goals. In the first set of questions, student leaders were asked not to make a comparison to the average but rather to rank their organizational goals and personal goals in relation to the organizational and personal goals of other students at the university:

*The Director of Student Activities has decided to distribute funds to the current officially recognized student organizations, one of which is your organization. There are 100 such organizations. If the Director wants to distribute the funds based on the **importance of***

---

74 Cited in "This year's freshmen at 4-year colleges: A statistical profile," *The Chronicle of Higher Education* (February 3, 2006). The results can be found in John H. Pryor, Sylvia Hurtado, Victor B. Saenz, Jennifer A. Lindholm, William S. Korn, Kathryn M. Mahoney, *The American Freshman: National Norms for Fall 2005* (Los Angeles: University of California Higher Education Research Institute, 2005), 173. Studies also confirm the better-than-average effect in leaders. A *BusinessWeek* survey of people in management found that 90 percent of respondents think they perform in the top 10 percent. At the executive level, the result is 97 percent (Peter Coy, "Ten Years From Now...A *BusinessWeek* poll indicates big changes are ahead in tomorrow's workplace," *BusinessWeek* [August 20, 2007]).

75 For the complete findings of this and related studies, see Crystal L. Hoyt, Terry L. Price, and Alyson Emrick, "Leadership and the More-Important-Than-Average Effect." Manuscript in preparation.

*each organization's goals, where in the ranking should your organization be put for the distribution of funds? 1 = **most important** organizational goals and 100 = **least important** organizational goals (one organization per ranking)* ————.

*The Director of the Career Development Center has decided to award "personal development" grants to the leaders of the current officially recognized student organizations, one of which is your organization. There are 100 such organizations. If the Director wants to distribute the grants based on the **importance of each leader's personal goals**, as distinguished from his or her organization's goals, where in the ranking should you be put for the distribution of grants? 1 = **most important** personal goals and 100 = **least important** personal goals (one leader per ranking)* ————.

As we expected, bias triumphed over mathematical possiblity. The mean scores for importance were nowhere close to what should be the average – 50 percent. Student leaders held their organizational goals to be near the top 10 percent in terms of importance, and they put their personal goals near the top 20 percent in terms of importance.

A second set of survey questions used a different strategy to discover how student leaders think about the importance of their organizational and personal goals:

*The goals of my **student organization** are best described as being... (circle one)*

|   | Unimportant | Somewhat important | Important | Very important | Extremely important |
|---|---|---|---|---|---|

*What percentage of the student organizations on campus have goals that are best described as being:*

|   | Unimportant | Somewhat important | Important | Very important | Extremely important |
|---|---|---|---|---|---|

*Enter percentages here:*

*My **personal goals** are best described as being... (circle one)*

|   | Unimportant | Somewhat important | Important | Very important | Extremely important |
|---|---|---|---|---|---|

*What percentage of students on campus have personal goals that are best described as being:*

| Unimportant | Somewhat important | Important | Very important | Extremely important |
|---|---|---|---|---|

*Enter percentages here:*

Based on responses to these questions, leaders' organizational goals and personal goals are best described as being "very important." These results would not present a problem if student leaders believed that the organizational and personal goals of others were also very important. There is certainly no inconsistency in saying that everyone has very important goals. However, again supporting the more-important-than-average effect, leaders rated the organizational goals and personal goals of others as being merely "important."

A third set of survey questions employed a Likert scale to test for the same effect:

| Strongly disagree | Disagree | Somewhat disagree | Neither agree nor disagree | Somewhat agree | Agree | Strongly agree |
|---|---|---|---|---|---|---|
| 1 | 2 | 3 | 4 | 5 | 6 | 7 |

*Using the scale in the table, indicate the extent to which you agree with the following statements by writing the **number** in the space provided:*

_____ *"The goals of my student organization are important."*
_____ *"The goals of the average student organization on campus are important."*

_____ *"My personal goals are important."*
_____ *"The personal goals of the average student on campus are important."*

Here, too, student leaders were committed to the above-average importance of their organizational goals and personal goals. With respect to the importance of their own goals, the responses of leaders are best described as "agree." Yet student leaders thought less well of the goals of the others. With respect to the importance of other students' organizational goals and personal goals, the responses of leaders are best described as "somewhat agree." The difference between how leaders view the importance of their own goals and how they view the importance of the goals of others again provides evidence for the more-important-than-average effect.

The results of our study also support the claim that *being a leader* affects a person's view of how important his organizational goals are. In other words, leaders are not only susceptible to the more-important-than-average effect but also show a greater bias than non-leaders. First, when subjects were asked to rank their organizational goals on a descending scale of importance (where "1" denotes "most important organizational goals" and "100" denotes "least important organizational goals"), student leaders attributed greater importance to their organizational goals than did non-leaders.

Second, the difference between how respondents described their organizational goals (as being important, very important, or extremely important) and how they described the organizational goals of other students was greater for leaders than for non-leaders. Leaders rate their own organizational goals significantly higher than non-leaders rate their organizational goals.

Third, *being a leader* had an effect on participant responses to the Likert-style questions: The difference between the extent to which respondents agreed with the claims "the goals of my student organization are important" and "the goals of the average student organization on campus are important" was greater for leaders than for non-leaders. In other words, compared with non-leaders, leaders agreed more strongly with the claim "the goals of my student organization are important."

## THE JUSTIFICATORY FORCE OF LEADERSHIP

The necessity-based justification assumes that leaders have to break the rules to achieve goals that are not simply important but *very* or, perhaps, *extremely* important. This assumption rests on two claims. First, it must be true that the goal cannot be reached without breaking moral rules. Leaders probably overestimate the extent to which immorality is necessary to achieve their ends. In some cases, breaking the rules may be the only means to the desired end. But in many other cases, leaders use talk of necessity as shorthand for conveying the fact that rule breaking is simply the easiest route to success. In these cases, rule-breaking behavior is sufficient for reaching the goal, but not necessary. Rule breaking is one, but not the only, way for leaders to achieve what they want to achieve.

Second, the argument from necessity is hardly convincing when leaders engage in rule-breaking behavior to achieve ends that are only of average importance. So the necessity-based justification also rests on the claim that the goals to which leaders are committed are exceptionally important. This claim exposes the necessity-based justification to the criticism that it overlooks the more-important-than-average effect. In the study described in the previous section, student leaders expressed the belief that their goals were significantly more important than average. In fact, leaders were more susceptible to this bias than non-leaders. The results of this study are a testament to just how much more important than average student leaders believe their goals to be. But their beliefs defy mathematical possibility. All leaders of student organizations can no more have goals that are more important than average than all the children of Garrison Keillor's fictional Lake Wobegon can be above average.[76] The second claim on which the necessity-based argument rests is even more questionable than the first.

The fact that the more-important-than-average effect applies not only to personal goals but also to organizational goals complicates the moral psychology of leadership. While organizational goals give leaders an added source of justification, leaders' commitments to these goals are subject to the same biases about importance that distort the way we think about our goals more generally. This kind of commitment to organizational goals and, specifically, the *justificatory force* of these goals makes leadership ethics distinctive.[77]

In ethics, an appeal to the importance of one's personal goals carries little justificatory weight in an argument for breaking the moral rules.[78] One of the primary purposes of morality is to adjudicate between the personal goals of individuals, each of whom is committed

---

[76] This contention assumes in each case, of course, that there is not some external group to which the comparison is being made.
[77] See Terry L. Price, *Understanding Ethical Failures in Leadership* (New York: Cambridge University Press, 2006).
[78] See Chapter 3.

to the importance of his goals. However, moral theory is typically much more receptive to appeals to the good of the group. Because ethics often aims to get us to think more about the group and less about ourselves, appeals to organizational goals are readily distinguished from motivations such as naked self-interest and from personal grabs for power.

Organizational goals thus provide leaders with an alternative justificatory framework, one that is relatively immune to standard moral criticisms. The findings of our study on student leaders suggest that leaders are well positioned to try to justify their behavior with this kind of argument. Given assumptions about the moral primacy of the group, it is easy to see why leaders might think their organizational goals have special justificatory force.

The claim that leaders are overly committed to the importance of their organizational goals generates an interesting explanation of ethical failures in leadership. According to this explanation, immoral leaders do not always put personal goals ahead of organizational goals. Leaders also fail ethically when they act on mistaken beliefs about the importance of their organizational goals. In short, they have an inflated view of the justificatory force of the group goals to which they are committed. Another way to put this point is to say that selfishness may not be the central problem in leadership ethics.

Everyday leaders are generally wrong to think that the importance of their ends gives them a situational justification to break the rules. The ends of leadership have special justificatory force only if these ends really are of exceptional importance. The main argument of this chapter is that the goals of everyday leadership are not important in this way. This is not to deny that some goals may indeed meet this condition. In fact, Chapter 8 considers the argument that ends such as "the greater good" are important enough to justify rule-breaking behavior by leaders. First, however, Chapter 7 addresses the claim that a leader's role in a particular group, community, or society is sufficient to justify the exceptions he makes of himself, regardless of the importance of its members' goals.

# 7

## Membership and Moral Particularity

Standard moral theories aim to eradicate, or at least limit, partiality in moral decision making. For instance, Kant's deontological ethics requires that we act on demands of reason that apply equally to all rational agents, not simply on more particular reasons that can be applied only to us. It does not matter whether these particular reasons advance self-interest or group interest. In this way, Kantian ethics strictly limits the extent to which people can put themselves or their groups ahead of others.

In Chapter 8, we will see that consequentialist theories such as utilitarianism are also committed to impartiality, as evidenced – for example – by the utilitarian requirement that we count the utility, or happiness, of all agents equally. According to this view, the fact that one course of action would contribute to my own utility, or to that of members of my group, is morally irrelevant, except insofar as these contributions promote what the utilitarian ultimately seeks to maximize – namely, *overall* utility.

Both Kantianism and utilitarianism rest on a fundamental assumption about moral agency – that agents can be addressed independently of their circumstances, relationships, and allegiances. A commitment to this assumption implies that leaders cannot use the special importance of their groups' ends to justify rule-breaking behavior. No rational agents can endorse as generally true, in any objective sense, the idea that their group's ends are more important than the ends of all (or even most) other groups. Without this kind of impartial assessment of value, leaders will be unable to justify breaking the moral rules to privilege the particular ends of their groups.

The *communitarian* alternative to deontological and consequentialist moral theories encourages us to think about moral justification in a different way. According to this view, what counts as a justification for any moral agent depends on particular facts about that agent. Because value is defined not in some objective, third-party sense but rather by membership in particular organizations, communities, or states, group members must look to "social meanings" to determine what morality requires of them.[1] What socially situated agents have reason to do will depend upon who they are. In short, it will depend on their "moral identity."[2] And the starting point for a determination of who they are is their "membership in communities."[3]

Communitarian thinkers who accept this picture of moral identity reject the "modern individualism" of Kantian and utilitarian ethics, as well as the liberal political theory to which they give rise.[4] Communitarian standard-bearer Alasdair MacIntyre tells us, "From the standpoint of individualism I am what I myself *choose* to be."[5] Individualism misses the fact that identity rests not on our choices but on our social circumstances. In the end, so too does morality itself:

What the good life is for a fifth-century Athenian general will not be the same as what it was for a medieval nun or a seventeenth-century farmer. But it is not just that different individuals live in different social circumstances; it is also that we all approach our own circumstances as bearers of a particular social identity. I am someone's son or daughter, someone else's cousin or uncle; I am a citizen of this or that city, a member of this or that guild or profession; I belong to this clan, that tribe, this nation. Hence what is good for me has to be the good for one who inhabits these roles. As such, I inherit from the past of my family, my city, my tribe, my nation, a variety of debts, inheritances,

---

[1] For a discussion of social meanings, see Michael Walzer, *Spheres of Justice: A Defense of Pluralism and Equality* (New York: Basic Books, 1983).
[2] Alasdair MacIntyre, *After Virtue: A Study in Moral Theory*, 2nd ed. (Notre Dame, IN: University of Notre Dame Press, 1984), 220.
[3] MacIntyre, *After Virtue*, 221.
[4] MacIntyre, *After Virtue*, 220.
[5] MacIntyre, *After Virtue*, 220 (emphasis added).

rightful expectations and obligations. This is in part what gives my life its own moral particularity.[6]

Who we are significantly determines what is good for us and ultimately what behaviors are right in our particular social condition.

Communitarians conclude that liberal moral and political theory fails because it conceives of moral agents primarily as choosers, essentially free from the contingency and particularity of human relationships. John Rawls's work in *A Theory of Justice*, which was discussed in Chapter 5, serves as a prime example of how the liberal position generates a political morality that neglects community.[7] Here we need only recall the conditions under which the principles of justice are chosen: "Among the essential features of [the hypothetical] situation is that no one knows his place in society, his class position or social status..."[8] According to the communitarian critique, a conception of moral identity that sees agents as radically individuated – as completely free to adopt or sever ties with others – ignores the fact that our true selves are so immersed in our relationships that we cannot abstract away from communal membership.[9]

Communitarianism thus offers a potential response to Chapter 6's argument against rule breaking by leaders. All this response has to show is that justification derives not from autonomous choice but rather from the moral particularity that characterizes the relationships in which leaders find themselves. As such, these relationships can justify rule-breaking behavior even if group ends cannot be endorsed as exceptionally important by all rational agents. Leaders do not need to appeal to notions of objective value to justify pursuit of their goals. Such an appeal mistakenly assumes that we are unconnected choosers, rationally deciding what groups we might join or lead.

Because communitarian leaders use the ends of their organization, community, or state to justify their behavior, what these leaders have

---

[6] MacIntyre, *After Virtue*, 220.

[7] See Michael Sandel, *Liberalism and the Limits of Justice* (Cambridge: Cambridge University Press, 1982), for a communitarian critique of John Rawls's liberalism.

[8] John Rawls, *A Theory of Justice* (Cambridge, MA: Belknap Press of Harvard University Press, 1971), 12.

[9] MacIntyre does deny "that the self has to accept the moral *limitations* of the particularity of those forms of community" (*After Virtue*, 221). His admission that the self is not identical to the community makes room for some form of autonomous evaluation.

reason to do must be judged from an internal perspective – that is, from within the group. If the communitarian view of moral agency is correct, it is simply too much to ask leaders to offer an externally convincing justification for doing what they have to do to achieve group goals. Indeed, a leader will sometimes be justified in breaking the rules "because he has special obligations to his group."

ROLES IN EVERYDAY LIFE

Robert Solomon's work on "corporate roles" is the business ethics incarnation of communitarianism.[10] Like communitarianism more generally, it seeks to show why partiality is permissible – indeed, required – according to a proper conception of morality. As Solomon puts it, "[P]eople that work for [corporations] are . . . citizens of (at least) two communities at once, and one might think of business ethics as getting straight about that dual citizenship."[11]

Solomon's aim is to make business ethics practical by applying the insights of communitarian moral and political theory to the corporate context.

It is the situatedness of corporate roles that lends them their particular ethical poignancy, the fact that an employee or an executive is not just a person who happens to be in a place and is constrained by no more than the usual ethical prohibitions. To work for a company is to accept a set of particular obligations . . . There may be general ethical rules and guidelines that cut across most positions but, as these get more general and more broadly applicable, they also become all but useless in concrete ethical dilemmas . . . [B]usiness ethics presumes concrete situations and particular people and their places in organizations. There is little point to an ethics that tries to transcend all such particularities and embrace the chairman of the board as well as a middle manager, a secretary, and a factory worker.[12]

Just as we cannot make sense of the duties we have as individuals without an adequate understanding of the moral implications of membership in a particular family or nation, so we cannot determine our

[10] Robert Solomon, *Ethics and Excellence: Cooperation and Integrity in Business* (New York: Oxford University Press, 1992).
[11] Solomon, *Ethics and Excellence*, 103.
[12] Solomon, *Ethics and Excellence*, 162.

duties in the business community unless we attend to the meanings of our roles within the corporation.

Solomon's "Aristotelean approach" to business ethics constitutes an alternative to Kantian applied ethics.[13] In fact, Solomon calls Kant "a kind of disease in ethics."[14] In its attempt to derive duties from "abstract ratiocination, [a] principle of contradiction, or *a priori* formulations of the categorical imperative," Kant's moral philosophy leaves business people "empty-handed."[15] All Kant has to offer corporate managers is "'don't lie,' 'don't steal,' 'don't cheat' – elaborated and supported by the most Gothic non-econometric construction ever allowed in a company training center."[16]

The practical impotence of Kant's approach, Solomon claims, is a necessary implication of its *universalism*.[17] Kant has nothing useful to say about the actual ethical challenges faced by business people because he excludes the *particular* features of the contexts in which they work. As a result, corporate executives are left with a laundry list of tired – and some might say obvious – prohibitions. Kant's deontological view simply cannot come to terms with the fact that our duties "are defined by our roles in a community (for example, a corporation)."[18]

The first thing to notice about communitarian business ethics is that corporate roles are importantly different from the roles to which standard arguments in communitarian moral and political theory appeal. Recall that the communitarian critique of Rawls's theory takes issue with the liberal assumption that our moral identities are simply the outcome of voluntary choice. According to the communitarian account, this assumption betrays a failure to notice, for example, that we have duties of family and country despite the fact that the roles from which these duties are derived are in no significant sense voluntarily incurred. We do not choose our parents, and most of us still acquire our political membership by birth alone. In other words, we are born into families and nation-states.

---

[13] Solomon, *Ethics and Excellence*, 162.
[14] Solomon, *Ethics and Excellence*, 114.
[15] Solomon, *Ethics and Excellence*, 114 (emphasis added).
[16] Solomon, *Ethics and Excellence*, 114.
[17] Solomon, *Ethics and Excellence*, 114. See my discussion in Chapter 2.
[18] Solomon, *Ethics and Excellence*, 114.

The force of this insight about fundamental aspects of our ethical lives explains the ascendancy of communitarian moral and political theory as an alternative to liberalism. This insight, however, does not easily extend to our everyday business lives. Corporate roles are hardly characterized by the absence of choice, and we should not think of them in this way. The analogy between family roles or political citizenship, on the one hand, and occupational roles, on the other, may have been apt at some points in our history – most recently, say, with respect to the responsibilities of the American family farmer – but the similarities between such roles are now too weak to support communitarian business ethics, especially in current corporate contexts.[19] People *choose* to adopt the particular corporate roles they inhabit. In our everyday business lives, corporate roles – including positions of leadership – are voluntarily adopted in a way that our roles as sons and daughters or citizens are not.

Even Solomon admits as much: "Whether we do well, whether we like ourselves, whether we lead happy productive lives, depends to a large extent on the companies we *choose*...To my business students today, who are all too prone to choose a job on the basis of salary and start-up bonus alone, I always say, 'to live a decent life *choose* the right company.'"[20] People also choose whether to maintain their corporate roles or to sever ties with companies to take on other roles. With the demise of the notion of lifetime employment, it is no longer true – if it ever was – that employment relations are characterized by anything like the permanency of parent–child or citizen–state relations.

Perhaps as much as any other endeavor, business lends itself to the liberal's preoccupation with choice in moral and political analysis. People acquire business duties associated with particular roles because they have chosen to take on and maintain these roles. It is precisely the voluntary nature of business – represented, for example, by the central role played by contracts – that gives business its individualistic rather than communitarian character. An individual's participation in corporate life, especially at the executive level, must be understood

---

[19] Even modern militaries now rely upon an all-volunteer force.
[20] Solomon, *Ethics and Excellence*, 148 (emphases added). But see his discussion at 78–79.

first and foremost as the result of choice. Choice, not the role itself, ultimately grounds the relevant duties.

Solomon recognizes the difficulties involved in trying to approach all ethical problems *from within the role itself*, admitting that "people in business inevitably play several roles or wear several hats at once, and these roles may clash with one another as they may clash with more personal roles based on family, friendship, and personal obligations."[21] But he overlooks the source of these difficulties. Many moral duties exist prior to voluntarily assumed corporate obligations. Sometimes the moral duties in the background of the choice – for example, the duty not to lie or break promises – precludes justifiably adopting the corporate role in the first place. In these cases, the focal point of moral concern cannot be restricted to what happens within these roles. An appeal to one's corporate role and its duties misses the real origin of the conflict – unjustifiable choice.

So, how should we respond to people who find themselves in situations in which their corporate roles generate duties that conflict with other demands of morality? The corporate executive in the ethics training workshop may be just such an individual. As Solomon pictures the situation, here the executive sits, stuck with particularized duties, and all he gets is universal prohibitions against lying, stealing, and cheating.[22] Worse still, if Solomon is right, the particularities of the executive's role occasion legitimate doubt as to whether there really are any universal prohibitions. Although some moral imperatives apply "across most positions," universals look "all but useless" from the executive's perspective.[23]

Distinguishing between *given* and *chosen* roles takes much of the sting out of executives' complaints about the inapplicability of moral absolutes of the kind advocated by Kant. Once we recognize the voluntary nature of corporate roles in everyday business life, it no longer makes sense to see business duties as being forced upon executives. The appropriate attitude of the individual in the workshop is not,

---

[21] Solomon, *Ethics and Excellence*, 166. He does not leave these questions completely unresolved, appealing instead to Aristotle's notion of practical wisdom (174–179). I discuss practical wisdom in Chapter 4.

[22] Solomon, *Ethics and Excellence*, p. 114.

[23] Solomon, *Ethics and Excellence*, p. 162.

"How dare you give me a list of prohibitions that conflict with the duties of my role!" In some cases at least, ethics training should lead her to say, "Look what I've gotten myself into!" For it is the executive who chose this role.

The applicability of Kantian ethics in the business world turns not simply on its systematic enumeration of general moral imperatives but also on its capacity to show executives how they are bound by morality no matter what their corporate role. In other words, Kant's ethics gives us the *content* of morality, expressed in part by proscriptions such as Solomon's "'don't lie,' 'don't steal,' 'don't cheat.'"[24] But Kant also has something to teach executives about the *scope* of morality – namely, that moral prohibitions apply regardless of the demands of one's corporate role.[25] A central lesson of a Kantian approach to corporate ethics is that the business ends with which corporate roles are associated do not justify breaking the rules. The ends of business are like any other ends we might voluntarily choose to adopt. Sometimes they conflict with morality and force us to choose between role expectations and the rules of morality. What the corporate executive often needs to learn – or, at least, be reminded of – is that business ends do not release her from the moral rules.

One might object that there is another sense in which business is a quintessentially communitarian context and, accordingly, that the duties derived from corporate roles have independent moral weight. Although the voluntary nature of these roles distinguishes them from family roles or political roles, executives who take on corporate roles – like family members and citizens – are engaged in what are undeniably *collective* activities. Executives work with others – ordinarily stockholders and employees – to produce an excellent product, provide a needed service, or simply turn a profit.

Does the collective nature of business activities imply that executives are no longer bound by moral rules? There is little reason to think so. Just as it is wrong for people to break the rules to pursue their individual ends, it is wrong for them to break the rules when they are working in concert with others. A rule breaker working on the behalf

---

[24] Solomon, *Ethics and Excellence*, 114.
[25] See Chapter 1 and Terry L. Price, *Understanding Ethical Failures in Leadership* (New York: Cambridge University Press, 2006), ch. 1.

of the group enjoys no special dispensation based on the mere fact that the activity in which he is engaged is a collective one.

An ambiguity in the expression "collective activity" potentially causes the confusion. In addition to taking the expression to mean that people are working together to achieve some end, we might be tempted to assume that this end is somehow part of the common good or the good of all. This significantly stronger understanding of collective activity might do more moral work in an argument for the claim that leaders are sometimes justified in breaking the rules.[26] For now, suffice it to say that the communitarian appeal to the weaker notion of collective activity fails to justify rule-breaking behavior by leaders. Morality gives people significant freedom to engage in both individual and collective activities, but only within the constraints of common rules that apply to all actors.

## A KANTIAN ACCOUNT OF SPECIAL OBLIGATIONS

Can leadership ethics accommodate the moral particularity of the corporate context? Fortunately, accepting the idea that ethical universals trump role expectations is not incompatible with accepting the idea that there are also duties associated with corporate roles and, furthermore, that these duties have significant moral weight. In fact, there are good moral reasons to embrace these duties. In the ethically robust relationships of business and professional life, we indeed owe group members more than what they might expect from our basic compliance with moral rules.

Communitarians are correct that corporate roles are characterized by a "particular ethical poignancy" and that we should not see the executives in these roles as "constrained by no more than the usual ethical prohibitions."[27] But they are wrong in thinking that moral particularity requires a dismissive attitude toward ethical universals. Because "more than the usual ethical prohibitions" can mean "in addition to" instead of "in lieu of," corporate executives might be constrained *both* by ethical universals *and* by particular role expectations – at least as

---

[26] In the next chapter, I consider the argument that leaders are justified in breaking the rules for the greater good.

[27] Solomon, *Ethics and Excellence*, 162.

long as the role expectations are consistent with the rules of morality. We must therefore consider the possibility that a fundamentally impartial theory of leadership ethics can also make room for the partiality of special obligations within corporate contexts.

The special obligation of business leaders that merits first mention is the one derived from the relationship between corporate executives and stockholders. As Milton Friedman puts it in his famous paper "The Social Responsibility of Business Is to Increase Its Profits," the corporate executive should "conduct the business in accordance with [his employer's] desires, which generally will be to make as much money as possible while conforming to the basic rules of the society, both those embodied in law and those embodied in ethical custom."[28] Friedman's defense of profit maximization for stockholders is sometimes read by students as a manifesto for amoralism in business. However, it is clear that Friedman sees corporate executives as being rigidly bound by the rules of morality. Most notably, profit must be pursued within constraints such as rules against "deception or fraud."[29]

Friedman's critics nevertheless suggest that he misses additional moral requirements by giving too much weight to the interests of stockholders. For example, Edward Freeman questions the "assumption of the primacy of the stockholder" and proposes a much broader conception of the parties to whom executives have special obligations.[30] Freeman concludes that we must

revitalize the concept of managerial capitalism by replacing the notion that managers have a duty to stockholders with the concept that managers bear a fiduciary relationship to stakeholders. Stakeholders are those groups who have a stake in or claim on the firm. Specifically I include suppliers, customers, employees, stockholders, and the local community, as well as management in its role as agent for these groups.[31]

---

[28] Milton Friedman, "The Social Responsibility of Business Is to Increase Its Profits," in *Ethical Issues in Business: A Philosophical Approach*, eds. Thomas Donaldson, Patricia H. Werhane, and Margaret Cording (Upper Saddle River, NJ: Prentice Hall, 2002), 33.

[29] Friedman, "Social Responsibility of Business," 38.

[30] Edward Freeman, "Stakeholder Theory of the Modern Corporation," in *Ethical Issues in Business: A Philosophical Approach*, eds. Thomas Donaldson, Patricia H. Werhane, and Margaret Cording (Upper Saddle River, NJ: Prentice Hall, 2002), 38.

[31] Freeman, "Stakeholder Theory," 39.

In short, executives have special obligations not just to stockholders but to all "groups and individuals who benefit from or are harmed by, and whose rights are violated or respected by, corporate actions."[32]

On the stakeholder account, our special obligations will depend on what constitutes a benefit and what constitutes a harm. The moral scope of concern changes radically, for instance, if people can be harmed by all kinds of inaction – that is, by the things that organizational decision makers choose not to do and even the omissions that are never considered as possibilities. Here, I do not have in mind the negative implications of inaction such as the failure to reduce pollution, which clearly affects people's interests in a morally relevant way, but the negative implications of inaction such as the failure to move a plant to a community or country that would benefit greatly from the added jobs. Do these effects constitute harms to potential recipients?

We certainly want a leader's moral calculations to consider both the costs to the community that loses an important source of employment and the benefits to the community that gets much-needed opportunities for work. But must business leaders also consider the interests of people in all possible localities that might benefit from a new plant? If there are no limits on the kinds of inaction that can harm people, then the scope of concern must be widened to include these stakeholders. Business leaders would have to take into consideration not only the interests of people directly affected by organizational activities but also the interests of anyone who might be benefited in any way by a decision to pursue a different course of action. In effect, everyone would become a stakeholder. Just as we cannot be friends with everyone we know, we cannot have special obligations to everyone we affect.

Kenneth Goodpaster rejects even more limited characterizations of stakeholder membership on the grounds that they "[cut] management loose from certain well-defined bonds of stockholder accountability."[33] As Goodpaster puts it, allowing special obligations to stakeholders dilutes "management's *fiduciary* duty to the stockholder, essentially the duty to keep a profit-maximizing promise..."[34] Goodpaster's

[32] Freeman, "Stakeholder Theory," 41.
[33] Kenneth E. Goodpaster, "Business Ethics and Stakeholder Analysis," *Business Ethics Quarterly* 1 (1991): 63.
[34] Goodpaster, "Business Ethics and Stakeholder Analysis," 63.

main insight is that this *promise* is the source of the partiality of special obligations that corporate executives owe to stockholders. Executives have promised to give priority to stockholders' financial interests, whereas executives have made no such promise to other stakeholders. Treating the interests of all stakeholders equally would be incompatible with discharging the most straightforward special obligation that can be attributed to corporate executives – to act as agents on behalf of stockholders in financial matters.

Efforts to understand all corporate relations in terms of this fiduciary model give rise to an economic system in which there are no special obligations at all:

> [I]f we treat other stakeholders on the model of the fiduciary relationship between management and the stockholder, we will, in effect, make them into quasi-stockholders. We can do this, of course, if we choose to as a society. But we should be aware that it is a radical step indeed. For it blurs traditional goals in terms of entrepreneurial risk-taking, pushes decision-making towards paralysis because of the dilemmas posed by dividend loyalties and, in the final analysis, represents nothing less than the conversion of the modern private corporation into a public institution and probably calls for a corresponding restructuring of corporate governance (e.g., representatives of each stakeholder group on the board of directors).[35]

Goodpaster is careful, however, to make sure that his narrower understanding of the special obligations of executives does not leave other stakeholders morally at risk. In addition to having fiduciary obligations to stockholders, executives are bound by "morally significant *nonfiduciary* obligations . . . to those whose freedom and well-being is affected by their economic behavior."[36] In other words, executives must follow ordinary moral rules.

An appeal to the promises between executives and stockholders is consistent with a Kantian understanding of moral particularity in corporate contexts. By virtue of these promises, the corporate executive owes a moral debt to stockholders that he does not owe to other individuals to whom he has made no such promise.[37] "Keep your promises"

---

[35] Goodpaster, "Business Ethics and Stakeholder Analysis," p. 66.

[36] Goodpaster, "Business Ethics and Stakeholder Analysis," 67. Goodpaster's view does not differ greatly from Milton Friedman's. Goodpaster tells us that "Milton Friedman must be given a fair and serious hearing" (69).

[37] In the next two sections, I discuss constraints on the kinds of promises executives can make.

constitutes an ethical universal, and the special obligation arises when there is a promise to a particular person or group of people. Violation of the universal rule thus depends on the presence of a special obligation on the part of the person who makes a promise. According to this Kantian approach, there is a relationship of interdependence between the ethical universal and the special obligation.

Contrary to what the communitarian critique of Kant suggests, then, we do not need to abandon liberal moral and political assumptions to make sense of moral particularity. Contracts, and the promises they represent, are a very rich source of special obligations, especially within corporate contexts. In fact, there are clear contractual relationships between corporations and many groups typically characterized as stakeholders. Understanding the nature of these relationships between business actors will help us fill out a Kantian account of the special obligations of corporate executives.

Corporations have relationships with suppliers, employees, and customers that they do not have with other groups affected by their business activity. In typical cases, businesses promise to provide payment to suppliers, wages and benefits to employees, and products to customers in exchange for materials, labor, and payment, respectively. So, while corporate executives do not have a fiduciary relationship with these stakeholders in the same way that they have a fiduciary relationship with stockholders – that is, executives cannot be expected to act in the best financial interests of suppliers, employees, and customers – corporate executives nevertheless have a special *moral* relationship with these stakeholders. Indeed, it is fair to say that contracts between corporations and stakeholders give rise to a fiduciary relationship in the more general sense that it is one of "confidence and trust."[38]

This relationship generates special obligations between corporate executives and stakeholders. Such obligations will differ among – and even within – the various stakeholder groups, depending upon the nature of the contracts. The relationships between corporate executives and suppliers are not identical to the relationships between corporate executives and stockholders, and there can also be different contractual relationships with different employees. What the various stakeholder groups, as well as different individuals within these groups,

---

[38] *Merriam-Webster's Collegiate Dictionary*, electronic edition, version 1.2 (1994–1996).

receive is determined – to some extent at least – by their perceived contributions to the organization.

This is not to suggest that what stakeholders such as suppliers, employees, and customers receive in exchange for their contributions is all that they are owed by morality; as we have seen, stakeholders are also owed the protection of moral rules that govern all human relations.[39] The point is rather that contractual relationships with stakeholders oblige corporate executives to do *more than* discharge the duties of ordinary morality but, in many cases, *less than* what they must do for stockholders. What stakeholders such as suppliers, employees, and customers are *specially* owed, in addition to what they are *universally* owed, depends on the nature of their particular agreements. The only way to get greater moral particularity would be to release corporate executives from universal ethical requirements.

This application of Kant's ethics to corporate contexts takes us from an *interest-based* determination of obligations to stakeholders – according to which corporate executives have special obligations to anyone whose interests are affected by the corporation – to a *contractual* understanding of these obligations. In so doing, it is in keeping with much of Norman Bowie's "A Kantian Approach to Business Ethics."[40] Bowie draws on the contractual nature of business to support his claim that Kant's ethics "does not prohibit commercial transactions."[41] For example, in his discussion of layoffs, he writes:

American[s] have been deeply concerned about the massive layoffs created by the downsizing of corporations in the early and mid-1990s. Are these layoffs immoral? A naive Kantian response would label them as immoral because, allegedly, the employees are being used as mere means to enhance shareholder wealth. However, that judgment would be premature. What would be required from a Kantian perspective is an examination of the employer/employee relationship, including any contractual agreements. So long as the relationship was neither coercive nor deceptive, there would be nothing immoral about layoffs.[42]

---

[39] For additional requirements, see Chapter 5 and the final section of this chapter.
[40] Norman Bowie, "A Kantian Approach to Business Ethics," in *A Companion to Business Ethics*, ed. Robert E. Frederick (Oxford: Blackwell Publishers, 1999), 3–16. See also Norman Bowie, *Business Ethics: A Kantian Perspective* (Oxford: Blackwell Publishers, 1999).
[41] Bowie, "A Kantian Approach to Business Ethics," 7.
[42] Bowie, "A Kantian Approach to Business Ethics," 8.

Clearly, layoffs do not benefit all parties to the exchange. It is the agreement between employers and employees, not the fact that the decision would be in the best interests of all involved, that grounds the Kantian justification of the executive's decision.[43]

In other places, however, Bowie's defense of the morality of business also appeals to the interest-based characterization of duties to stakeholders. In claiming that "[n]o one is used as merely a means in a voluntary economic exchange *where both parties benefit*,"[44] he inaccurately describes the grounds of the duty. Contrary to what Bowie says, people are used as mere means whenever they do not consent to economic exchanges – no matter what the benefit. Furthermore, Kantian ethics permits economic exchanges when they are consensual, regardless of whether one or both of the parties fail to benefit from the exchange. So, even if we assume that perceived self-interest motivates economic exchanges and, accordingly, that such exchanges are typically to the benefit of the parties involved in them, the consensual nature of the exchanges, not the effect on people's interests, serves as the Kantian rationale for allowing the exchanges in the first place.

Bowie's interpretation of Kant also takes too strong a view of the special obligations executives have to include employees in the governance of the corporation:

Kantian moral theory also requires worker participation; indeed, it requires a vast democratization of the work place . . . Consent also requires that the individuals in an organization endorse the rules that govern them. As a minimum condition of democratization, Kantian moral philosophy requires that each person in an organization be represented by the stakeholder group to which he or she belongs, and that these various stakeholder groups must consent to the rules and policies which govern the organization.[45]

---

[43] It would have been better for Bowie to say that layoffs "*might* not be immoral" or that there is "nothing *necessarily* immoral about layoffs." Some such qualification is necessary to cover potential positive duties that employers have to employees. For example, if there is a less drastic means for fulfilling financial obligations, then it would seem that this alternative ought to be pursued even if layoffs would not violate the employment contract. Bowie correctly notes, for example, that "business organizations and practices should be arranged so that they contribute to the development of human rational and moral capacities, rather than inhibit the development of these capacities" ("A Kantian Approach to Business Ethics," 8.).

[44] Bowie, "A Kantian Approach to Business Ethics," 7 (emphasis added).

[45] Bowie, "A Kantian Approach to Business Ethics," 12.

This argument draws on two distinct Kantian requirements. First, Kant thinks that the moral rules must be ones that could be endorsed by rational agents. These rules must lend themselves to universalization.[46] Second, because the moral rules prohibit coercion, Kantian ethics also requires that employees consent to the conditions of employment.

Together, these requirements tell us that a determination of the rules of morality must appeal to the reason of all rational agents – including employees – and that the justification of the employment relationship rests on employee consent. But the requirements do not tell us that employees must be able to determine organizational rules and policies. In other words, democratic participation in business is not a direct implication of Kantian ethics. Whether there is a more extensive special obligation of employee participation in *corporate* governance – as opposed to governance in Kant's *kingdom of ends*[47] – depends on the nature of the employment agreement itself.

## CONTINGENCY AND SPECIAL OBLIGATIONS

Kant characterizes the requirements of morality as categorical, not hypothetical.[48] Unlike reason's other demands on action, ethical universals are binding independently of the particular ends to which agents are committed. Categorical imperatives thus lack the kind of contingency that characterizes hypothetical imperatives. Whereas hypothetical imperatives direct agents to pursue the means to an end *only if* the agents in question want to achieve the end, categorical imperatives bind agents regardless of any effects on the achievement of the agents' ends.

In contrast to ethical universals, special obligations share some of the contingency of hypothetical imperatives. Special obligations are contingent in two ways. Contracts are binding only if they are *voluntarily* and *justifiably* adopted. First, a corporate executive cannot be financially obliged to pursue stockholder interests without giving

---

[46] Immanuel Kant, *Groundwork of the Metaphysic of Morals*, trans. H. J. Paton (New York: Harper and Row Publishers, 1964), 88.

[47] Kant, *Groundwork*, 100–102.

[48] Kant, *Groundwork*, 82. See my discussion in Chapter 2.

his word that he will do so. Second, he cannot be bound by a promise to do what the moral rules do not permit him to do.[49] Special obligations are thus contingent on both choice and compliance with the moral rules.

Does this contingency make special obligations akin to hypothetical imperatives? First, consider the executive's promise to act in the financial interests of stockholders. In most cases, making such a pledge is contingent on the expected contribution that adopting the corporate role will have for the achievement of the executive's ends. As such, promising constitutes a case of acting on a hypothetical imperative. Reason directs the executive to make the promise *only if* he wants to achieve a particular set of ends. But this kind of contingency – the contingency of choice – applies to promise-*making* behavior, not to promise-*keeping* behavior. While it is up to the executive as to whether he makes a promise that can be justifiably made, it is not up to him as to whether he should keep this promise once he has made it. The requirement that he keep the promise is categorical in nature.

Second, notice that whether a promise binds an executive is contingent on the relationship between the promised behavior and other pre-existing duties and obligations. The executive cannot be bound to do *whatever* is necessary to maximize profits. He is required to act in accordance with the demands of profit *only if* the moral rules allow the requisite behavior. The reach of the promise is itself constrained by morality. But, here again, the contingency in question – the contingency associated with the justifiable adoption of a promise – is connected to the issue of whether the executive should *take on* a promise. The issue is whether he can *make* the promise, not whether he should *keep* it.

This second kind of contingency is straightforward *moral* contingency.[50] Whether an executive's promise to stockholders can be justifiably adopted is contingent on morality, not simply on his desires

---

[49] Goodpaster, "Business Ethics and Stakeholder Analysis," 68.
[50] The first kind of contingency also has a moral component. Special obligations cannot be forced upon people against their will. In addition, because Kant holds that agents have duties to themselves just as they have duties to other agents, whether an executive can take on a special obligation – in the normative sense that it is justifiable to do so – will sometimes depend on that executive's ends and projects. In other words, duties to himself might preclude a special obligation.

or ends. He can adopt the promise – in the sense that it is morally justifiable to do so – only if pre-existing duties and obligations allow the promised behavior. Understanding special obligations in this way makes their contingent features consistent with Kant's absolute prohibition on promise *breaking*. If an executive chooses to make a promise that can justifiably be made, then he ought to keep it – period. The moral requirement is thus categorical, not hypothetical.

This attempt to solidify the moral bonds between executives and stockholders might nevertheless leave us wondering whether Kantian special obligations really capture the moral particularity of the corporate context. What kind of relationship can executives have with stockholders if their behavior is constrained by ethical universals as well as other obligations? The moral contingency associated with promises – albeit, the *making* of promises – significantly limits the development and maintenance of special relationships, in effect subordinating them to all other moral relationships. Ultimately, the primary moral relationships would be between the executive and anyone else to whom he owes something morally. Because the executive has duties to everyone by virtue of impartial morality, so the objection goes, the moral relationship between executives and stockholders must necessarily be characterized as secondary.

The advocate of the Kantian account of special obligations has to admit that the moral rules will substantively regulate the kinds of relationships that executives can have with stockholders. For example, these rules leave executives with no discretion to lie, cheat, or steal in order to turn a profit, regardless of any standing contractual relationships with stockholders. Prohibitions against these behaviors apply at all times and in all circumstances, regardless of the effects that conformity to the prohibitions might have on an executive's ends or the ends of others. Nor can executives appeal to stockholder interests to violate the trust embodied in other contractual relationships. With no room for exceptions to these moral rules, executives will be constrained both in what they can agree to do in pursuit of stockholder ends and in what corporate roles they can adopt.

Executives are also bound by other universal ethical requirements – for example, the duty to help others in need.[51] Does this requirement

---

[51] Kant, *Groundwork*, 90–91.

generate similarly substantial constraints on executives in their pursuit of stockholder ends? After all, executives have at their disposal a wealth of resources that would go a long way toward helping people to whom they may have no special obligations – both members of the local community and people around the world. It is also true that executives are typically in a position to help stakeholders to whom they already have special obligations. Suppliers may need to bring in additional revenue, employees might stand to earn higher wages, and customers would like to buy products at lower prices.

A demanding view of our duties to help people in need would trivialize the corporate executive's special obligation to stockholders. Advocates of the executive–stockholder relationship would rightly complain that a moral theory that makes discharging special obligations subject to carrying out a demanding duty of beneficence might as well dispense with special obligations altogether. Because there will always be people who could use the help that an executive could provide, there will hardly be any occasions on which the executive might carry out the behaviors required by his corporate role.

Fortunately, Kantians are not forced to accept this picture of corporate life. The duty of beneficence is derived from a contradiction in will, as opposed to a contradiction in conception.[52] We have a duty to help others achieve their ends not because we cannot conceive of a world in which no one helps anyone, but because we cannot will such a world. An attempt to will a world in which no one helps anyone would contradict what we have already willed – that someone help us when we are in need. According to this derivation, the duty to help others achieve their ends is therefore a broad duty, as opposed to a strict duty, which means that the duty must be discharged only some of the time and only in some circumstances. As we have seen, Kant does not provide much direction for determining when we ought to discharge our broad duties. Broad duties thus leave executives with significant discretion in how they carry out the behaviors that these duties require.

Bowie, quoting J. W. Marriott Jr.'s justification of the hotel chain's employment program for welfare recipients, provides an excellent

---

[52] Kant, *Groundwork*, 91. See my discussion in Chapter 2 of the derivation of this duty.

example of Kantian reasoning about the requisite consistency between special obligations and broad duties. Marriott explains:

We're getting good employees for the long term but we're also helping these communities. If we don't step up in these inner cities and provide work, they'll never pull out of it. But it makes bottom line sense. If it didn't we *wouldn't* do it.[53]

To put the quotation in Kantian language, Marriott might have said, "If it didn't make bottom line sense, then we *couldn't* do it." Expressing the justification this way better reflects the moral contingency that characterizes broad duties. Were Marriott unable to discharge the broad duty to help people in need by hiring welfare recipients and *at the same time* meet its special obligations to stockholders, the company *could* not – in the normative sense – continue the program. Discharging the broad duty is subordinate to keeping the promise made to stockholders.

## THE OVERCOMMITTED LEADER

As we have seen, broad duties differ from strict duties such as the duty to keep a promise in that the former, unlike the latter, do not have to be discharged at all times and in all circumstances. The indeterminacy that characterizes the broad duties makes it impossible to know exactly when such duties must be discharged. In other words, while an executive might be in a position to know that a broad duty *could* be discharged in his particular circumstances, he would not be in a position to determine whether it *must* be discharged in these circumstances.

Still, the broad duties must be discharged at some times and in some circumstances. So leaders cannot avoid their broad duties altogether by having a long list of projects and by using promises to generate multiple special obligations. The corporate roles a leader can justifiably adopt and maintain must allow him to discharge his broad duties, just as these roles must allow him to discharge any strict duties represented by moral rules against deception and coercion. A leader's pursuit of his own projects must therefore make general room for

---

[53] Bowie, "A Kantian Approach to Business Ethics," 13 (emphasis added). Bowie cites D. Millbank, "Hiring welfare people, hotel chain finds, is tough but rewarding," *Wall Street Journal* (October 31, 1996).

discharging broad duties, and the promises he makes to others must assume that the promised behavior would not make it unreasonably difficult for him to discharge these duties at some times and in some circumstances.

Simply put, being overcommitted does not get leaders off the moral hook. As Kant might tell us, given what a person must will as a rational agent, he cannot will – without contradiction – a world in which people are so overcommitted to their own projects and special obligations that they cannot engage in non-contractual behavior to help others achieve their ends. Accordingly, executives can be expected to work to create lifestyles in which they can discharge broad duties such as the Kantian duties to help people develop their rationality and pursue their ends.[54]

Such duties call upon executives to go beyond the dictates of their contractual relationships with suppliers, employees, and customers. Contracts with these stakeholders specify what they are owed as a matter of the strict duties associated with special relationships – in essence, what executives promised they would do. Contracts do not specify what stakeholders are owed by virtue of broad duties that *bind* all rational agents. Moreover, these broad duties *protect* other rational agents, not just stakeholders. As such, executives must discharge broad duties even with respect to those individuals with whom they have no contractual relationships.

Unfortunately, the overcommitted world is the world in which many people now live. For a lot of us, it is easy to think of times when we would have helped someone in need had it not been for the fact that we were particularly busy with obligations at work or at home.[55] How many times have we said to ourselves, "Were it not for the meeting I must attend, or the fact that I am already late for a family engagement, I would gladly stop to help the person stranded at the side of the road?" Conversely, it is quite difficult to think of times when we had nothing – or even very little – we were supposed to do, let alone to think of times at which such freedom miraculously coincided with someone's needing our help.

---

54 See Bowie, "A Kantian Approach to Business Ethics," 8.
55 See John M. Darley and C. Daniel Batson, "'From Jerusalem to Jericho': A Study of Situational and Dispositional Variables in Helping Behavior," *Journal of Personality and Social Psychology* 27 (1973): 100–108.

In fact, our lives can be so scheduled that we are often unable to come to the help of our friends, much less strangers. We should not be surprised to find that leaders who work in corporate contexts are especially susceptible to being overcommitted in precisely this way – with all the attendant moral consequences. Business competition, as well as the schedule it demands, can promote the belief that broad duties simply do not apply to executives. In other words, executives can come to believe that the importance of their work justifies breaking moral rules that require them to help others. In some cases, leaders are so busy that they fail to recognize that there are such rules in the first place.

This variety of moral blindness is evident in articles on "balance" in the popular business press. In these articles, what typically gets balanced is work and family life, not work and the broad duties. Perhaps discussions of balance ignore broad duties because CEOs, who put in an average of twelve hours a day, have a hard enough time meeting their special obligations to employers and family members.[56] In fact, some "work seven-day weeks, 18 hours a day"[57] because "CEOs today... have a little over two years, or sometimes less, to prove their worth to stakeholders."[58] For many of these executives, there simply is not enough time in the waking day for anything other than work, not even family.

Many executives are best seen as "married to work" and, as a consequence, rely heavily on spouses for "support and family maintenance."[59] As Stanford Business School professor Debra Myerson puts it, "Most jobs – particularly senior level jobs – are still based on the notion that people have someone behind them, that there is a division of labour... There's no notion that people have responsibilities outside work."[60] Keith Ferrazzi, CEO of consulting firm Ferrazzi Greenlight and author of *Never Eat Alone (and Other Secrets to Success, One Relationship at a Time)*, adds that CEOs are really *at work* even when

[56] Tim Stevens, "Striking a balance," *Industry Week* (November 20, 2000); Peter McLaughlin, "Fit to be CEO: How some CEOs link fitness and performance," *Chief Executive* (September 2006).

[57] Julie Daum and Spencer Stuart, "The fifth annual route to the top: The family factor," *Chief Executive* (February 2000) (www.chiefexecutive.net).

[58] Michael Landa, "What's happening to CEOs?" *CMA Management* (November 2001).

[59] Daum and Stuart, "The fifth annual route to the top."

[60] Alison Beard, "The return of the stay-at-home-spouse," *Financial Times* (October 6, 2000).

they are supposedly *at home*: "'CEO Time' is a zone of operations in which the switch-board is always open ... How could a company function if its CEO left every night at 6 PM sharp for dinner or insisted that he or she could not be reached at home before 6:30 AM or after 10 PM?"[61]

Practitioners recommend a range of strategies for managing the conflicting commitments that are most salient to them. When Harry M. Jansen Kraemer Jr. was CEO of medical products company Baxter International Inc., he regularly left work to attend to the needs of his family, and he urged his employees to follow his lead.[62] At the other end of the spectrum, Sherwin Williams CEO Christopher Conner says, "Ideally you protect both sides, business and personal, but most times I come down on the side of the business."[63] To justify missed family obligations, Conner suggests that his work habits model the attitude people should have toward a "noble cause" and, in so doing, gives his children "another dose of ... commitment."[64] Ferrazzi advises us that we should reject the goal of balancing altogether and replace it with the notion of "blending."[65] He says that "[t]he first rule is to let personal and professional lives overlap ... Overlapping the different pockets of your life can actually have benefits even beyond time management."[66]

To the extent that these strategies work, they allow CEOs to meet special obligations associated with their corporate roles as well as obligations to their families. But it is doubtful that any of these strategies

---

61  Keith Ferrazzi, "Why 'balance' is b.s.: For CEOs, blending work and home makes sense," *Chief Executive* (August-September 2005). Given the constant accessibility of today's CEOs, it is somewhat surprising that a recent survey by the Association for Executive Search Consultants found that only 59 percent of senior executives said "that new technologies, such as a Blackberry or mobile phone, had reduced their leisure time" (Chris Silva, "Senioritis: Work-Life Concerns Impede Senior Executive Promotions," *Employee Benefit News* [October 1, 2006]). One wonders whether this response is best explained by the fact that new technologies free executives from the physical workplace or by the fact that there was little leisure time to be reduced in the first place.

62  Michael Arndt, "How does Harry do it? Baxter is thriving as CEO Kraemer makes sure he and his employees have plenty of time for family," *Business Week* (July 22, 2002).

63  Stevens, "Striking a balance."

64  Stevens, "Striking a balance."

65  Ferrazzi, "Why 'balance' is b.s."

66  Ferrazzi, "Why 'balance' is b.s."

will be entirely successful. Kraemer resigned from Baxter at the beginning of 2007, citing the company's "terrible" performance.[67] Sherwin Williams CEO Connor's advice neglects duties on one side of the work/personal life balance. Whereas Kraemer's departure signals that he may not have lived up to reasonable expectations of profitability, Connor's description of the life of the overcommitted CEO comes across as more of a rationalization than a justification. Is paint really a noble enough cause to make up for family sacrifices? We should also note that Ferrazzi's embrace of "overlapping pockets" brings new ethical worries of its own. Here we need only remember Dennis Koslowski's failure to respect the boundaries between work at Tyco and family life.

These strategies are also silent on the duties that CEOs have to themselves. For instance, although the wealth, power, and fame sometimes associated with leadership would seem to put executives in a good position to take care of their physical well-being, many senior executives are unable to find enough time to look after their own health. Drawing on a study by William Mercer Associates, McLaughlin reports that "73% of the senior executives surveyed were physically inactive, 40% were obese, and 75% had two or more risk factors for cardiovascular disease."[68]

It is little wonder, then, that executives sometimes fail to acknowledge – let alone discharge – the broad duties. By all accounts, their lives are so scheduled that there is no room for doing anything other than meeting the obligations of work and personal life – and there is hardly room for that. As one executive puts it:

I ... schedule everything – yoga, haircut, workout. If it's in my planner, I'll do it. If it's not, that slot will be taken up with another appointment, usually business-related.[69]

Likewise, Michael Volkema, when he was CEO of Herman Miller Furniture, had "a centralized calendar, kept at work," to which his family had access and could add engagements.[70] According to Volkema, "I got great counsel early on in taking this responsibility – that I treat my

[67] "Company news; Baxter says chief executive will resign," *New York Times* (January 10, 2007).
[68] McLaughlin, "Fit to be CEO."
[69] Ferrazzi, "Why 'balance' is b.s."
[70] Stevens, "Striking a balance."

son's tennis match the same way as I treat a meeting with an institutional investor."[71]

Special obligations lend themselves to this kind of scheduling. Some broad duties can also be discharged in this way. For example, an executive might fit employee mentoring or regular community service into his schedule. But the realities of the demands on a CEO's time at work and at home may explain why many executives seem to have little experience in the volunteer world. When volunteering after retirement, as one non-profit manager puts it, many former executives "have grandiose ideas of their own skills, and they just end up causing trouble."[72] Horror stories include the retiree who demanded "a corporate account and a credit card," new computers, and "plenty of one-on-one contact with the executive director."[73]

Even if the executive is not too busy to schedule volunteer work, overcommitment will mean that she is rarely in a position to help people when they most need it. Many opportunities to discharge this duty do not conform to a schedule, especially to the tight schedule of the CEO. Occasions to help employees, community members, and strangers often arise unexpectedly, and busy executives will be unable to act on these opportunities to discharge their broad duties if their corporate roles and family lives rarely, if ever, allow for deviations from the schedule.

The ethical problem faced by business leaders, then, is not an absence of moral particularity in corporate contexts. Kantian ethics makes plenty of room for special obligations between executives and stockholders, as well as between executives and stakeholders. The problem is rather that current demands of corporate life call for too much moral particularity. Although morality must allow for special obligations, these obligations cannot prevent executives from discharging more general duties of the strict or broad variety.

One way to put this point is to say that everyday leadership ethics places restrictions on the extent to which leaders can be *partial* to the people to whom they owe special obligations. A leader's commitment

[71] Stevens, "Striking a balance."
[72] Jason Tanz and Theodore Spencer, "Candy striper, my ass! A culture clash is looming as a high-powered wave of retiring executives meets the genteel world of volunteerism," *CNNMoney.com* (August 14, 2000).
[73] Tanz and Spencer, "Candy striper, my ass!"

to the members of his group and to the pursuit of their ends justifies him in breaking neither the moral rules prohibiting deception and coercion nor the moral rules requiring helping behavior and the development of the rationality of others. The next chapter addresses the question of whether rule-breaking behavior can be justified by *impartial* moral considerations such as the good of all.

# 8

# The Greater Good

THE CHALLENGES OF COSMOPOLITAN LEADERSHIP

Some moral theories deny that groups – for example, organizations or nation-states – can justifiably privilege their own goals and projects. According to these *cosmopolitan* moral theories, the particular ends to which group members are committed are ultimately subordinate to more general social ends such as human welfare. Unlike communitarianism, this cluster of theories is immune to the criticism that it contributes to psychological biases such as "in-group favoritism."[1] Whereas the communitarian argument encourages leaders to justify their behavior by appeal to the moral particularity of special relationships, cosmopolitan justifications appeal only to reasons that apply to rational actors more broadly.

At the foundation of the cosmopolitan approach is the idea that reasons of partiality – for example, "this is *my* group" – must be replaced with an impartial consideration of interests, thereby extending moral concern well beyond group members to include all of human society. Cosmopolitanism thus allows us to revive the argument that the importance of a leader's ends might justify rule-breaking behavior. When this kind of leader breaks the rules, she does so not

---

[1] See David M. Messick, "Social Categories and Business Ethics," *Business Ethics Quarterly: Special Issue, Ruffin Series* 1 (1998): 149–172.

because she holds a mistaken view about the exceptional importance of organizational goals but rather "because it was for a higher cause."

To justify rule-breaking behavior by an appeal to the greater good, a cosmopolitan leader must show that her ends really are higher than ordinary organizational goals. In other words, this justification for rule breaking requires ends that are *morally superior* to other ends; otherwise, the leader's justification cannot be distinguished from the often-exaggerated views leaders have about the importance of organizational goals.[2] The leader must also show that the ends at which she aims are greater in the sense of being *broader* than ordinary organizational goals. If the good that ultimately comes of her rule-breaking behavior is restricted to her own group, then her justification will be subject to the charges of partiality that are leveled against communitarian leadership.[3]

When combined, the requirements of moral superiority and breadth create an important set of challenges for the advocate of cosmopolitan appeals to the greater good. These challenges are ultimately *epistemic* in nature. First, how do cosmopolitan leaders *know* which end can be identified with the greater good? For example, should leaders aim for the higher end of freedom, or equality of opportunity, or poverty reduction, or global peace? Second, how do cosmopolitan leaders *know* which means serve the greater good? For example, should leaders break the rules to achieve higher ends? This chapter analyzes two cosmopolitan approaches to answering these questions.[4]

## MILL'S UTILITARIANISM

John Stuart Mill (1806–1873) claims that there is one end that can be generalized across groups and societies – in other words, that one moral purpose is set apart from all others.[5] According to Mill, happiness – or utility – is the ultimate end of morality. Unlike the

---

[2] See Chapter 6.

[3] See Chapter 7.

[4] For a cosmopolitan approach based in religion, see Douglas A. Hicks, *Inequality and Christian Ethics* (Cambridge: Cambridge University Press, 2000).

[5] John Stuart Mill, *Utilitarianism*, ed. George Sher (Indianapolis: Hackett Publishing Company, 1979).

egoist, however, Mill does not think that our individual happiness is the final object of moral concern.[6] Neither our own happiness nor the happiness of the members of our own group has any special moral significance for decision making or action. Rather, the good for all is derived by summing up the good for each individual. Because "each person's happiness is a good to that person, . . . the general happiness, therefore, [is] a good to the aggregate of all persons."[7] Utilitarianism demands that we act in ways that maximize overall utility in society.

Mill is also committed to a particular conception of what constitutes happiness. For humans, some pleasures – namely, "the pleasures of the intellect, of the feelings and imagination, and of the moral sentiments" – have a higher value than mere bodily pleasures or physical sensations.[8] Here, Mill is careful to distinguish his defense of utilitarianism from that of predecessors who overstate the value of the lower pleasures and, in so doing, make it too easy to reject this theory "as a doctrine worthy only of swine."[9] Properly understood, utilitarian moral theory is sensitive not only to the *quantity* of pleasures but also to the *quality* of pleasures.[10] In this way, the theory makes sense of the fact that, as Mill famously puts it, "It is better to be a human being dissatisfied than a pig satisfied; better to be Socrates dissatisfied than a fool satisfied."[11]

How do we know which pleasures constitute the higher pleasures? Mill claims that we need only ask "if there be one to which all or almost all who have experience of both give a decided preference."[12] To make sense of his argument, we might consider an analogous method that is commonly used to make a value judgment. When people want to determine the comparative quality of a pair of films, they do not ask a person who has seen only one of the two movies to judge which of the two is of superior quality. Because of this person's inexperience, she is in no position to make an educated judgment of relative value. Similarly, judgments about whether the pleasures

---

[6] Mill, *Utilitarianism*, 11.
[7] Mill, *Utilitarianism*, 35–36.
[8] Mill, *Utilitarianism*, 8.
[9] Mill, *Utilitarianism*, 7.
[10] Mill, *Utilitarianism*, 11–12.
[11] Mill, *Utilitarianism*, 10.
[12] Mill, *Utilitarianism*, 8.

of "competently"[13] reading Plato are higher than the pleasures of watching football, chugging beer, and munching nachos must be made by someone who has experienced both kinds of pleasures. Mill claims that pleasures of the mind will win out in this comparative exercise, vouchsafing their role as higher pleasures in a proper characterization of happiness.

Because happiness is the ultimate end, Mill denies that moral rules are absolute. For instance, it is sometimes permissible to violate the prohibition on deception. Mill writes:

> [T]hat even this rule [of veracity], sacred as it is, admits of possible exceptions is acknowledged by all moralists; the chief of which is when the withholding of some fact (as of information from a malefactor, or of bad news from a person dangerously ill) would save an individual (especially an individual other than oneself) from great and unmerited evil, and when the withholding can only be effected by denial... It is not the fault of any creed, but of the complicated nature of human affairs, that rules of conduct cannot be so framed as to require no exceptions, and that hardly any kind of action can safely be laid down as always obligatory or always condemnable.[14]

Here we can read Mill as offering a justification for deception. Breaking the moral rule against deception can be justified when it is the required means to avoiding some great harm.

For example, lying would be justified in the stock classroom case of the Nazi on the doorstep. A bald-faced lie is probably the only way to deter the Nazi and save the lives of the Jews hiding inside the house. The passage from Mill also suggests that some kinds of medical paternalism might be justified.[15] If giving a patient an accurate picture of his condition would clearly make the patient worse off, then doctors may be justified in withholding information regarding the prognosis, or even in lying to the patient about his chances for recovery.

Despite his concessions to the possibility of justified rule breaking, Mill plainly thinks that everyday exception making must be limited:

[13] Mill, *Utilitarianism*, 8.
[14] Mill, *Utilitarianism*, 22–25.
[15] This point is seemingly contrary to what we find in another famous tract from Mill, *On Liberty*, ed. Elizabeth Rapaport (Indianapolis: Hackett Publishing Company, 1978),12.

[I]n order that the exception may not extend itself beyond the need, and may have the least possible effect in weakening reliance on veracity, it ought to be recognized, and, if possible, its limits defined; and if the principle of utility is good for anything, it must be good for weighing these conflicting utilities against one another, and marking out the region within which one or the other preponderates.[16]

From this passage we can glean a necessary condition on justified deception. Lying is justified only if it is consistent with preservation of truthful relations in society. Why worry about truth? The answer, of course, points to the consequences of deception for overall utility.

Mill offers two main lines of argument regarding the disutility of lying, each of which is meant to show that utilitarianism does not imply a rejection of moral "principle."[17] Both arguments raise concerns about the *indirect* effects of violating the moral prohibition on deception, as opposed to more standard, *direct* effects on the deceived person. In cases in which rule breaking might be justified, we can assume that costs in terms of direct effects are offset by the benefits of rule breaking – either to other parties (as in the Nazi case) or to the person who is deceived (as in the medical paternalism case). In contrast, indirect effects move beyond consequences for these parties to include costs that, though they may not be readily apparent to the individual considering the rule-breaking behavior, are nonetheless relevant to a utilitarian calculation.

The first argument from indirect effects highlights the negative influences on the character of the agent who engages in deceptive behavior. The primary importance of these effects, however, is not their potential disutility for the agent himself. Rather, given Mill's necessary condition on justified deception, we must be concerned with the consequences that having a duplicitous character might have for overall utility in society. We can refer to these influences as *dispositional* effects. What are these effects of violating the rule against deception? As Mill puts it, "[T]he cultivation in ourselves of a sensitive feeling on the subject of veracity is one of the most useful, and the enfeeblement of that feeling one of the most hurtful, things to which our conduct

---

[16] Mill, *Utilitarianism*, 23.
[17] Mill, *Utilitarianism*, 22.

can be instrumental."[18] In short, lying undermines habits of action that are ultimately utility maximizing.

We have all been told that one lie leads to another because additional deception is necessary to cover up for the earlier lie. But Mill seems to be offering a distinct argument about motivation – that telling the first lie makes it all the easier to tell the second, and so on. Breaking the rule against lying thus damages our moral sensibilities. Accordingly, even if deception would be justified by utility calculations that take into account the direct effects on the parties in the situation, the exception can nevertheless be wrong because it increases the likelihood of future exception making in situations in which a rule violation would not be justified by the facts of the case.

Does this dispositional argument against exception making work? Unfortunately, it appears that Mill has landed on the wrong disposition. The utilitarian would be better served by a disposition to promote utility than by a disposition to tell the truth.[19] If it is psychologically possible to have – as well as act upon – such a disposition, then it is unclear why the utilitarian would trade the utility-maximizing disposition for something akin to sentimentality about moral rules. In other words, a utility-maximizing disposition would seem to be preferable to a rule-following disposition. The argument from dispositional effects thus fails to show that utilitarianism has the resources to constrain deceptive behavior in everyday life.

The second argument from indirect effects focuses on the tension between rule breaking and maintenance of the more general system of rules that define moral practices within a society. Mill suggests that violating prohibitions such as the principle of veracity undermines the trust that serves as the foundation of human society: "[A]ny, even unintentional, deviation from truth does that much toward weakening the trustworthiness of human assertion, ... the principal support of all present social well-being."[20] We can refer to these effects as *institutional* effects. If telling a lie would have serious institutional repercussions, then – according to Mill's necessary condition on justified deception – this behavior would not be justified.

---

[18] Mill, *Utilitarianism*, 22.
[19] Mill himself defends the possibility of a utilitarian disposition (*Utilitarianism*, 17).
[20] Mill, *Utilitarianism*, 22.

Is it true that in everyday life a single individual's behavior has the capacity to undermine trust within society? In reality, the health of the institution of truth telling depends not on the behavior of any one person but on collective behavior. In other words, the moral rule against deception stands or falls regardless of how particular individuals behave with respect to the institution of truth telling. As a consequence, Mill cannot use the institutional argument to limit the everyday exception-making behavior of the person who has good reason to think that she can promote utility by telling a lie. If she is a good utilitarian, she will certainly hope that most others generally abide by the principle of veracity, and she will take special care to ensure that her example does not cause too many others to make exceptions of themselves. However, from the utilitarian perspective, the individual liar can correctly conclude that her rule-breaking behavior does not do "that much toward weakening" the foundations of human society.[21]

A variation on the institutional argument makes no appeal to the costs associated with violations of moral rules in particular cases. In this argument, Mill applauds the fact that there are "things which people forebear to do from moral considerations, though the consequences in the *particular* case might be beneficial," claiming that "it would be unworthy of an intelligent agent not to be consciously aware that the action is of a class which, if practiced *generally*, would be generally injurious, and that this is the ground of the obligation to abstain from it."[22] That is, considerations of disutility associated with the *general* practice of rule breaking can outweigh considerations of utility associated with rule breaking in the *particular* case.

Here, to make sense of Mill's argument, we must understand "beneficial in the particular case" to mean "all-things-considered utility maximizing." Otherwise, there would be no need for Mill to fall back on the utility of the general practice. That is, if we assume that there is only *some* benefit in breaking a moral rule – say, that the action would be utility maximizing were it not for the indirect effects of the action – then Mill could simply say so and reject the rule-breaking behavior on

---

[21] In *extreme* circumstances, the behavior of a single leader has the capacity to undermine social trust, especially trust in political institutions. Here we might think of former President Richard Nixon's behavior in Watergate. Even in this kind of case, however, it is a pattern of behavior that taints the institution.

[22] Mill, *Utilitarianism*, 19 (emphases added).

the grounds that the principle of utility condemns it outright in these circumstances. The fact that Mill is forced to make recourse to the disutility of the *general* practice of rule breaking to "ground the obligation to abstain from it" shows that he thinks that it can be wrong to break a moral rule even when doing so would be all-things-considered utility maximizing in the *particular* case.

To its credit, this variation on the institutional argument does not rely on the false premise that rule-breaking behavior in the particular case always has high indirect costs. However, this version of the argument raises serious questions about the nature of Mill's utilitarianism. The argument seems to portray Mill as a *rule* utilitarian rather than as an *act* utilitarian. Rule utilitarianism holds that our behavior ought to conform to rules that – if followed by everyone – would maximize utility, whereas act utilitarianism holds that we ought to do the action that maximizes utility in the particular circumstances. Given Mill's clear assertion that exceptions to the rules are sometimes justified, he cannot be a rule utilitarian. Why, then, does Mill think we should sometimes follow the rule when breaking it would be all-things-considered utility maximizing in the particular case?

## A UTILITARIAN VIEW OF EVERYDAY LEADERSHIP

Mill is trying to limit exceptions to the moral rules, not to exclude them altogether. So, a utilitarian defense of reliance on moral rules in everyday life need not insist that these rules can never be violated to maximize utility in particular cases. Rather, it must show only that in many particular cases in which utility could be maximized by rule breaking, people should nevertheless follow the rule. The difficulty is to distinguish between these two kinds of cases.

Mill certainly seems to believe that we can separate out a sphere of everyday ethics in which the rules of morality apply even when the actions they demand are not utility maximizing in the particular case. As we might expect, "marking out the region" ultimately requires an appeal to the principle of utility itself.[23] What considerations of utility constitute reasons to follow general moral rules even when "the consequences [of breaking them] in the particular case might

[23] Mill, *Utilitarianism*, 23.

be beneficial?"[24] Mill's statement of utilitarian theory allows us to develop two arguments against rule breaking in everyday leadership. Both arguments point to problems with using rule-breaking behavior as a means to overall utility maximization. These utilitarian objections to rule breaking fare better than Mill's dispositional and institutional arguments against deception.

The first argument starts from Mill's assumption that overall utility fails to provide practical grounds for action in everyday life.

[I]t is a misapprehension of the utilitarian mode of thought, to conceive it as implying that people should fix their minds upon so wide a generality as the world, or society at large. The great majority of good actions are intended not for the benefit of the world, but for that of individuals, of which the good of the world is made up; and the thoughts of the most virtuous man need not on these occasions travel beyond the particular persons concerned, except so far as is necessary to assure himself that in benefiting them he is not violating the *rights*, that is, the legitimate and authorized expectations, of anyone else. The multiplication of happiness is, according to the utilitarian ethics, the object of virtue: the occasions on which any person (except one in a thousand) has it in his power to do this on an extended scale – in other words to be a public benefactor – are but exceptional; and on these occasions alone is he called on to consider public utility; in every other case, private utility, the interest or happiness of some few persons, is all he has to attend to. Those alone the influence of whose actions extends to society in general need concern themselves habitually about so large an object.[25]

In everyday life, overall utility is better served by a concern for the people we can directly affect. Because overall utility is not a practical guide for everyday action, we cannot use it to justify rule-breaking behavior.

This argument does not deny that we are psychologically capable of developing a concern for "society in general." Given the assumption that some individuals have a duty to be concerned with overall utility, it must indeed be psychologically possible for them to do so. Here, we might think about high-profile leaders who use their political power or financial resources for the global good. Mill's claim is an empirical one – that most people (and, we might add, most *leaders*) do not have the kind of influence necessary to make significant contributions to

---

[24] Mill, *Utilitarianism*, 19.
[25] Mill, *Utilitarianism*, 18–19 (emphasis added).

the utility of others, except for those with whom they regularly interact in everyday life. Because peoples' actions do not have greater reach, it would diminish overall utility for them to act with a greater scope of concern.

This view of utilitarianism makes the theory compatible with everyday leadership. In everyday life, leaders do not normally aim at the maximization of overall utility, say, by establishing justice or ending world poverty. Heroic leaders aside, people engaged in everyday leadership are primarily concerned with the pursuit of more particular goals and projects that they and others find valuable. The efforts of everyday leaders also show marked partiality for followers and group members. Utilitarians make sense of the particularism and partiality in leadership by pointing to their effects on utility. Overall utility would not be better served if everyday leaders were to drop the goals and projects of their groups and show concern for society as a whole. According to this argument, everyday leadership has an important role to play in the utilitarian "moral division of labor."[26] The maximization of overall utility depends on the accomplishment of particular ends as well as on genuine attention to the interests of the people who have these ends.

If everyday leaders are not bound by the universalism and impartiality that characterizes the principle of utility, are they now free to make exceptions of themselves for the good of their groups? In other words, does utilitarianism allow rule breaking to sneak in through the back door?

Mill's answer is that adopting a narrower scope of concern in everyday life implies respect for the "rights" of others. Initially we might think that these rights would have to be derived from an application of the principle of utility in each particular case. But Mill cannot mean that he wants us to understand the argument in this way. If the rights of others were derived from individual applications of the principle of utility, then the argument would imply that moral agents are permitted to concern themselves with the advancement of the interests of "particular persons," as opposed to those of "society at large," *only if* their actions do not conflict with overall utility. People would have to determine what overall utility demands *before* they would know that they

---

[26] Thomas Nagel, *Equality and Partiality* (Oxford: Oxford University Press, 1991), ch. 6.

were justified in concentrating on the good of group members and not on overall utility. Surely Mill is not saying that decisions in everyday ethics need not consider the good of society as a whole unless the good of society as a whole demands otherwise!

Mill's reference to rights must rather be to "the legitimate and authorized expectations" associated with general moral rules. An appeal to moral rules not only maintains the coherence of the argument but also supports a utilitarian account of particularism and partiality in everyday leadership. Utility is maximized by allowing leaders to pursue goals and projects other than utility maximization and by allowing them to focus on the interests of followers and group members. However, this account emphasizes that we can expect utility maximization only if the behavior of everyday leaders is constrained by general moral rules. As a consequence, utilitarianism can allow only so much particularism and partiality in everyday leadership. Everyday leaders cannot break the moral rules for the good of the group.

Other utilitarians would claim that the cosmopolitanism at the heart of utilitarian moral theory demands that we adopt a cosmopolitan attitude about the obligations of everyday life. For example, Peter Singer, a contemporary utilitarian, writes:

If we accept any principle of impartiality, universalizability, equality, or whatever, we cannot discriminate against someone merely because he is far away from us (or we are far away from him). Admittedly, it is possible that we are in a better position to judge what needs to be done to help a person near to us than one far away, and perhaps also to provide the assistance we judge to be necessary. If this were the case, it would be a reason for helping those near to us first . . . This may once have been a justification for being more concerned with the poor in one's own town than with famine victims in India. Unfortunately for those who like to keep their moral responsibilities limited, instant communication and swift transportation have changed the situation. From a moral point of view, the development of the world into a "global village" has made an important, though still unrecognized, difference to our moral situation.[27]

Singer's point is that it is no longer true that the role of "public benefactor" is limited to a minority of heroic leaders. In wealthy societies,

---

[27] Peter Singer, "Famine, Affluence, and Morality," *Philosophy and Public Affairs* 1 (1972): 232.

almost everyone is in a position to make great contributions to overall utility by focusing their moral attention not on those closest to them but, instead, on the neediest people around the world.

Singer's disagreement with Mill is empirical, and it can be traced to the different times in which they are working.[28] Both Singer and Mill accept the principle of utility, but the world has changed dramatically since Mill wrote *Utilitarianism.* Thanks to cable television and its twenty-four hour news cycle, we know almost immediately where our resources could do great good. And thanks to credit cards and reliable international relief agencies, we can offer almost instantaneous assistance.[29] One way to put Singer's point is to say that most of us in the modern world can be much more than everyday leaders.

What are the implications of Singer's empirical disagreement with Mill's view of everyday ethics? Does adopting a broader scope of moral concern mean that everyday leaders should rely less on moral rules and, in each particular case, act strictly on what they take to be the dictates of the principle of utility? Perhaps city leaders ought to divert tax revenues to help needy residents in a neighboring city or CEOs ought to take it upon themselves to use corporate funds for famine relief. Singer certainly does not advocate anything this extreme. In fact, his recommendation that "we ought to be campaigning for entirely new standards for both public and private contributions to famine relief" makes it look as though his position is consistent with both democratic processes and the rules embodied in a system of private property.[30] Yet he does claim that "[f]rom the moral point of view, the prevention of the starvation of millions of people outside our society must be considered at least as pressing as the upholding of property norms within our society."[31]

If the proper utilitarian perspective for everyday leaders is one that "look[s] beyond the interests of [their] own societ[ies],"[32] and – we might add – their own groups within each society, serious conflicts

---

[28] Terry L. Price and Douglas A. Hicks, "A Framework for a General Theory of Leadership," in *The Quest for a General Theory of Leadership,* eds. George R. Goethals and Georgia L. J. Sorenson (Cheltenham, UK: Edward Elgar, 2006), 134.

[29] Peter Singer, "The Singer solution to world poverty," *New York Times Magazine* (September 5, 1999).

[30] Singer, "Famine, Affluence, and Morality," 240.

[31] Singer, "Famine, Affluence, and Morality," 237.

[32] Singer, "Famine, Affluence, and Morality," 237.

are bound to arise between the principle of utility and commonly held moral rules. Singer's version of utilitarianism thus has the potential to justify rule breaking by everyday leaders. But it does so at great expense. By challenging all particularism and partiality, this utilitarian perspective does away with everyday leadership as we know it. As a result, we would have to revolutionize everyday leadership, just as Singer suggests we ought to make radical revisions to our view of our ordinary moral responsibilities.[33]

Mill's version of utilitarianism allows us to develop a second argument against rule breaking by everyday leaders. This argument also suggests that there are good utilitarian reasons not to rely directly on the principle of utility in everyday life. The committed utilitarian who is motivated by Singer's universal and impartial considerations faces serious barriers to knowing what utilitarianism demands. How does a leader identify the action – among all possible actions – that would maximize overall utility?

Here Mill claims that we must rely on the knowledge contained in our moral practices:

During [the past duration of the human species] mankind have been learning by experience the tendencies of actions; on which experience all the prudence as well as all the morality of life are dependent . . . [M]ankind must by this time have acquired positive beliefs as to the effects of some actions on their happiness; and the beliefs which have thus come down are the rules of morality for the multitude, and for the philosopher until he has succeeded in finding better. That philosophers might easily do this, even now, on many subjects; that the received code of ethics is by no means of divine right; and that mankind have still much to learn as to the effects of actions on the general happiness, I admit or rather earnestly maintain. The corollaries from the principle of utility, like the precepts of every practical art, admit of indefinite improvement, and, in a progressive state of the human mind, their improvement is perpetually going on. But to consider the rules of morality as improvable is one thing; to pass over the intermediate generalization entirely and endeavor to test each individual action directly by the first principle is another.[34]

In other words, even if we assume that it is within the power of everyday leaders to have significant effects on overall utility, there is still

---

[33] Singer, "Famine, Affluence, and Morality," 230.
[34] Mill, *Utilitarianism*, 23–24.

substantial cause to worry about whether breaking the rules will positively or negatively affect overall utility.

Mill's insight is that we should not be optimistic that people will correctly identify utility-maximizing opportunities for rule breaking. In fact, because the moral rules passed down through history have a kind of epistemic superiority to individual judgment, including that of leaders, we can expect a net disutility to be associated with "test[ing] each individual action directly by the principle."[35] In everyday leadership, rule following, not rule breaking, is the correct means to the greater good.

## TRANSFORMING LEADERSHIP

James MacGregor Burns's 1978 book *Leadership* made him the father of leadership studies.[36] In this work, Burns develops a normative theory of leadership, working primarily from examples of heroic leaders in politics, reform movements, and public opinion: Franklin Roosevelt, Mahatma Gandhi, James Madison, and many others.[37] These *transforming* leaders, Burns thinks, are distinguished by the fact that they are "more concerned with *end-values*, such as liberty, justice, equality" than with "*modal values*, that is, values of means – honesty, responsibility, fairness, the honoring of commitments."[38] In short, they are more concerned with cosmopolitan values than with moral rules.

Burns does not suggest that the modal values are unimportant, only that they are less important than the end-values. He writes, "Fairness, civility, tolerance, openness, and respect for the dignity of others undergird and legitimate the elaborate system of due process that characterizes decent relations among human beings."[39] Like Mill, that is, Burns is committed to the idea that the modal values are merely *instrumentally* important in virtue of their connection to the end-values. For example, Burns emphasizes that "insufficient attention to means can corrupt the ends."[40]

---

[35] Mill, *Utilitarianism*, 24.
[36] James MacGregor Burns, *Leadership* (New York: Harper and Row Publishers, 1978).
[37] Burns uses "heroic leadership" in a different sense in *Leadership* (243–248).
[38] Burns, *Leadership*, 426.
[39] Burns, *Leadership*, 430.
[40] Burns, *Leadership*, 426.

For Burns, the notions of "collective purpose" and "social change" have moral priority in his normative theory of leadership, and the achievement of such ends – not strict rule-following behavior – serves as the best indicator of successful leadership.[41] When there is an irresolvable conflict between the moral rules and the legitimate goals of transforming leadership, Burns comes down on the side of the greater good.[42]

The significant discretion Burns gives leaders to choose end-values over modal values shows that he has much greater confidence than Mill in the epistemic abilities of leaders. What is the source of this confidence? According to Burns, transforming leadership *"operates at need and value levels higher than those of the potential follower."*[43] Here, Burns's appeal to "hierarchies of wants and needs" and "stages and levels of moral development"[44] refers to the work of Abraham Maslow and Lawrence Kohlberg in developmental psychology.[45] Compared with followers, the transforming leader works from "higher levels of motivation and morality."[46]

First, drawing on Maslow's theory of a motivational hierarchy, Burns holds that the transforming leader seeks to satisfy people's lower-level needs – for example, basic physical requirements – so that their higher-level social needs to be equal, contributing members of a community can then be met. Second, Burns uses Lawrence Kohlberg's sequence of moral development to make transforming leadership cosmopolitanism. This form of leadership moves people *away from* an ethics of self-interest, partiality, and blind conformity *toward* conceptions of morality that reject particularity and embrace universal moral principles.

---

41 Burns, *Leadership*, 3.
42 As far as I know, Burns does not explicitly make this claim in his vast writings. However, he has confirmed in conversation that it is an implication of a correct interpretation of his theory.
43 Burns, *Leadership*, 42.
44 Burns, *Leadership*, 30.
45 See A. H. Maslow, *Motivation and Personality* (New York: Harper and Brothers, 1954); Lawrence Kohlberg, *Essays on Moral Development*, Vol.1 : *The Philosophy of Moral Development* (San Francisco: Harper and Row, 1981); and Lawrence Kohlberg, *Essays on Moral Development*, Vol. 2 : *The Psychology of Moral Development* (San Francisco: Harper and Row, 1984).
46 Burns, *Leadership*, 20.

Transforming leaders are thus able to effect social change because "in the sequence of the moral stages," their values "take on increasingly the qualities of more broadly and socially defined morality."[47] As a result of their motivational and moral maturity, they are more likely to make the correct judgments about value. In contrast, people struggling to satisfy needs for sustenance, shelter, and security, or at low levels of moral development, are hardly in a position for successful pursuit of the common good.

Is Burns entitled to the assumption that transforming leaders are somehow epistemically privileged? Can we assume that their superior motivational and moral maturity decreases the need for strict adherence to the moral rules? Notice that Burns is very reluctant to trust leaders who base their judgments about what they ought to do on "lesser values and 'responsibilities'" as opposed to "overriding, general welfare-oriented values."[48]

[T]he concept of responsibility could easily be stretched to authorize the kind of opportunism that we associate, for example, with nineteenth-century "rugged individualism." If leaders are encouraged to follow immediate, specific, calculable interests, they can end up serving their narrow, short-run interests alone, rationalizing the consequences in terms of responsibility to themselves, to their families, or to a relatively narrow group. Leaders holding this ethic, or representing people holding this ethic, would act amid such a plethora of responsibilities as to legitimate both high-minded and self-serving behavior... Worse, leaders might lack useful standards for distinguishing between the two sets of alternatives.[49]

Burns's argument against relying on the responsibilities associated with the modal values is that when these responsibilities become disconnected from the end-values, leaders are unable to adjudicate between particular and partial commitments and, moreover, unable to know when these commitments ought to be set aside for the greater good. Because modal values alone are insufficient to determine what morality requires, leaders would be tempted to use special obligations and "responsibilities" to justify whatever choice they make.

We might expect that transforming leaders, who work at higher levels of motivational and moral development, would not be similarly

---

[47] Burns, *Leadership*, 429–430.
[48] Burns, *Leadership*, 46.
[49] Burns, *Leadership*, 45.

susceptible to this kind of indeterminacy about value. However, almost four hundred pages later in his treatise, Burns asks:

Dare we speculate about these end-values and ultimate purposes? Only to a degree. Probably the worldwide debate over principle and purpose will focus even more directly, over the decades ahead, on the mutually competing and supporting values, the paradoxical trade-offs, of liberty and equality . . . How these values will be defined; how they will relate to one another in hierarchies of principles or priorities of purposes; how 'subvalues' – liberty as privacy, for example, or equality, or equality of opportunity – will support or contradict subvalues; how idiosyncratic talent and freedom of innovation will be protected under the doctrine of liberty of expression – these and many other questions can only be roughly answered. Fortunately, analysts can proceed on the basis of reason and logic as well as empirical data collection and analysis. One of the remarkable intellectual developments of recent years has been the rise in the quality and quantity of the investigation across national borders of peoples' needs, aspirations, and values at the same time that scholars have been reanalyzing concepts of equality in terms of the principles of "justice."[50]

But how, then, can leaders be guided by the end-values – indeed, privilege them over the modal values – if they have no way of knowing what the greater good is?

Regardless of what value-conflicts actually dominate our public discussion, the central truth of Burns's passage is that judgments based on the end-values are subject to no less moral indeterminacy than judgments based on the modal values.[51] This concession – namely, that there are bound to be conflicts among end-values – is at odds with Burns's critique of leadership moralities grounded in the modal values. His appeal to "empirical data collection and analysis" concerning people's values does not serve as an adequate response to these conflicts. Empirical research in ethics tells us how people think about values, but what people think about values is hardly a reliable indicator of the morality of these values. Indeed, the strongly descriptive foundation of Burns's theory constitutes one of its primary weaknesses as a normative theory of leadership. For example, the assumption that cognitive development proceeds as Kohlberg suggests does not prove that

---

[50] Burns, *Leadership*, 431–432.
[51] Burns cannot be criticized for failing to predict that – in the decades to come, especially after September 11 – the central value conflict might be between liberty and *security*, not liberty and equality.

the values associated with Kohlberg's highest stages of moral development reflect the correct morality.

Burns's recourse to "scholarly" investigation puts his account on slightly firmer ground, and it is reminiscent of Mill's recommendation that we leave the conflicts between moral rules and overall utility to the philosopher.[52] Yet Burns ultimately does not take this route. Instead, he leaves the resolution of conflicts between values – and conflicts *within* values – to transforming leaders themselves:

> Leaders who appeal to followers with simplistic slogans such as Equality, Progress, Liberty, Justice, Order are neither offering a guide to followers on where leaders really stand nor mobilizing followers to seek explicit objectives; they are seeking the widest possible consensus on the basis of the thinnest – or least thoughtful – consensus. They are not acting as leaders as we have defined leadership. Leaders who act under conditions of conflict within hierarchies of needs and values, however, must act under the necessity of *choosing* between certain *kinds* of liberties, equalities, and other end-values.[53]

Howard Prince similarly countenances moral discretion for leaders in the face of a plurality of values: at the highest stages of moral development, a leader recognizes that "there are a variety of possible value systems," and recognition of this fact requires "operat[ing] from a set of universal moral principles" that apply "irrespective of specific laws or rules . . . [W]hile it is well and good to live up to the rules of society, . . . there are exceptions."[54]

On what basis should transforming leaders choose between various value systems to justify rule-breaking behavior? Commitment to the collective good is hardly sufficient to enable transforming leaders to adjudicate between the Burnsian end-values. Such a commitment also does little to alleviate tensions between theoretical competitors such as libertarianism and egalitarianism or between moral principles such as the utilitarian's "greatest good for the greatest number" and the Kantian's "respect for the dignity of man."[55]

---

[52] Mill, *Utilitarianism*, 23.
[53] Burns, *Leadership*, 432 (second emphasis mine).
[54] Howard T. Prince II, "Moral Development in Individuals," in *The Leader's Companion: Insights on Leadership Through the Ages*, ed. J. Thomas Wren (New York: Free Press, 1995), 487.
[55] Prince, "Moral Development in Individuals," 487.

The problem is that transforming leaders are left with a *"variety* of possible value systems" and "a *set* of universal moral principles."[56] Yet, according to Burns, they must choose. It is this "necessity"[57] of choice that puts transforming leaders in a morally dangerous situation. Given the indeterminate ranking of end-values, what is to stop the transforming leader from exaggerating the importance of his particular conception of the greater good and, as a consequence, overestimating the justificatory force of the end-values to which his group happens to be committed?

The two previous chapters highlighted the tendency of leaders to overestimate both the importance of the particular ends of their groups and the moral weight of partial commitments to group members. For this reason, we turned to the greater good as a potentially stronger justification for rule breaking by leaders. The greater good is supposed to transcend value conflicts between particularistic ends and allow us to adjudicate between the claims of different groups. But if the higher ends at which leaders aim are pluralistic, not monistic, we must be prepared for similar kinds of conflicts.

We should be similarly prepared for biased resolutions of these conflicts. The dangers of partiality and particularity often extend beyond the self-interested concerns of leaders or group members. Leaders can be overly partial and particularistic even with respect to the collective-minded goals of their groups. In other words, they can inappropriately privilege seemingly impartial and universal goals such as capitalist freedom or poverty reduction just as they can inappropriately privilege naked self-interest or the interests of the group. Because no one can rightly claim knowledge of the greater good, leaders are not justified in breaking the moral rules to resolve these conflicts of value in an effort to advance what happens to be a favored conception.

## THE GREATER GOOD IN POLITICS AND ORGANIZATIONS

Late in a 2007 Republican presidential primary debate in South Carolina, Fox News correspondent Britt Hume asked a series of

---

[56] Prince, "Moral Development in Individuals," 487 (emphases added).
[57] Burns, *Leadership*, 432.

questions designed to force candidates to face the necessity of having to act on a higher value.

The questions in this round will be premised on a fictional, but we think plausible scenario involving terrorism and the response to it. Here is the premise: Three shopping centers near major U.S. cities have been hit by suicide bombers. Hundreds are dead, thousands injured. A fourth attack has been averted when the attackers were captured off the Florida coast and taken to Guantanamo Bay, where they are being questioned. U.S. intelligence believes that another larger attack is planned and could come at any time...How aggressively would you interrogate those being held at Guantanamo Bay for information about where the next attack might be?[58]

In this kind of scenario, can the president make a claim of *strong necessity* – that what he has to do is justified by the greater good of human life and welfare?[59]

Many of the Republican candidates thought so. For them, the fact that the president is confronted with a matter of human survival – namely, a decision affecting the lives and welfare of scores of people – was sufficient to justify the use of "enhanced interrogation techniques," if not torture, on the prisoners.[60] For example, Representative Ron Paul of Texas responded to the necessity of the situation by pointing out that although "[n]obody's for the torture...the president has the authority to do that. If we're under imminent attack, the president can take that upon himself to do it."[61]

Rudy Giuliani, who was mayor of New York City at the time of the September 11 attacks, made it clear that he was open to "every method they could think of," reminding his audience, "I've seen what can happen if you make a mistake about this, and I don't want to see another 3,000 people dead in New York or any place else."[62] Representative Tom Tancredo of Colorado agreed that the appropriate choice among values was obvious:

Well, let me just say that it's almost unbelievable to listen to this in a way. We're talking...about it in such a theoretical fashion. You say that...nuclear

---

[58] "Republican presidential primary debate sponsored by the South Carolina Republican Party and Fox News Channel," *Federal News Service* (May 15, 2007).
[59] See my discussion of strong necessity in Chapter 6.
[60] "Republican presidential primary debate."
[61] "Republican presidential primary debate."
[62] "Republican presidential primary debate."

devices have gone off in the United States, more are planned, and we're wondering about whether waterboarding would be a – a bad thing to do? I'm looking for "Jack Bauer" at that time, let me tell you . . . [W]e are the last best hope of Western civilization . . . [W]hen we go under, Western civilization goes under.[63]

However, the responses of both candidates exaggerate the necessity of the situation. Giuliani bases his defense of "enhanced interrogation techniques" on a misleading insinuation that it was our failure to use these techniques in the past that led to great harm.[64] And, to justify the strength of his position on what amounts to torture, Tancredo introduces a nuclear component to the scenario, invokes the fantasy television program *24*, and moves the discussion from matters of life and death to the survival of Western civilization itself. Talk about the greater good!

In contrast, Senator John McCain of Arizona, who was a prisoner of war in Vietnam for more than five years, rejected enhanced interrogation techniques, claiming that they are the moral equivalent of torture. McCain's argument had both virtue theory and consequentialist components. First, consistent with the virtue theorist's approach, he argued that we do not want to be the kind of people who use these methods: "It's not about the terrorists, it's about us. It's about what kind of country we are."[65]

Second, McCain gave several consequentialist considerations against torture. Enhanced interrogation techniques do more harm than good because of their effects on "world opinion"; the techniques do not work because prisoners are motivated to "tell you what they think you want to know" rather than the truth; and, finally, torture puts our own soldiers at greater risk of facing the same kind treatment when they are captured.[66]

Giuliani and other candidates ignored these less obvious costs, just as many advocates of strong necessity arguments for military action are inclined to ignore costs in human lives – both of soldiers and civilians. For example, even if we accept the premise that the war in Iraq was

---

[63] "Republican presidential primary debate."
[64] "A question of torture: Excepting John McCain, Republican candidates for president seem to favor it, *Washington Post* (May 17, 2007).
[65] "Republican presidential primary debate."
[66] "Republican presidential primary debate."

necessary to prevent a terrorist attack on the same scale as September 11, the number of American troops killed – not to mention the deaths of other soldiers and Iraqi civilians – already exceeds the loss of life on September 11.

Perhaps the most interesting part of McCain's response, however, was his characterization of the subject of Hume's question as "a million-to-one scenario."[67] Contrary to Hume's introduction of the case, the candidates were not asked about "a plausible scenario." As Andrew Sabl characterizes torture dilemmas often used in the ethics classroom, "[R]eal-world cases... don't look like that."[68] McCain similarly notes in his response that the "procedures for interrogation in the Army Field Manual... would be adequate in 999,999 of cases."[69] Although this statement makes it sound as though the procedures might not be adequate in Hume's one-in-a-million case, McCain's objections to the use of torture in the scenario as it is presented imply that officials ultimately ought to abide by the rules even in the most extreme cases.

The inappropriateness of greater good justifications is more obvious still when we consider the everyday organizational context in which they are regularly applied. Everyday leaders are much more likely to find themselves confronted with unmotivated employees than to face terrorists intent on destroying their cities. Still, the much lower stakes of everyday leadership have not discouraged attempts to apply the insights of cosmopolitan theories such as transforming leadership to organizational contexts. For example, the work of Bernard Bass, the chief organizational advocate of transformational leadership, suggests that Burns's vision of self and community presents an equally attractive framework for getting employees to put organizational objectives ahead of self-interest.[70]

---

[67] "Republican presidential primary debate." Interrogation expert Colonel Stuart Herrington comments that in the "real world" he did not come across a single "ticking time bomb scenario... in interrogations in three wars of hundreds of people" (Stuart Herrington, "TV torture changes real interrogation techniques," *Fresh Air with Terry Gross* [October 10, 2007]).

[68] Andrew Sabl, "Torture as a case study: How to corrupt your students," *Chronicle of Higher Education* (November 11, 2005). According to Sabl, "Professors worship at the alter of 'maybe'" with the result that students become "unreliable defenders of what should be moral certainties."

[69] "Republican presidential primary debate."

[70] Bernard Bass, *Leadership and Performance Beyond Expectations* (New York: Free Press, 1985).

Critics such as Richard Couto rightly charge that this particular application of transformational leadership trivializes Burns's foundational theory.[71] Most importantly, Burns's conception of the higher good involves "actual social change."[72]

By social change I mean here *real change* – that is, a transformation to a marked degree in the attitudes, norms, institutions, and behaviors that structure our daily lives ... The leadership process must be defined, in short, as carrying through the decision-making stages to the point of concrete changes in people's lives, attitudes, behaviors, institutions ... In seeking to change social structures in order to realize new values and purposes, leaders go far beyond the politicians who merely cater to surface attitudes. To elevate the goals of humankind, to achieve high moral purpose, to realize major intended change, leaders must thrust themselves into the most intractable processes and structures of history and ultimately master them.[73]

This hardly sounds like everyday organizational leadership. In fact, what Burns is describing does not sound like everyday political leadership. Here, his vision of transforming leadership is more in keeping with the grand, historical examples of leadership that give life to his theory.

It is somewhat curious, then, that transformational leadership has had its greatest influence in organizational theory. The organizational context is perhaps least able to claim that there is some higher purpose at work. Organizational objectives are "greater" only in the sense that they sometimes prove worthier than the pursuit of self-interest by particular individuals. But there is no reason to think that collective goals invariably – or even typically – deserve priority over the interests of individuals. For example, it is false that a company's profit always – or usually – takes moral precedence over the interests employees have in pursuing individual projects outside of work.

The obvious problem is that organizational goals do not meet the superiority or breadth requirements of cosmopolitan arguments from the greater good. In everyday ethics, the ends of organizations are particular and partial, not general and impartial. In this respect, they are no different from the ends pursued by most other groups. As a

[71] Richard Couto, "The Transformation of Transforming Leadership," in *The Leader's Companion: Insights on Leadership Through the Ages*, ed. J. Thomas Wren (New York: Free Press, 1995), 102–107.

[72] Burns, *Leadership*, 3.

[73] Burns, *Leadership*, 414, 421.

consequence, it is morally misleading to suggest that followers ought to allow themselves to be transformed for the greater good embodied in the organization.

In the end, the commitments followers have to the organization are rightly a function of their views of the instrumental and intrinsic value of organizational goals. Views about the value of organizational goals – like views about higher causes such as welfare and liberty – will vary among different organizations and even among members of the same organization. This value pluralism explains why leaders cannot appeal to the greater good, especially in everyday leadership, to justify rule-breaking behavior.

# 9

# Everyday Leadership Ethics

## MORAL THEORY IN EVERYDAY LIFE

This book addresses what I have suggested is the central question of leadership ethics: *Do the distinctive features of leadership justify rule-breaking behavior?* We are now in a position to answer this question for everyday leaders by drawing together the conclusions of various chapters and extrapolating from them to articulate a view of everyday leadership ethics.

To this end, let us again consider the leader who lies to followers. Here we might think specifically of a student leader in a campus organization, a politician in city government, or a CEO of a corporation. Like any moral agent who thinks that she should be allowed to break the rules, the everyday leader must convince us that we ought to look differently upon her behavior than we look upon the behavior of people who break the rules without justification. No moral agent can concede that the facts of both cases are identical in all morally relevant respects and, at the same time, urge that she deserves special dispensation.[1] Justification involves giving reasons, and justification of behavior that is typically considered to be immoral requires good *moral* reasons.

[1] Terry L. Price, *Understanding Ethical Failures in Leadership* (New York: Cambridge, 2006), ch. 3.

The most straightforward way for the leader to make her case for justification would be to pair the action she proposes with the behavior of people whose rule-breaking behavior we have every reason to think was justified. Consider how such a justification might proceed. In ethics classes, the standard test for the moral rule against deception is the Nazi on your doorstep. Would you be justified in lying to the Nazi to save the lives of Jews hiding inside your house? This kind of example is meant to draw out the intuition that there are exceptions even to the most basic moral rules. Surely morality allows us to deceive Nazis to protect innocent human beings.

Suppose, then, that the everyday leader who lies to followers raises this extreme case in defense of her behavior. Does the Nazi example enable her to make the argument that she is justified in breaking the rules? No. The everyday leader can hardly claim – at least not with a straight face – that her circumstances make her relevantly similar to people who risked their lives to confront the Nazis! Fortunately, everyday life is not stocked with Nazi-like characters. All the extreme case tells us is that the prohibition on lying is not absolute. By itself, the case does not serve as any kind of justification at all for exception making in everyday life. The everyday leader needs something more if her justification is to be successful.

It is little wonder, though, that leadership ethics nevertheless works from extreme cases. Applied ethicists are often trained as moral philosophers, and moral philosophers – like philosophers more generally – delight in the extreme case. Part of the explanation for this reaction points to philosophical methodology. Argumentation in philosophy generally proceeds by the method of counterexample. The moral theorist poses a claim that is universal in nature – say, that everyone has a reason to be moral or that lying is always wrong – and the test of the claim is whether it stands up to potential counterexamples.

For purely philosophical purposes, it can be pretty much irrelevant whether such cases actually exist in reality. The moral philosopher deals primarily in the prescriptive, not the descriptive, so his intellectual curiosity will not be satisfied by the fact that there are no empirically realized counterexamples to a claim. Rather his question is whether the claim is true in all conceivable cases. If we can imagine any case in which a person has no reason to be moral or a case in which lying would be permissible, then the theory from which the universal claims are derived must be rejected or qualified, even if no cases of this extremity have ever occurred or are likely to occur.

However, in the context of everyday leadership, once we recognize the challenge of using the ethics of the extreme case as a model, Kantian prohibitions on lying, promise breaking, and other forms of rule breaking have a renewed attractiveness. The extremity of the cases necessary to constitute clear counterexamples to absolutist prohibitions actually increases the plausibility of moral absolutism in the everyday lives of leaders. Of course, the student of leadership ethics will not be surprised that a Kantian approach does not make room for everyday exception making. How could a theory associated with the thought of Immanuel Kant allow people to go around thinking that they deserve special moral treatment?

But Kantian ethics is not alone in raising serious challenges to exception making in everyday life. For example, rule breaking is hardly in keeping with the practices of the virtuous individual. Virtue theory holds that the right action is always a properly habituated and moderated response to the situation in which an agent finds herself. As Aristotle puts it, the virtues ensure that when we feel a certain way or engage in particular actions, we do so "at the right times, about the right things, towards the right people, for the right end, and in the right way."[2] So, while it is true that the virtuous individual might be able to use moral judgment to identify true occasions for rule breaking, she respects the fact that she is not in an extreme case – in everyday life at least – and that exception making would be excessive in these circumstances. Because the virtuous response to ordinary circumstances is properly habituated and moderated, the behavior of the virtuous individual cannot be exceptional.[3]

Other moral theories similarly reject exception-making behavior in everyday life. For example, Hobbes's social contract theory gives pride of place to keeping one's word, especially when one has the

[2] Aristotle, *Nicomachean Ethics*, trans. Terence Irwin (Indianapolis: Hackett Publishing Company, 1985), 44 [1106b21–23].

[3] It is also difficult to see how we can rely on the virtuous person to determine when rule breaking would be justified in the extreme case. The more extreme the circumstances, the less likely it is that leaders can rely simply upon "practiced virtues" to come to a correct decision (Robert Solomon, "Victim of Circumstances? A Defense of Virtue Ethics in Business," *Business Ethics Quarterly* 13 [2003]: 53).

assurances of civil society.[4] In fact, for Hobbes, promises are binding *even in the state of nature* if there has already been first performance by the other party to the exchange – that is, if the other party has done what he said he would do.[5] In civil society, it is only in the most extreme circumstances – those involving life and death – that a promise is not binding (for example, when one promises to give one's life to the sovereign or to obey the sovereign without a guarantee that one's life will be protected).[6]

Not even the flexibility of utilitarianism, a theory that identifies the exact principle on which exception making is sometimes justified, puts us in a position to betray our commitments to the moral rules in anything but the most extreme cases. Overall utility is not best served by allowing individuals to decide for themselves when everyday exception making would be utility maximizing.[7]

A defense of rule breaking in everyday leadership would therefore have to show not only that moral theory allows exceptions to the rules in extreme cases such as the Nazi example but also that there is something morally special about everyday leadership. Is everyday leadership special in this sense?

As it turns out, several morally relevant features of leadership extend to its everyday practice. For instance:

Leadership functions with its own set of norms.
Leaders sometimes give greater priority to their goals than to morality.
Leaders have the power to do what others cannot do.
Leaders are different from followers.
Leadership is a relationship of consent.
Leaders must respond to necessity.
Leadership is a special moral relationship between leaders and followers.
Leaders sometimes pursue higher moral causes.

Each of these features serves as a potential reason to distinguish between rule-breaking behavior by everyday leaders and other kinds

---

[4] Thomas Hobbes, *Leviathan*, ed. Richard Tuck (Cambridge: Cambridge University Press, 1991).

[5] Hobbes, *Leviathan*, 102.

[6] Hobbes, *Leviathan*, 151, 153.

[7] See my discussion of John Stuart Mill's views in Chapter 8.

of exception making in everyday life. Collectively, these reasons also play an important role in the moral psychology of leadership. Like all leaders, everyday leaders sometimes think they have to break the rules to achieve their ends. The question, then, is whether the distinctive features of leadership justify rule-breaking behavior in everyday life.

## THE REJECTION OF MORAL EXCEPTIONALISM

People sometimes say that leaders have their own code of ethics. There are at least two ways to understand this claim. The first understanding suggests that leaders are committed to basic moral beliefs that differ from our own moral beliefs. As a result of cultural background or upbringing, a leader might reject commonly held assumptions about morality – for example, that it is morally wrong to lie, break promises, or refuse to help people in need. This *relativist* way of thinking about the moral beliefs of leaders is not plausible in the context of everyday leadership. Only in the most extreme cases would we expect to find a leader who is mistaken about the foundational rules of morality.

According to a second, more plausible way of thinking about the moral beliefs of leaders, the leader who deviates from an ethical requirement is not committed to a different set of rules, but rather believes that his rule breaking can be justified by the special features of leaders, the circumstances leaders face, or leaders' relationships with followers. This version of the claim that leaders have their own code of ethics characterizes everyday exception making by leaders in terms of *moral exceptionalism*, not moral relativism. The basic demands of morality are not in contention. These demands simply do not apply with the same force to leaders.

Is there a convincing case for moral exceptionalism in everyday leadership? One argument for rule breaking in this context draws our attention to the fact that some leaders care more about their goals than they care about morality. Why should anyone act according to the dictates of morality when doing the morally right thing conflicts with what they most value? Surely it would be inconsistent of a leader to act against what is best by her lights.

According to this *amoralist* strategy, determining that an action constitutes unethical behavior does not make the behavior irrational – at least for a leader who does not particularly care about doing what is ethical. If we insist that, despite her values, she should nevertheless conform to the moral rules, this leader is bound to ask us to say more about the sense in which she should do what ethics requires. When we reply that we mean she *morally* should do so, the leader is well within her rights to inform us that we have told her nothing new. She already understands that ethics tells us what people *morally* should and should not do. This kind of leader sees no reason why *she* should do what ethics requires when ethics does not matter much to her.

We must admit that there is very little to say to the leader who concedes that, in her reasoning, morality plays second fiddle to achieving her goals. Yet we can make this admission and nevertheless deny that the amoralist strategy is available in most cases of everyday leadership. It is no more plausible to think that everyday leaders believe that morality has little or no force for them than to think that everyday leaders hold radically different views about the basic demands of morality. Everyday leaders are no more amoralists than they are relativists.

A better explanation of rule breaking in everyday contexts holds that leaders are sincerely committed to the same morality as the rest of us. Lying, promise breaking, and other violations of the moral rules are generally wrong, and these leaders do not want to do what is wrong. They simply believe that exception making by leaders can be compatible with morality. In other words, everyday leaders sometimes think that they are morally justified in breaking the rules.

Does the *power* of everyday leaders justify their rule-breaking behavior? Whereas it is in the *self-interest* of most people to obey the basic demands of morality, everyday leaders can sometimes use their power to get away with exception making. Moreover, when leaders have enough power, there can be terrible effects on anyone who tries to stop them from pursuing their self-interest. But power is not sufficient for moral justification. The fact that leaders *can* engage in rule-breaking behavior does not imply that it is permissible for them to do so.

What people *can* do has only limited relevance for what they are permitted to do. We could hardly ask everyday leaders to abide by the moral rules if it were psychologically impossible for them to do so. We might therefore allow exceptions for leaders who break the rules when they are unable, or when it is unreasonably difficult for them, to do otherwise. However, we cannot allow exceptions for everyday leaders who break the rules because power makes it easy for them to act egoistically and get away with it.

Still less does the ability of leaders to get away with breaking the rules imply that they *should* engage in rule-breaking behavior to advance their self-interest. An egoistic justification of rule breaking in everyday leadership would have to prove a very controversial claim – that the self-interest of everyday leaders matters more than the interests of other people, including followers. Moral rules that apply equally to leaders and followers are appealing precisely because they ensure that no moral agents unjustifiably put their interests ahead of the interests of others just because they can do so.

Perhaps leaders are better than other people and, as a consequence, deserve significant moral leeway. Here the critical question is, "Better in what way?" To justify rule breaking, this argument cannot simply show that everyday leaders have special skills and talents that differentiate them from followers. It is safe to assume that everyday leaders are better than other people at the specific tasks associated with their leadership positions. Otherwise, why would leaders be in these positions? But these non-moral differences between leaders and followers are not directly relevant to moral justification. A trait-based justification of rule breaking by everyday leaders would have to defend a much stronger claim that leaders are *morally* better than other people. In other words, the argument would have to establish that everyday leaders are superior in *virtue*.

If we assume that everyday leaders are virtuous, we can rest assured that when they make exceptions of themselves, they are justified in doing so. According to the virtue theorist, we can appeal to nothing other than the behavior of the virtuous person to determine what actions are justified.[8] Ultimately, in the context of everyday leadership, this view is incomplete on two counts. First, even if virtuous people make exceptions only when they are justified, everyday leaders have no way of knowing whether they are virtuous! In fact, we know enough about ordinary human psychology to conclude that leaders will overestimate their virtuousness, just as they overestimate the strength of their other positive qualities.

Second, the trait-based justification of exception making tells us nothing about how everyday leaders decide when to follow the moral

---

[8] Julia Annas, "Being Virtuous and Doing the Right Thing," *Proceedings and Addresses of the American Philosophical Association* 78, 2 (November 2004): 67.

rules and when to break them. Discrimination on the part of the virtuous leader requires an appeal not to his own justificatory traits – that is, to whether he is virtuous or not – but rather to the justificatory features of situations. Because the virtuous leader breaks the rules only in some circumstances, we need to know what it is about the situations that grounds a justification for rule breaking. The claim that everyday leaders are virtuous does not answer this question.

Can followers *consent* to rule breaking by everyday leaders? After all, followers might more readily achieve their ends if they allow leaders to break moral rules such as the prohibitions on lying and promise breaking. But surely followers are hardly in any position to consent to the rule-breaking behavior of leaders that affects non-group members. Although followers may have great interests in this kind of behavior because of the competitive advantage it potentially brings to the group, their consent would do nothing to justify the behavior of their leaders. All consent does in this case is to make followers more responsible for potentially immoral treatment of non-group members.

There are also good consent-based reasons to think that followers cannot permit leaders to break the moral rules, even when the rule-breaking behavior is limited to interactions between leaders and followers. For example, allowing employers to lie and make false promises to employees would call into question employees' continued consent to membership in the group. Because the relationship between leaders and followers is a series of voluntary exchanges over time, we must understand consent as an ongoing process, not a one-time encounter in which followers relinquish the protections of morality, especially the protections that make consent possible. The process of leadership requires some moral rules – for example, the prohibitions on lying and promise breaking – that set the parameters of the exchanges but are not themselves subject to the exchanges. In other words, followers cannot forego the moral protections that make consent possible.[9]

Is there something about everyday leadership situations that forces leaders to make exceptions of themselves and, in some cases, encourages followers to permit their exception-making behavior? One answer is that although everyday leaders do not have to confront Nazis, they

---

[9] See John Stuart Mill's discussion of slave contracts in *On Liberty*, ed. Elizabeth Rapaport (Indianapolis: Hackett Publishing Company, 1978), 101.

do have to respond to *necessity*. We expect leaders, including everyday leaders, to be successful. They are thus faced with the necessity of goal achievement. Whether this necessity justifies everyday leaders in breaking the rules depends upon the importance of group goals. If the goals of everyday leadership are to play a role in the justification of exception making, they must stand out as especially important – short of matters of life and death perhaps, but surely significantly more important than the goals to which other everyday leaders are committed.

We can expect everyday leaders to make wildly inaccurate appraisals of the importance of their goals. Initial empirical evidence suggests that they are especially susceptible to the "more-important-than-average effect."[10] In short, everyday leaders are more likely than non-leading group members to think that their goals are more important than average. Of course, some everyday leaders will have more-important-than-average goals – at least compared with other everyday leaders. The problem, however, is that everyday leaders cannot be trusted to make these assessments for themselves.

Everyday leaders therefore have a choice. They must either abide by the moral rules or prove that their goals are indeed more important than average. Proving that their goals are especially important is not a promising strategy because other everyday leaders are similarly confident in their beliefs about the importance of achieving their group goals. A better strategy is to follow the moral rules that apply to all everyday leaders.

An alternative justification of exception making in everyday leadership suggests that a leader's obligations are determined by the *special role* he plays as a group member. According to this justification, the everyday leader need not abstract away from his leadership position and decide what he should do as though he were identical to all other moral agents. Because roles are a constitutive part of our moral identity, no leader is morally identical to anyone else. A leader is a member of a particular group, and, furthermore, he has a special role within this group. This role brings with it the burden of particular moral responsibilities – especially to group members – that others do not have.

[10] Crystal L. Hoyt, Terry L. Price, and Alyson Emrick, "Leadership and the More-Important-Than-Average Effect." Manuscript in preparation.

This argument from role responsibilities ignores the fact that the obligations of everyday leadership are not simply foisted upon people. Unlike other role responsibilities – say, of family or country – the obligations of everyday leadership are normally voluntarily assumed. In other words, it is an exercise of free choice that puts everyday leaders in positions of leadership. Therefore, even if the leadership role requires rule breaking in the pursuit of group goals, the everyday leader cannot pretend that the demand for justification ends with an appeal to his position.

The obvious question to ask all everyday leaders is whether their roles were justifiably adopted, given the moral rules, and whether these roles can be justifiably maintained within the constraints of morality. An affirmative answer to this question assumes consistency between the role responsibilities and the other duties that everyday leaders have as moral agents. The appeal to leadership roles merely raises, but does not resolve, questions about the justification of rule breaking in everyday life.

Some leaders try to transcend the partiality of role responsibilities. The ends at which they aim are morally better and significantly broader than the relatively trivial ends other leaders pursue in virtue of their positions in distinct groups. Leadership relations are therefore redefined to make them sensitive to what really matters morally, as well as to make them maximally inclusive. Because these leaders want to achieve what is objectively good and, moreover, what is good for all of us – not just what is good for the people with whom they have a special relationship – this line of argument stands the best chance of vindicating moral exceptionalism in everyday leadership. How could what is really the greater good fail to have special force in a justification for rule breaking?

There are serious problems, however, with applying this final strategy of justification to the context of everyday leadership. First, everyday leaders – no less than others – face substantial epistemic barriers: How do leaders *know* what *ends* are morally superior to other ends and what *means* are best suited for the achievement of these ends? Given these epistemic constraints, moral rules are ultimately necessary to adjudicate between parties who disagree about what is objectively good, even when the parties are sincere in their commitments to doing what really is good for all of us. Rule following will also play an important instrumental role in achieving the greater good, whatever it turns out to be.

Second, everyday leaders are not charged with the maximization of overall utility or grand social change. Their ends are the more ordinary, but nevertheless rich and significant, goals associated with personal excellence and success in organizational life. In fact, because particular and partial ends are the point of everyday leadership, it is hard to imagine how we might function in everyday life with recourse only to the general and impartial ends that constitute the greater good.

## KANTIANISM FOR EVERYDAY LEADERS

None of the morally relevant features of leadership distinguishes rule-breaking behavior by everyday leaders from other cases of immorality in everyday life. Where does that leave us? We are now in a position to conclude that everyday leadership is not morally special. Leaders are not justified in breaking the rules in everyday life.

This answer suggests that everyday leaders should rethink their view of themselves, their place in the moral community, and the importance of their goals. These leaders must come to terms with their status as the moral equals of other rational agents and accept the implications of this kind of equality for the pursuit of their individual and collective projects. In essence, everyday leaders should develop a Kantian respect for the rules of morality.

A Kantian view of everyday leadership ethics nevertheless makes room for many of the essential components of leadership. First, while it is true that everyday leaders cannot pursue their own goals and projects without regard for the ends of others, morality does not require leaders to abandon or sacrifice their own ends to help achieve what other people think is valuable. As long as everyday leaders act within the constraints of the moral rules, it is permissible for them to privilege the goals and projects to which they are committed. This does not mean that leaders can simply ignore the needs of other rational agents and their equal moral status. Indeed, leaders have a duty to help people achieve their ends and develop as autonomous agents.[11]

---

[11] See Chapters 2 and 7.

But such duties are significantly less demanding than leaders' duties not to use immoral means such as lying and promise breaking to advance their ends. Duties of beneficence are less stringent because people must be able to discharge them without undermining their status as rational agents. If leaders constantly set their own goals aside to help others, they lose something essential to their identity as project pursuers – namely, their projects! Kant's moral philosophy thus creates a context within which everyday leaders can put their own goals and projects first. This context is defined both by strict constraints on the means of leadership and by significantly weaker, but nonetheless important, expectations that leaders will contribute to the good of others.

Second, Kantianism for everyday leaders creates moral space for hierarchical relationships between leaders and followers. A close examination of the relationship between trait theory and virtue ethics shows that everyday leaders are in no position to see themselves as morally superior to followers or to anyone else. But a justification of hierarchy does not need to establish the moral superiority of leaders. What it needs to show is that followers consent to some individuals having relatively greater influence, authority, or power in group contexts. Sometimes the reasoning behind the consent of followers will appeal to the traits of leaders. For example, the leader–follower relationship may be the result of the fact that a particular group member is most qualified to help the group achieve its ends.

Alternatively, hierarchy can be a straightforward response to needs for efficiency and accountability. Maybe the leader is no more qualified than any other member of the group, but group members recognize that goal achievement requires someone to have the responsibilities of leadership. Social life depends on these kinds of hierarchical relationships, and they pervade the public, private, and non-profit sectors. The Kantian view can accommodate this kind of hierarchy in everyday leadership without forsaking a commitment to the equal moral status of all rational agents. Organizational differentiation does not imply any kind of moral inequality – in particular, it does not imply the moral inequality associated with differential application of moral rules.

Third, the Kantian view of everyday leadership allows leaders to behave with partiality toward group members. There is something of a contradiction in the idea that everyday leadership should aspire to complete generality and impartiality. What would be the purpose of a relationship between leaders and followers in which the leader treats the goals and interests of group members no differently than she treats the goals and interests of outsiders? Everyday leadership as we know it would be impossible without the special commitment that leaders have to the groups within which they exercise leadership. One of the most attractive features of Kant's ethics is that it has the moral resources to support this central commitment of the leader–follower relationship. Leaders promise to work to achieve group goals, and this promise must be treated like any other promise a rational agent makes. If the promised behavior does not conflict with other duties that the leader has, there is a categorical prohibition on breaking the promise.

Of course, non-group members deserve the kind of respect that is fitting for any rational agent. Leaders have a duty not to deceive, cheat, coerce – or otherwise bypass the rationality of – non-group members. In addition, the fact that some people are outsiders does not release everyday leaders from their duty to provide help to these individuals when they are in need. Here, the reasoning is similar to that in Kant's more general argument for a duty of beneficence. Because we must will that outsiders sometimes help us achieve our ends, it would be inconsistent of us to refuse to help outsiders on the basis of group membership. The Kantian view of everyday leadership can support all of these claims and, at the same time, hold that leaders owe followers more than they owe non-group members.

Fourth, Kantianism for everyday leaders concedes the possibility of extreme situations in which it is difficult to know whether a violation of the moral rules would be justified. Would torture be permissible to prevent another September 11 terrorist attack? Does the war on terrorism justify infringements of civil liberties? These questions and others like them are of great theoretical and practical importance. Getting them right will determine, among other things, whether a leader is a villain or a hero. Yet these hard questions should not be the focus of everyday leadership, and our struggles to find the right way to answer them cannot serve as a model for thinking about how everyday leaders ought to act.

The Kantian view of everyday leadership moves leaders away from the models of villainous and heroic leadership by reminding them that their circumstances are not so special after all. In so doing, this view requires everyday leaders to rethink the role of rule breaking in everyday leadership. If everyday leadership is not exceptional, exception making cannot be justified. By differentiating organizational ends from the grand goals that may justify rule breaking in heroic leadership, everyday leaders are poised to work within the context of moral rules to carry out the individual and collective projects that characterize our day-to-day lives. Kantianism for everyday leaders thus requires that we rethink everyday leadership. It does not require that we give it up.

# Select Bibliography for Students

Annas, Julia. "Virtue Ethics." In *The Oxford Handbook of Ethical Theory*, ed. David Copp, 515–36. Oxford: Oxford University Press, 2006.

Aristotle. *Nicomachean Ethics*, trans. Terence Irwin. Indianapolis, IN: Hackett Publishing Company, 1985.

Avolio, Bruce J., and Edwin E. Locke. "Contrasting Different Philosophies of Leader Motivation: Altruism Versus Egoism." *Leadership Quarterly* 13 (2002): 169–91.

Bass, B. M., and R. E. Riggio. *Transformational Leadership*. 2nd edition. Mahwah, NJ: Lawrence Erlbaum, 2006.

Bass, Bernard M. *Bass and Stogdill's Handbook of Leadership: Theory, Research, and Managerial Applications*. 3rd edition. New York: Free Press, 1990.

—— *Leadership and Performance Beyond Expectations*. New York: Free Press, 1985.

Bass, Bernard M., and Paul Steidlmeier. "Ethics, Character, and Authentic Transformational Leadership Behavior." *Leadership Quarterly* 10 (1999): 181–217.

Bowie, Norman. *Business Ethics: A Kantian Perspective*. Oxford: Blackwell Publishers, 1999.

Buchanan, Allen E. "Justice as Reciprocity versus Subject-Centered Justice." *Philosophy and Public Affairs* 19 (1990): 227–52.

Burns, James MacGregor. *Leadership*. New York: Harper and Row Publishers, 1978.

—— *Transforming Leadership: A New Pursuit of Happiness*. New York: Atlantic Monthly Press, 2003.

Ciulla, Joanne B. "Leadership Ethics: Mapping the Territory." *Business Ethics Quarterly* 5 (1995): 5–24.

—— ed. *The Ethics of Leadership*. Belmont, CA: Wadsworth/Thomson Learning, 2003.

—— ed. *Ethics, the Heart of Leadership.* 2nd edition. Westport, CT: Praeger, 2004.

Ciulla, Joanne B., Terry L. Price, and Susan E. Murphy, eds. *The Quest for Moral Leaders: Essays in Leadership Ethics.* Cheltenham, UK: Edward Elgar, 2005.

Darley, John M., and C. Daniel Batson. "'From Jerusalem to Jericho': A Study of Situational and Dispositional Variables in Helping Behavior." *Journal of Personality and Social Psychology* 27 (1973): 100–108.

Donaldson, Thomas, Patricia H. Werhane, and Margaret Cording, eds. *Ethical Issues in Business: A Philosophical Approach.* Upper Saddle River, NJ: Prentice Hall, 2002.

Doris, John. *Lack of Character: Personality and Moral Behavior.* Cambridge: Cambridge University Press, 2002.

Feinberg, Joel, and Russ Shafer-Landau, eds. "Psychological Egoism." *Responsibility: Readings in Some Basic Problems of Philosophy.* 10th edition. Belmont, CA: Wadsworth Publishing Company, 1999.

Flanagan, Owen. *Varieties of Moral Personality: Ethics and Psychological Realism.* Cambridge, MA: Harvard University Press, 1991.

Fletcher, Joseph. *Situation Ethics: The New Morality.* Philadelphia: Westminster Press, 1966.

Foot, Philippa. *Virtues and Vices and Other Essays in Moral Philosophy.* Oxford: Basil Blackwell, 1978.

Glover, Jonathan. *Humanity: A Moral History of the Twentieth Century.* New Haven, CT: Yale University Press, 2000.

Goethals, George R., Georgia Sorenson, and James MacGregor, eds. *Encyclopedia of Leadership.* Thousand Oaks, CA: Sage Publications, 2004.

Greenleaf, Robert K. *Servant Leadership: A Journey into the Nature of Legitimate Power and Greatness.* New York: Paulist Press, 1977.

Hill, Thomas E. Jr. *Autonomy and Self-Respect.* Cambridge: Cambridge University Press, 1991.

Hobbes, Thomas. *Leviathan,* ed. Richard Tuck. Cambridge: Cambridge University Press, 1991.

Hollander, E. P. *Leaders, Groups, and Influence.* New York: Oxford University Press, 1964.

Johnson, Craig E. *Meeting the Ethical Challenges of Leadership: Casting Light or Shadow.* Thousand Oaks, CA: Sage Publications, 2001.

Jones, David H. *Moral Responsibility in the Holocaust: A Study in the Ethics of Character.* New York: Rowman and Littlefield Publishers, 1999.

Kant, Immanuel. *Groundwork of the Metaphysic of Morals,* trans. H. J. Paton. New York: Harper and Row Publishers, 1964.

—— *Practical Philosophy,* trans. Mary J. Gregor. Cambridge: Cambridge University Press, 1996.

Kellerman, Barbara. *Bad Leadership: What It Is, How It Happens, Why It Matters.* Boston: Harvard Business School Press, 2004.

Lipman-Blumen, Jean. *The Allure of Toxic Leaders: Why We Follow Destructive Bosses and Corrupt Politicians – and How We Can Survive Them.* Oxford: Oxford University Press, 2005.

Locke, John. *Two Treatises of Government*, ed. Peter Laslett. Cambridge: Cambridge University Press, 1988.

Ludwig, Arnold M. *King of the Mountain: The Nature of Political Leadership.* Lexington: University of Kentucky Press, 2002.

Ludwig, Dean C., and Clinton O. Longenecker. "The Bathsheba Syndrome: The Ethical Failure of Successful Leaders." *Journal of Business Ethics* 12 (1993): 265–73.

Machiavelli, Niccolò. *The Prince*, ed. Quentin Skinner and Russell Price. Cambridge: Cambridge University Press, 1988.

MacIntyre, Alasdair. *After Virtue: A Study in Moral Theory.* 2nd edition. Notre Dame, IN: University of Notre Dame Press, 1981.

Marturano, Antonio, and Jonathan Gosling, eds. *Leadership: The Key Concepts.* London: Routledge, 2008.

Messick, David M., and Max H. Bazerman. "Ethical Leadership and the Psychology of Decision Making." *Sloan Management Review* 37, 2 (1996): 9–22.

Milgram, Stanley. *Obedience to Authority: An Experimental View.* New York: Harper and Row Publishers, 1974.

Mill, John Stuart. *Utilitarianism*, ed. George Sher. Indianapolis, IN: Hackett Publishing Company, 1979.

Nisbett, Richard, and Lee Ross. *Human Inference: Strategies and Shortcomings of Social Judgment.* Englewood Cliffs, NJ: Prentice-Hall, 1980.

Plato. *Republic*, trans. G. M. A. Grube. Indianapolis, IN: Hackett Publishing Company, 1992.

Price, Terry L. *Understanding Ethical Failures in Leadership.* New York: Cambridge University Press, 2006.

Rachels, James. *The Elements of Moral Philosophy.* New York: Random House, 1986.

Rawls, John. *A Theory of Justice.* Cambridge, MA: Belknap Press of Harvard University Press, 1971.

Rousseau, Jean-Jacques. *The Social Contract and Discourses*, trans. G. D. H. Cole. London: J. M. Dent Ltd., 1973.

Sandel, Michael J. *Liberalism and the Limits of Justice.* Cambridge: Cambridge University Press, 1982.

Schoeman, Ferdinand, ed. *Responsibility, Character, and the Emotions: New Essays in Moral Psychology.* Cambridge: Cambridge University Press, 1987.

Singer, Peter. "Famine, Affluence, and Morality." *Philosophy and Public Affairs* 1 (1972): 229–43.

Solomon, Robert C. *Ethics and Excellence: Cooperation and Integrity in Business.* New York: Oxford University Press, 1992.

Walzer, Michael. "Political Action: The Problem of Dirty Hands." *Philosophy and Public Affairs* 2 (1973): 160–80.

—— *Spheres of Justice: A Defense of Pluralism and Equality.* New York: Basic Books, 1983.

Werhane, Patricia H. *Moral Imagination and Management Decision-Making.* New York: Oxford University Press, 1999.

Wren, J. Thomas, ed. *The Leader's Companion: Insights on Leadership Through the Ages*. New York: Free Press, 1995.

Wren, J. Thomas, Douglas A. Hicks, and Terry L. Price. *The International Library of Leadership*. Cheltenham, UK: Edward Elgar, 2004.

Yukl, Gary. *Leadership in Organizations*. 6th edition. Upper Saddle River, NJ: Prentice Hall, 2002.

# Works Cited

Alicke, M. D., and O. Govorun. "The Better-than-Average Effect." In *The Self in Social Judgment*, eds. M. D. Alicke, D. A. Dunning, and J. I. Krueger, 85–106. New York: Psychology Press, 2005.

Allport, F. H. *Social Psychology*. Cambridge, MA: Riverside Press, 1924.

Alter, Jonathan, and Eleanor Clift. "You didn't reveal your pain: Clinton reflects on the turmoil of his childhood." *Newsweek*, March 30, 1992.

Annas, Julia. "Being Virtuous and Doing the Right Thing." *Proceedings and Addresses of the American Philosophical Association* 78, 2 (November 2004): 61–75.

—— "Virtue Ethics." In *The Oxford Handbook of Ethical Theory*, ed. David Copp, 515–36. Oxford: Oxford University Press, 2006.

Aristotle. *Nicomachean Ethics*, trans. Terence Irwin. Indianapolis, IN: Hackett Publishing Company, 1985.

—— *The Politics*, trans. T. A. Sinclair. New York: Penguin Books, 1981.

Arndt, Michael. "How does Harry do it? Baxter is thriving as CEO Kraemer makes sure he and his employees have plenty of time for family." *Business-Week*, July 22, 2002.

Avolio, Bruce J., and Edwin E. Locke. "Contrasting Different Philosophies of Leader Motivation: Altruism Versus Egoism." *Leadership Quarterly* 13 (2002): 169–91.

Badaracco, Joseph L., Jr. *Defining Moments: When Managers Must Choose between Right and Right*. Boston: Harvard Business School Press, 1997.

Barnett, Randy E. *The Structure of Liberty: Justice and the Rule of Law*. Oxford: Oxford University Press, 1998.

Bass, Bernard M. *Bass and Stogdill's Handbook of Leadership: Theory, Research, and Managerial Applications*. 3rd edition. New York: Free Press, 1990.

—— *Leadership and Performance Beyond Expectations*. New York: Free Press, 1985.

Bass, Bernard M., and Paul Steidlmeier. "Ethics, Character, and Authentic Transformational Leadership Behavior." *Leadership Quarterly* 10 (1999): 181–217.

Beard, Alison. "The return of the stay-at-home-spouse." *Financial Times*, October 6, 2000.

Bebchuk, L., and Y. Grinstein. "The Growth of Executive Pay." *Oxford Review of Economic Policy* 21 (2005): 285–303.

Berkowitz, Sean M. "Quotation of the day." *New York Times*, May 26, 2006.

Blum and Weprin Associates, Inc. "The inner life of Americans: Views on spirituality, identity, sexuality, anxiety, and more." Survey for *New York Times*, March 13–16, 2000. http://asnic.utexas.edu/~bennett/_310/Wolfepoll.htm.

Blumenthal, Ralph, Maureen Balleza, and Audrey La. "Ex-university head in Texas on trial for money misuse." *New York Times*, September 17, 2007.

Bowie, Norman. *Business Ethics: A Kantian Perspective.* Oxford: Blackwell Publishers, 1999.

—— "A Kantian Approach to Business Ethics." In *A Companion to Business Ethics*, ed. Robert E. Frederick, 3–16. Oxford: Blackwell Publishers, 1999.

—— "A Kantian Theory of Leadership." *Leadership and Organization Development Journal: Special Issue on Ethics and Leadership* 21 (2000): 185–93.

Brown, Marvin T. *Corporate Integrity: Rethinking Organizational Ethics and Leadership.* Cambridge: Cambridge University Press, 2005.

Buchanan, Allen E. *Ethics, Efficiency, and the Market.* Totowa, NJ: Rowman and Allanheld, 1985.

—— "Justice as Reciprocity versus Subject-Centered Justice." *Philosophy and Public Affairs* 19 (1990): 227–52.

Buchanan, Allen, Dan W. Brock, Norman Daniels, and Daniel Wickler. *From Chance to Choice: Genetics and Justice.* Cambridge: Cambridge University Press, 2000.

Burns, James MacGregor. *Leadership.* New York: Harper and Row Publishers, 1978.

—— *Roosevelt: The Lion and the Fox.* New York: Harcourt Brace, 1956.

—— *Transforming Leadership: A New Pursuit of Happiness.* New York: Atlantic Monthly Press, 2003.

Carruthers, Peter. *The Animals Issue.* Cambridge: Cambridge University Press, 1992.

Catan, Thomas. "Late-running nation told to wake up and start living in English time." *Times of London*, February 28, 2007.

Ciulla, Joanne B. "Leadership Ethics: Mapping the Territory." *Business Ethics Quarterly* 5 (1995): 5–24.

"Company news; Baxter says chief executive will resign." *New York Times*, January 10, 2007.

Conger, Jay A. "Oh Lord, Won't You Buy Me a Mercedes-Benz: How Compensation Practices are Undermining the Credibility of Leaders." In *The Quest for Moral Leaders: Essays in Leadership Ethics*, eds. Joanne B.. Ciulla, Terry L. Price, and Susan E. Murphy, 80–97. Cheltenham, UK: Edward Elgar, 2005.

Couto, Richard. "The Transformation of Transforming Leadership." In *The Leader's Companion: Insights on Leadership Through the Ages*, ed. J. Thomas Wren, 102–07. New York: Free Press, 1995.

Cowell, Alan. "Adventures change. Danger does not." *New York Times*, June 4, 2006.

—— "'Dead' climber's survival impugns Mount Everest ethics." *New York Times*, May 28, 2006.

Coy, Peter. "Ten years from now . . . A BusinessWeek poll indicates big changes are ahead in tomorrow's workplace." *BusinessWeek*, August 20, 2007.

Darley, John M., and C. Daniel Batson. "'From Jerusalem to Jericho': A Study of Situational and Dispositional Variables in Helping Behavior." *Journal of Personality and Social Psychology* 27 (1973): 100–108.

Daum, Julie, and Spencer Stuart. "The fifth annual route to the top: The family factor." *Chief Executive*, February 2000.

Dawes, Robyn M., Alphons J. van de Kragt, and John M. Orbell. "Not Me or Thee but We: The Importance of Group Identity in Eliciting Cooperation in Dilemma Situations: Experimental Manipulations." *Acta Psychologica* 68 (1988): 83–97.

"Dear Abby: Rude cell phone patrons should learn etiquette." *Richmond Times-Dispatch*, November 22, 2005.

"The decline of American civilization, or at least its manners." Associated Press/Ipsos, October 14, 2005. http://poll.orspub.com/.

Devlin, Patty. "Valuing Servants' Ends: A New Theory of Ethical Service." Senior Honors Thesis, Jepson School of Leadership Studies, University of Richmond, 2004.

Doris, John. *Lack of Character: Personality and Moral Behavior*. Cambridge: Cambridge University Press, 2002.

Eichenwald, Kurt. "Kurt Eichenwald discusses the collapse of energy giant Enron." *Fresh Air with Terry Gross*, January 17, 2002.

Fabrikant, Geraldine, Patrick McGeehan, and David Cay Johnston. "Executives take company planes as if their own." *New York Times*, May 10, 2006.

Fain, Paul. "Faculty group votes no confidence in president of Indiana State U." *Chronicle of Higher Education*, May 5, 2006.

Feinberg, Joel. "Psychological Egoism." In *Responsibility: Readings in Some Basic Problems of Philosophy*, eds. Joel Feinberg and Russ Shafer-Landau, 10th edition, 493–505. Belmont, CA: Wadsworth Publishing Company, 1999.

Ferrazzi, Keith. "Why 'balance' is b.s.: For CEOs, blending work and home makes sense." *Chief Executive*, August-September 2005.

Flanagan, Owen. *Varieties of Moral Personality: Ethics and Psychological Realism*. Cambridge, MA: Harvard University Press, 1991.

Fletcher, Joseph. *Situation Ethics*. Philadelphia: Westminster Press, 1966.

Foot, Philippa. "Morality as a System of Hypothetical Imperatives." In *Virtues and Vices and Other Essays in Moral Philosophy*, 157–73. Oxford: Basil Blackwell, 1978.

Frankfurt, Harry G. "Freedom of the Will and the Concept of a Person." *Journal of Philosophy* 68 (1971): 5–20.

Freeman, R. E. "Stakeholder Theory of the Modern Corporation." In *Ethical Issues in Business: A Philosophical Approach*, eds. Thomas Donaldson, Patricia H. Werhane, and Margaret Cording, 38–48. Upper Saddle River, NJ: Prentice Hall, 2002.

French, John R. P. Jr., and Bertram Raven. "The Bases of Social Power." In *Studies in Social Power*, ed. Dorwin Cartwright, 150–67. Ann Arbor, MI: Institute for Social Research, 1959.

Friedman, Milton. "The Social Responsibility of Business is to Increase Its Profits." In *Ethical Issues in Business: A Philosophical Approach*, eds. Thomas Donaldson, Patricia H. Werhane, and Margaret Cording, 33–38. Upper Saddle River, NJ: Prentice Hall, 2002.

Gilbert, Daniel. *Stumbling on Happiness*. New York: Alfred A. Knopf, 2006.

Gillespie, Norman. "The Business of Ethics." *University of Michigan Business Review* 27 (1975): 1–4.

Glover, Jonathan. *Humanity: A Moral History of the Twentieth Century*. New Haven, CT: Yale University Press, 2000.

Goethals, G. R. "Social Comparison Theory: Psychology From the Lost and Found." *Personality and Social Psychology Bulletin* 12 (1986): 261–78.

Goethals, G. R., D. W. Messick, and S. T. Allison. "The Uniqueness Bias: Studies of Constructive Social Comparison." In *Social Comparison Contemporary Theory and Research*, eds. J. Suls and T. A. Wills, 149–76. Hillsdale, NJ: Erlbaum, 1991.

Goodpaster, Kenneth E. "Business Ethics and Stakeholder Analysis." *Business Ethics Quarterly* 1 (1991): 53–74.

Greenleaf, Robert K. *Servant Leadership: A Journey into the Nature of Legitimate Power and Greatness*. New York: Paulist Press, 1977.

Haney, Craig, Curtis Banks, and Philip Zimbardo. "Interpersonal Dynamics in a Simulated Prison." *International Journal of Criminology and Penology* 1 (1973): 69–97.

Harman, Gilbert. "Moral Philosophy Meets Social Psychology: Virtue Ethics and the Fundamental Attribution Error." *Proceedings of the Aristotelian Society* 99 (1999): 315–31.

—— "No Character or Personality." *Business Ethics Quarterly* 13 (2003): 87–94.

Harvey, Van A. "Is There an Ethics of Belief?" *Journal of Religion* 49 (1969): 41–58.

Hegel, Georg Wilhelm Friedrich. *Reason in History: A General Introduction to the Philosophy of History*, trans. Robert S. Hartman. New York: The Liberal Arts Press, 1953.

Heifetz, Ronald A. *Leadership Without Easy Answers*. Cambridge, MA: Belknap Press of Harvard University Press, 1994.

Hermanson, Dana. "Executive Compensation and Corporate Governance." *Internal Auditing* 21, 2 (2006): 36–38.

Herrington, Stuart. "TV torture changes real interrogation techniques." *Fresh Air with Terry Gross*, October 10, 2007.

Hicks, Douglas A. *Inequality and Christian Ethics*. Cambridge: Cambridge University Press, 2000.

—— *Religion and the Workplace: Pluralism, Spirituality, Leadership.* Cambridge: Cambridge University Press, 2003.

Hill, Thomas E. Jr. "Servility and Self-Respect." In *Autonomy and Self-Respect,* 4–18. Cambridge: Cambridge University Press, 1991.

Hobbes, Thomas. *Leviathan,* ed. Richard Tuck. Cambridge: Cambridge University Press, 1991.

Hollander, E. P. *Leaders, Groups, and Influence.* New York: Oxford University Press, 1964.

"Hot topic: Are CEOs worth their weight in gold?" *Wall Street Journal,* January 21, 2006.

Howell, Jane M., and Bruce J. Avolio. "The Ethics of Charismatic Leadership: Submission or Liberation?" *Academy of Management Executive* 6, 2 (1992): 43–54.

Hoyt, Crystal L., Terry L. Price, and Alyson Emrick. "Leadership and the More-Important-Than-Average Effect." Manuscript in preparation.

Hume, David. "Off the Original Contract." In *Essays: Moral, Political, and Literary,* ed. Eugene F. Miller, 465–87. Indianapolis, IN: Liberty Fund, 1987.

Isen, A. M., and P. F. Levin. "Effect of Feeling Good on Helping: Cookies and Kindness." *Journal of Personality and Social Psychology* 21 (1972): 384–88.

Johnson, Craig E. *Meeting the Ethical Challenges of Leadership: Casting Light or Shadow.* Thousand Oaks, CA: Sage Publications, 2001.

Jones, David H. *Moral Responsibility in the Holocaust: A Study in the Ethics of Character.* New York: Rowman and Littlefield Publishers, 1999.

Jones, Edward E., and Richard E. Nisbett. "The Actor and the Observer: Divergent Perceptions of the Causes of Behavior." In *Attribution: Perceiving the Causes of Behavior,* eds. Edward E. Jones, David E. Kanouse, Harold H. Kelley, Richard E. Nisbett, Stuart Valins, and Bernard Weiner, 79–94. Morristown, NJ: General Learning Press, 1972.

Josephs, Leslie. "Peru trying to turn fashionably late into hopelessly passé." *Raleigh News and Observer,* February 25, 2007.

Kant, Immanuel. *Doctrine of Virtue: Part II of the Metaphysic of Morals,* trans. Mary J. Gregor. Philadelphia: University of Pennsylvania Press, 1964.

—— *Groundwork of the Metaphysic of Morals,* trans. H. J. Paton. New York: Harper and Row Publishers, 1964.

—— "On a Supposed Right to Lie from Philanthropy." In *Practical Philosophy,* trans. Mary J. Gregor, 605–15. Cambridge: Cambridge University Press, 1996.

Kanungo, Rabindra N., and Manuel Mendonca. *Ethical Dimensions of Leadership.* Thousand Oaks, CA: Sage Publications, 1996.

Kellerman, Barbara. *Bad Leadership: What It Is, How It Happens, Why It Matters.* Boston: Harvard Business School Press, 2004.

King, Martin Luther Jr. "Letter from the Birmingham City Jail." In *A Testament of Hope: The Essential Writings of Martin Luther King, Jr.,* ed. James Melvin Washington, 289–302. San Francisco: Harper and Row Publishers, 1986.

Kleinfield, N. R. "Life liberty and the pursuit of free box seats: One man's perks anger many, but to New Yorkers, corporate goodies are a right." *New York Times*, September 22, 2002.

Kohlberg, Lawrence. *Essays on Moral Development*. Vol. 1, *The Philosophy of Moral Development*. San Francisco: Harper and Row, 1981.

—— *Essays on Moral Development*. Vol. 2, *The Psychology of Moral Development*. San Francisco: Harper and Row, 1984.

Kurtz, Howard. "Bill Clinton's very personal reflections: In '60 Minutes' interview, ex-president calls affair 'terrible moral error.'" *Washington Post*, June 17, 2004.

Landa, Michael. "What's happening to CEOs?" *CMA Management*, November 2001.

Leader, Zachary. *The Life of Kingsley Amis*. New York: Pantheon Books, 2006.

Lentz, Harris M. III. *Encyclopedia of Heads of States and Governments 1900 through 1945*. Jefferson, NC: McFarland and Company, 1999.

Lindholm, Charles. *Charisma*. Cambridge, MA: Basil Blackwell, 1990.

Lipman-Blumen, Jean. *The Allure of Toxic Leaders: Why We Follow Destructive Bosses and Corrupt Politicians – and How We Can Survive Them*. Oxford: Oxford University Press, 2005.

Locke, John. *Two Treatises of Government*, ed. Peter Laslett. Cambridge: Cambridge University Press, 1988.

Ludwig, Arnold M. *King of the Mountain: The Nature of Political Leadership*. Lexington: University of Kentucky Press, 2002.

Ludwig, Dean C., and Clinton O. Longenecker. "The Bathsheba Syndrome: The Ethical Failure of Successful Leaders." *Journal of Business Ethics* 12 (1993): 265–73.

Machiavelli, Niccolò. *Discourses on the First Ten Books of Titius Livius*. In *Classics of Moral and Political Theory*, ed. Michael L. Morgan, 3rd edition, 467–87. Indianapolis, IN: Hackett Publishing Company, 2001.

—— *The Prince*, eds. Quentin Skinner and Russell Price. Cambridge: Cambridge University Press, 1988.

MacIntyre, Alasdair. *After Virtue: A Study in Moral Theory*. 2nd edition. Notre Dame, IN: University of Notre Dame Press, 1981.

Marks, G. "Thinking One's Abilities are Unique and One's Opinions are Common." *Personality and Social Psychology Bulletin* 10 (1984): 203–208.

Martz, Michael. "Judge faults Wilder on eviction; ruling lets school board sue over aborted move, validates City Hall lease." *Richmond Times-Dispatch*, November 6, 2007.

Marx, Karl. *Economic and Philosophical Manuscripts*. In *Selected Writings*, ed. Lawrence H. Simon, 54–97. Indianapolis, IN: Hackett Publishing Company, 1994.

Maslow, A. H. *Motivation and Personality*. New York: Harper and Brothers, 1954.

McClelland, David C. *Power: The Inner Experience*. New York: Irvington Publishers, 1975.

McCoy, Bowen H. "The Parable of the Sadhu." In *Ethical Issues in Business: A Philosophical Approach*, eds. Thomas Donaldson, Patricia H. Werhane, and Margaret Cording, 262–68. Upper Saddle River, NJ: Prentice Hall, 2002.

McGrath, Charles. "Norman Mailer, towering writer with a matching ego, dies at 84." *New York Times*, November 11, 2007.

McLaughlin, Peter. "Fit to be CEO: How some CEOs link fitness and performance." *Chief Executive*, September 2006.

Meiland, Jack W. "What Ought We to Believe? or The Ethics of Belief Revisited." *American Philosophical Quarterly* 17 (1980): 15–24.

*Merriam-Webster's Collegiate Dictionary*. Electronic edition, version 1.2. 1994–1996.

Messick, David M. "Social Categories and Business Ethics." *Business Ethics Quarterly: Special Issue, Ruffin Series* (1998): 149–72.

Messick, David M., and Max H. Bazerman. "Ethical Leadership and the Psychology of Decision Making." *Sloan Management Review* 37, 2 (1996): 9–22.

Milgram, Stanley. *Obedience to Authority: An Experimental View*. New York: Harper and Row Publishers, 1974.

Mill, John Stuart. *On Liberty*, ed. Elizabeth Rapaport. Indianapolis, IN: Hackett Publishing Company, 1978.

—— *Utilitarianism*, ed. George Sher. Indianapolis, IN: Hackett Publishing Company, 1979.

Millbank, D. "Hiring welfare people, hotel chain finds, is tough but rewarding." *Wall Street Journal*, October 31, 1996.

Miller, Dale T., and Rebecca K. Ratner. "Disparity Between the Actual and Assumed Power of Self-Interest." *Journal of Personality and Social Psychology* 74 (1998): 53–62.

Moody-Adams, Michele M. "Culture, Responsibility, and Affected Ignorance." *Ethics* 104 (1994): 291–309.

Morgenson, Gretchen. "The boss actually said this: Pay me less." *New York Times*, December 18, 2005.

Nagel, Thomas. *Equality and Partiality*. Oxford: Oxford University Press, 1991.

*New Oxford Annotated Bible: New Revised Standard Version*, ed. Michael D. Coogan. 3rd edition. Oxford: Oxford University Press, 2001.

Nietzsche, Friedrich. *Beyond Good and Evil: Prelude to a Philosophy of the Future*, trans. Walter Kaufmann. New York: Random House, 1966.

Nisbett, Richard, and Lee Ross. *Human Inference: Strategies and Shortcomings of Social Judgment*. Englewood Cliffs, NJ: Prentice-Hall, 1980.

*Oxford English Dictionary*. 2nd edition. Oxford: Oxford University Press, 1989.

Plato. *Republic*, trans. G. M. A. Grube. Indianapolis, IN: Hackett Publishing Company, 1992.

Price, H. H. "Belief and Will." *Aristotelean Society Supplementary Volume* 28 (1954): 1–26.

Price, Terry L. "Abuse, Privilege, and the Conditions of Responsibility for Leaders." In *The Quest for Moral Leaders: Essays in Leadership Ethics*, eds. Joanne B. Ciulla, Terry L. Price, and Susan E. Murphy, 65–79. Cheltenham, UK, and Northampton, MA, USA: Edward Elgar, 2005.

—— "The Ethics of Authentic Transformational Leadership." *Leadership Quarterly* 14 (2003): 67–81.

—— "Explaining Ethical Failures of Leadership." *Leadership and Organization Development Journal* 21 (2000): 177–84. Reprinted with revisions in *Ethics, the Heart of Leadership*, ed. Joanne B. Ciulla, 2nd edition (Westport, CT: Praeger, 2004), 129–46.

—— "Philosophical Approaches to Leadership." In *Leadership: The Key Concepts*, eds. Antonio Marturano and Jonathan Gosling, 126–27. London: Routledge, 2008.

—— "Philosophy." In *Encyclopedia of Leadership*, eds. George R. Goethals Georgia Sorenson, and James MacGregor Burns, 3:1195–99. Thousand Oaks, CA: Sage Publications, 2004.

—— "Responsibility." In *Leadership: The Key Concepts*, eds. Antonio Marturano and Jonathan Gosling, 141–43. London: Routledge, 2008.

—— "Transforming Leadership." In *Leadership: The Key Concepts*, eds. Antonio Marturano and Jonathan Gosling, 170–74. London: Routledge, 2008.

—— *Understanding Ethical Failures in Leadership.* New York: Cambridge University Press, 2006.

Price, Terry L., and Douglas A. Hicks. "A Framework for a General Theory of Leadership." In *The Quest for a General Theory of Leadership*, eds. George R. Goethals and Georgia L. J. Sorenson, 123–151. Cheltenham, UK: Edward Elgar, 2006.

Prince, Howard T. II. "Moral Development in Individuals." In *The Leader's Companion: Insights on Leadership Through the Ages*, ed. J. Thomas Wren, 484–91. New York: Free Press, 1995.

Pryor, John H., Sylvia Hurtado, Victor B. Saenz, Jennifer A. Lindholm, William S. Korn, and Kathryn M. Mahoney. *The American Freshman: National Norms for Fall 2005.* Los Angeles: University of California Higher Education Research Institute, 2005.

"A question of torture: Excepting John McCain, Republican candidates for president seem to favor it." *Washington Post*, May 17, 2007.

Rachels, James. *The Elements of Moral Philosophy.* New York: Random House, 1986.

Rand, Ayn. "The Ethics of Emergencies." In *Reason and Responsibility: Readings in Some Basic Problems of Philosophy*, eds. Joel Feinberg and Russ Shafer-Landau, 10th edition, 533–37. Belmont, CA: Wadsworth Publishing, 1999.

—— "Why Self-Interest is Best." In *The Ethics of Leadership*, ed. Joanne B. Ciulla, 44–52. Belmont, CA: Wadsworth/Thomson Learning, 2003.

Rawls, John. *A Theory of Justice.* Cambridge, MA: Belknap Press of Harvard University Press, 1971.

"Republican presidential primary debate sponsored by the South Carolina Republican Party and Fox News Channel." *Federal News Service*, May 15, 2007.

Richards, Ann. "Transcript of the keynote address by Ann Richards, the Texas treasurer." *New York Times*, July 19, 1988.

Rosenbaum, Ron. *Explaining Hitler: The Search for the Origins of His Evil.* New York: Random House, 1998.

Rousseau, Jean-Jacques. *A Discourse on the Origin of Inequality*. In *The Social Contract and Discourses*, trans. G. D. H. Cole, 31–126. London: J. M. Dent Ltd., 1973.
—— *The Social Contract*. In *The Social Contract and Discourses*, trans. G. D. H. Cole, 179–309. London: J. M. Dent Ltd., 1973.
Rubin, Harriet. "Ayn Rand's literature of capitalism." *New York Times*, September 15, 2007.
Sabl, Andrew. "Torture as a case study: How to corrupt your students." *Chronicle of Higher Education*, November 11, 2005.
Salazar, Carla. "This just in: Peru battles chronic lateness." *Seattle Times*, March 3, 2007.
Sandel, Michael J. *Liberalism and the Limits of Justice*. Cambridge: Cambridge University Press, 1982.
Sears, D. O., and C. L. Funk. "The Role of Self-Interest in Social and Political Attitudes." In *Advances in Experimental Social Psychology*, ed. M. P. Zanna, 24:2–19. New York: Academic Press, 1991.
—— "Self-Interest in Americans' Political Opinions." In *Beyond Self-Interest*, ed. J. J. Mansbridge, 147–70. Chicago: Chicago University Press, 1999.
Sheridan, C. L., and R. G. King. "Obedience to Authority with an Authentic Victim." *Proceedings of the American Psychological Association* 2 (1972): 165–66.
Silva, Chris. "Senioritis: Work-life concerns impede senior executive promotions." *Employee Benefit News*, October 1, 2006.
Singer, Peter. "Famine, Affluence, and Morality." *Philosophy and Public Affairs* 1 (1972): 229–43.
—— "The Singer solution to world poverty." *New York Times Magazine*, September 5, 1999.
Solomon, Robert C. "Ethical Leadership, Emotions, and Trust: Beyond 'Charisma.'" In *Ethics, the Heart of Leadership*, ed. Joanne B. Ciulla, 2nd edition, 83–102. Westport, CT: Praeger, 2004.
—— *Ethics and Excellence: Cooperation and Integrity in Business*. New York: Oxford University Press, 1992.
—— "Victims of Circumstances? A Defense of Virtue Ethics in Business." *Business Ethics Quarterly* 13 (2003): 43–62.
Stevens, Tim. "Striking a balance." *Industry Week*, November 20, 2000.
Stogdill, Ralph Melvin. "Personal Factors Associated with Leadership: A Survey of the Literature." *Journal of Psychology* 25 (1948): 35–71.
Strawson, Peter. "Freedom and Resentment." In *Perspectives on Moral Responsibility*, eds. John Martin Fischer and Mark Ravizza, 45–66. Ithaca, NY: Cornell University Press, 1988.
Tanz, Jason, and Theodore Spencer. "Candy striper, my ass! A culture clash is looming as a high-powered wave of retiring executives meets the genteel world of volunteerism." *CNNMoney.com*, August 14, 2000. http://www.money.cnn.com/.
Taylor, S. E., B. P. Buunk, and L. G. Aspinwall. "Social Comparison, Stress, and Coping." *Journal of Personality and Social Psychology Bulletin* 16 (1990): 74–89.

"This year's freshmen at 4-year colleges: A statistical profile." *The Chronicle of Higher Education*, February 3, 2006.

Tyler, T. R. "Justice, Self-Interest, and the Legitimacy of Legal and Political Authority." In *Beyond Self-Interest*, ed. J. J. Mansbridge, 171–79. Chicago: Chicago University Press, 1999.

Walker, Julian. "Chesterfield official paid $18,000 for flight." *Richmond Times-Dispatch*, February 21, 2006.

Walzer, Michael. "Political Action: The Problem of Dirty Hands." *Philosophy and Public Affairs* 2 (1973): 160–80.

—— *Spheres of Justice: A Defense of Pluralism and Equality*. New York: Basic Books, 1983.

Watson, Gary. "Responsibility and the Limits of Evil: Variations on a Strawsonian Theme." In *Responsibility, Character, and the Emotions: New Essays in Moral Psychology*, ed. Ferdinand Schoeman, 256–86. Cambridge: Cambridge University Press, 1987.

Werhane, Patricia H. *Moral Imagination and Management Decision-Making*. New York: Oxford University Press, 1999.

Wills, Gary. "Clinton's forgotten childhood." *Time*, June 8, 1992.

Wise, Steven M. *Rattling the Cage: Towards Legal Rights for Animals*. Cambridge, MA: Perseus Books, 2000.

Wolf, Susan. *Freedom Within Reason*. Oxford: Oxford University Press, 1990.

—— "Sanity and the Metaphysics of Responsibility." In *Responsibility, Character, and the Emotions: New Essays in Moral Psychology*, ed. Ferdinand Schoeman, 46–62. Cambridge: Cambridge University Press, 1987.

Wolfe, Alan. *Moral Freedom*. New York: W.W. Norton and Company, 2001.

Yukl, Gary. *Leadership in Organizations*. 6th edition. Upper Saddle River, NJ: Prentice Hall, 2002.

Zimmerman, Michael J. "Moral Responsibility and Ignorance." *Ethics* 107 (1997): 410–26.

# Index